Ireland:
A Colony Once Again

Ireland:
A Colony Once Again

By

Seán Ó Nualláin
Center for the Study of Language and Information,
Stanford University

CAMBRIDGE
SCHOLARS
PUBLISHING

Ireland: A Colony Once Again,
by Seán Ó Nualláin

This book first published 2012

Cambridge Scholars Publishing

12 Back Chapman Street, Newcastle upon Tyne, NE6 2XX, UK

British Library Cataloguing in Publication Data
A catalogue record for this book is available from the British Library

ISBN (10): 1-4438-4085-8, ISBN (13): 978-1-4438-4085-9

To the memory of Richard Strohman, late of UC Berkeley,
who always suspected he was really Irish;
and to my daughters Beth and Coralie, the future.

TABLE OF CONTENTS

PREFACE:
CRY, THE DEAR LAND!

It is worth clearing the ground by stating that this book is not primarily about Ireland.

That the country is Ireland, and the period the first two decades of the third millennium is irrelevant to this section. It deals, rather, with what types of evidence outside the purely historical and economic are allowed and what the theoretical structure underpinning this evidence is.

This preface will hint that a reduction to neuroscience may not be possible; this shall shortly be expanded upon. Yet there is strong evidence that much experimental work of the most morally debauched nature was undertaken by the CIA, inter alia, to attempt to break down psychological structures in the individual in order to reprogram them. There is preliminary evidence that certain of the CIA's coups like that in Chile attempted to extend this from the individual to the national level. We shall therefore apprise ourselves of any relevant neuroscience in the course of the book.

Secondly, we use some of the apparatus of contemporary postcolonial thought; "the other', alienation, inauthenticity, the welding back together of the Cartesian split between mind and matter. It is argued that one's "sense of place" should eschew this dualism. It is further argued that one of the critical aspects of neo-colonization is its violation of "sense of place" expectancies with catastrophic results. The book's specific program is about using the classical resources of Irish cultural nationalism to emerge from the current trap into a stable and just society.

It is further argued that "shock" treatment is in any case not applicable in a democracy. A democracy Ireland has remained, despite the threat posed by e-voting and a financial scam of such proportions that the national debt has quintupled in an attempt to deflate it(rather than undo it). Instead of shock treatment, what has been done is a more subtle nudging of the Irish away from feeling embodied in a particular locale as a particular indigenous population. The methods used were multifarious; massive immigration, with recent immigrants of all ethnicities labelled "new Irish" by all leading politically correct media; an assault on individuals attempting to create independent expressions of Irish culture through arts and scholarship; destruction of civil society structures, either by incorporating them into the state through agreements like "social partnership" or indirectly by refusing to give them the protection of the law; and so on.

This writer's background has been first, that amorphous set of disciplines called the "cognitive sciences" and, secondly, theoretical biology and experimental neuroscience. In contrast to many cognitive scientists, he believes it important to emphasise that, in his opinion, these disciplines as currently construed have next to nothing to say about political sociology. It is worth spending some time exploring why this is so.

Were it possible to describe mental processes solely in a set of differential equations or other such reductionist form, as the research program called "eliminative materialism" desires, both the cognitive and social sciences would quickly reduce to the null set. There would quite simply be no need for the former; the latter would become a kind of utilitarian "felicific calculus" where beneficial effects of varying policies for the populace (as distinct from citizenry) would be calculated by technocrats. It is worth noting, in this context, that eliminative materialism has ignored the fact of its claim-jump into the political arena. Liberal democracy requires freedom of conscience, even in the face of technocrats describing conscience as an illusion, whether necessary or not. The political will remain an ineluctable realm, whatever progress science makes.

In fact, due perhaps to their common origin in (Francis) Baconian science, the argument for the economization of life due to neoliberalism has a similar structure to that for eliminative materialism. Political argument, as construed by thinkers like Hannah Arendt, is replaced by the competition of various strategies for running the economy on free-market principles. The notion that there are human goals to which economic activity is subservient is, in general, not even considered. Remarkably, such an ethos as emerges from neoliberalism seems to cause economic as well as cultural devastation.

Both approaches are, above all, deeply naïve. Just as we can currently describe mind only with a set of guesses of greater and lesser levels of inspiration based on data that are still incomplete (and indeed largely inchoate), so also the collective action of a multitude of economic actors ranging in scale from the individual to the superstate (like the EU with its Euro) is very poorly understood. The "new economy" of the 1990's led to the series of economic crashes from 1998 to 2008. It is as foolish to rest a nation's welfare on this received wisdom as it is to bracket the joy and diversity of human existence in the eschatological hope of their being "explained".

Nor is that all. Previous attempts to reduce psychology impeded its progress, particularly once a coherent scientific realm common to humans and computers emerged from the functionalist ethos. Likewise, government by spreadsheet is totalising, and totally inept in that it cannot plan for disruptive technologies. Remarkably, early 21st century initiatives like Facebook, MySpace, Friendster, and the lesser known tribe.org all rested on the individual and her need for self-expression in a neoliberal world.

As construed in this book, the political must harness as much of the psychic energy of the people as possible, even at the expense of "precision". We are closer to Arendt than Milton Friedman. Political speech is processed by, and social forces experienced by, individual people. Yet these people are coalitions of selves; if not chronically split, at the very least multiply situated in identifications with nations, state, county, town, and so on. It may indeed be the case, a la Plato's Republic, that the individual projects onto the political stage the drama of her internal dynamics, with individual selves gaining power in the name of specific projects and ideas only to relinquish it in the greater history of the individual and political organism.

We shall indeed visit the various schools of thought that have explored coloniality through the prism supplied by phenomenology and, related by logical necessity, existentialism. For the moment, it will simply be stated that the colonial state is one in which the individual cannot comfortably identify with the place in which he lives, nor, as a consequence, with his body. In the vocabulary chosen here, the selves emerging from such identification will not be allowed gain purchase on the total energy of the organism. One would expect consumption of stupefecants, violence, suicide, and all the other symptoms of *anomie* to increase.

The colonising force, in turn, will wish to diminish the prestige of factors leading to a heightened sense of place; the national narrative and other aspects of the chthonic culture(particularly the artistic such, which can be controlled by its being objectified as intellectual property). It may also attempt a direct attack on sites that bear the imprint of the *genius loci*, while using a new type of colonial administrator to grab materially valuable resources. This preface will include several such examples. Finally, it will attempt to keep the populace busy in the service of globalized corporatism, and portray this kind of frenzied existence as the new patriotism.

It should be evident at this point that all the above are true of Ireland at the beginning of the third millennium CE. However, the standard narratives of nationalism are not true of Ireland; it is fundamentally susceptible to categorisation under the rubrics of a rekindled indigeneity rather than an invented nationalism. That there are aspects of Ireland's official national identity that are invented are beyond doubt; yet so also is the antiquity of the presence on the island of a relatively settled population, and the salience of the country in the colonial struggles of the 20th century.

The purpose of the book is not to rekindle any kind of myopic nationalism, let alone political violence in its service; it is rather to look at what happens when the centre fails to hold and a rather suspect economic theory presumes to become a national narrative. It must be stated from the start that even Fichte's extreme nationalism (see chapter 1) was in the service of a greater cosmopolitanism; likewise, any suggestions here about nationalism are put forward in an attempt to rescue it from its current meaninglessness.

This book also attempts, inter alia, to provide a foundation in cognitive science for social science concepts. It begins with the concept of selfhood, which is posited in the writer's experimental work as being founded on data-compression in the brain. In particular, our experience of selfhood qua identification derives from exclusion of data regarded by the organism either as irrelevant or as dangerous to its integrity. Our experience of ourselves as agents is largely a fiction in that we narrate continually, ascribing to ourselves the origins of actions that occurred automatically. However, there is a core of agency within each of us, while manifest perhaps in a conscious "won't" rather than "will".

The social is a higher category to the cognitive, which refers to the processing of information in the individual brain, and to the non-cognitive biological, yet is rooted in both. Insofar as the individual can construe herself as being the object of a norm or value, she is immersed in the social. This can be mediated as intersubjective, and not necessarily conscious, or – to be more precise - fully conscious. Social pressures can be exerted on the individual, with often devastating results. Some such are artifacts of colonisation; yet that is getting ahead of the story.

The expression of the social is primarily verbal, and that will be our first port of call. It can be argued that all human institutions are created by speech acts, whereby concepts previously abstract acquire rights and duties, and power over the individual; deontic powers. The particular types of speech acts involved are called performative utterances, which take the form "X institution shall...". And so it can be said, for example, that a certain limited company shall exist within a certain legislative framework for a certain amount of time, including for eternity.

Yet the words alone will not unravel the web in which critical theory finds that humans live. While it is perhaps excessive to state that behind the structure of modernity lies the mediaeval, there is undoubtedly ample room for projection, and indeed scapegoating. The contemporary critic might indeed go further and point to the access of torture and Christian crusade in the early years of the 21st century to suggest something altogether darker. Admixed with freedom of conscience are themes a great deal lower in the brain than the neocortex.

Nationalism famously epitomises these themes for many writers. Remarkably, the advent of global terror organizations has led to an attempt to rescue positive meanings for nationalism, referring to the influence that the enlightenment had in the creation of the 19th century nation-states. In this book, nationalism is proposed as unavoidable, and always to be seen as a step to a greater cosmopolitanism. In particular, nationalism is regarded as a synesthesia of sense of place through the modalities provided by state institutions, and a civil society that is recognisably autochthonous.

This definition of nationalism is obviously compatible with modern environmentalism. In countries that can demonstrate the existence of a long, relatively stable population, it can confront the notion of indigeneity with respect to genetic fact, and thus modern science, and the narratives that have sprung up around the facts of belonging to a particular place. It can also transform whatever violent political struggle has occurred to resecure possession of the place for the natives into a more pacific narrative.

Finally, it can combine several of the arguments above to combat neoliberal colonisation. The experience of recolonisation is experienced as a schism between identifications due to the formal nature of the social structure, and one's experience of one's body as belonging to a certain locus. In particular, the experience of being "othered" by the state is dislocation itself. The existence of a state apparat that does not hesitate to commit large sections of the population to conditions of alterity, this book argues, was apparent first in Ireland at the beginning of the third millennium, Common Era. As the first nation in the erstwhile British Empire to achieve (partial) modern independence, it is perhaps inevitable that Ireland was the first fully to be recolonised.

As this book was being written, two cases went through the High Court in Ireland. The first featured some rather Victorian punitive concepts, and frankly mediaeval logical leaps. Claiming state permission, the Anglo-Dutch Shell Corporation sought to put a gas pipeline taking gas from the Corrib field through the lands of some farmers around Rossport in County Mayo on Ireland's west Coast. This partly Gaelic-speaking area in question is one of the least densely populated parts of Europe. Five farmers refused to allow the pipeline through, claiming — correctly, as it happened — that the gas pressure planned for the pipeline was unprecedented in engineering history. They held out in the face of high court orders favouring Shell, and were committed to jail for contempt of court.

No-one has yet gone to jail, nor is anyone likely to do so, in the second case. It concerned an appeal against the building of a motorway near the hill of Tara, a site mythologised as the seat of Ireland's high kings. The minister of the environment, Dick Roche, acted against expert archaeological advice in proceeding with the motorway plans. The High Court granted leave to appeal against Roche's decision, but the appeal was turned down – as it turns out, by repudiating the grounds of the leave to appeal. Both these cases have potential significance far beyond their legal specifics.

The Rossport five, as they have become known, were repeatedly been brought back to the High Court and asked to "purge their contempt". A ceremonial grovel later, they would have been free men again. Yet, remarkably, it is Shell that was factually in breach of the law of the land and the men's behaviour now appears more akin to citizens' arrest than even civil disobedience. (They have been released, sans grovel). The permits granted to Shell were solely for preparatory work: it has now become clear that the company had welded together three km. of pipeline in flagrant breach of its permission.

There are two aspects to this case that deserve emphasis and will inform of central themes of this book. The behaviour of the Irish establishment has been truly extraordinary. The supporters of the Rossport five, in turn, have begun to reflect on the continuity of their movement with earlier egalitarian and democratic impulses in Irish history. Their placards now state that while their fellow Mayo man Michael Davitt took on the landlords in the late nineteenth century, they are taking on the corporations. In the upper house of parliament, the flamboyantly gay representative of Trinity College, David Norris, correctly pointed to Shell's behaviour in the Ogoniland culminating in the judicial murder of Ken Saro Wiwa. The placards began to echo this, pointing out that The Rossport five were lucky to be alive. Owens Saro Wiwa, Ken's brother, visited Ireland in support of them, and now distributes their literature on his world tours.

Not one organ of the Irish establishment has sought the jailing of Shell management for breaking the terms of the permissions granted them, and simultaneously insisting on the jailing of citizens who had themselves insisted that the law of the land be upheld. Rarely have the battle lines in Irish Politics been so clearly drawn. Specifically, the confrontation has caused to crystallise groups who see Ireland as a heaven for transnational corporations and, opposing them, those who see it as a nation of radical republicans – or, at the least, Jeffersonian citizens. The latter group see themselves as engaged in a struggle against Ireland's second colonisation; the former group seems prepared to invoke any shibboleth in order to maintain their pole position in Irish Society.

The Tara Skryne Case, as it has become known, did not heat up to anything like this temperature. Tara has perhaps the most potent mythology of place in Western Europe: a country whose dominant commodity for hundreds of years has been mythology cannot remain neutral on this issue for long. The received creation myth of the Irish envisages waves of settlers, starting with the fir Bolgs, Tuatha de Danann and finally the Milesians from the northern part of the Iberian Peninsula. (It should surprise no-one to find that in fact there may be a mitochondrial DNA link from the Irish to the Basques.) The Tuatha de Danann defeated the fir Bolgs at the second Battle of Moytura, and so established their claim to the island of Ireland. This claim was incarnated in stone pillars, and in particular at Tara the Liath Fail, or Stone of Destiny, spoke to attest the presence of the real high king of Ireland. This trope proved so powerful that British Celts came to see the provenance of the Stonehenge pillars as Ireland.

So Tara speaks both of political legitimacy and the mythologisation, making magical, of the Irish landscape. However, it is so close to Dublin that it was for a while potentially prime building land, or at worst a way station to prime building land. The value of the myth in a secularised time has been weighed against the potential price of the land, and has fallen short. Disenchantment in every sense is the appropriate response. To adapt Paton: Cry, the dear land! It was the reification of land in this way, pushing its value down and its price up, that put paid to Ireland as an independent state.

This book's content concerns a period in which a historical community with an attested history of freedom struggle experienced moral and eventually economic freefall. On November, 15, 2010, a Google search on the words "Ireland" and "default", with only documents which included both words looked up, yielded 55.100,000 hits; restricted only to the previous 24 hours, it was still over 1 million. The game was up, and had been for some time; economic sovereignty was gone, perhaps irretrievably. It was clear that the international financial community, through the press media it owned directly and indirectly, was forcing Ireland to submit to a regime of nationalization of private debt, and quarterly reports to the IMF. In fact, Ireland was to become an experiment in the implementation of economic theory like Pincohet's regime incarnated the Chicago school; not only were unsecured bondholders in Ireland's heretofore private banks to be paid back in full by the citizenry through the state, but this repayment was to be continued even after the banks were taken "into resolution", that is pronounced dead.

Thus, the root of the sovereign debt problem in Ireland from 2010, the mechanism through which the new colonial status was set in stone, was the transfer of debt incurred by private banks to the taxpayer through the mechanism of state. By means of irresponsible lending for property and other devices not yet fully clear, but which involved in at least one attested case an Austrian branch that did money-laundering for the Italian mafia, the Irish banks had run up hundreds of billions in debt, mainly to their European counterparts. German and British banks were both owed over $100 billion; Belgian banks were owed a sum exceeding 5% of that country's GDP. This vast reservoir of cash had not been used productively;

what happened rather resembles a coup d'état in that a super-privileged elite has been created by this money, and were still being kept in their Cap Ferrat mansions and $30 million Manhattan townhouses courtesy of the unwilling Irish taxpayer for years afterward. In early 2012, a high court case in London involving the Savoy group of hotels proved this.

It was clear that an Irish default, which is in any case almost certain, would have repercussions for the world financial system. Yet the Irish government's behavior since 2008 has been, by any standards, truly extraordinary. In general, the "senior" bondholders of the Irish banks' debt were held sacrosanct; while this may be standard financial practice, the same status being awarded to junior unsecured bondholders in banks undergoing "resolution' is unprecedented, and suggests something has gone very awry indeed. When confronted in Parliament at the end of 2010 with the argument that the Irish citizenry had "no moral or legal obligation" to bail out the likes of Citibank and Deutsches Bank, Ireland's Minister for finance, Brian Lenihan, rather gave the game away by replying that "Those who think we can unilaterally renege on senior bondholders against the wishes of the ECB are living in fantasy land".

Yet, of course, in the past decade, Argentina, Uruguay, and then Iceland have successfully renegotiated their debt in precisely the way that Lenihan repudiated out of hand. This book explores the cultural mindset of Lenihan and his colleagues as essentially resembling that of colonial officers passing out information piecemeal to the wogs. In fact, Lenihan inadvertently collapsed the government in 2010, finishing off his party as a force in Irish politics, by orchestrating a series of denials that a deal with the IMF was imminent. At the time, he was dying of cancer, and it is fair to say that the media showed some skill in rescinding what could have been serious economic debate by fatwas about giving scandal about the dead.

Since 2008, the government first guaranteed deposits and bondholders after emergency meetings in September, 2008. Remarkably, no attempt was made to renegotiate debt owed to bondholders by the obviously basket-case banks, which even the bondholders expected to happen. Instead, a national assets management bureau (NAMA) was set up, effectively perpetuating the privileges of many of the developers at the state's expense as loans on which these developers had not even been paying interest now became an issue for the public purse. In early 2009, Ireland's notorious mafia bank, Anglo-Irish, was nationalized, but it was made clear that depositors still had access to all their cash, regardless of their indebtedness. Scores of billions of state money was thrown into the bottomless pit of Anglo and Allied Irish Banks, before the latter was also effectively nationalized in an in camera session of Ireland's High court in late 2010, exploiting the expedited passage of banking laws not seen in peacetime countries.

The incoming government of 2011 had few real options. The central argument of this book is that what went on is an internal Irish problem, with a self-appointed elite exploiting evanescent liquidity in the international money markets to acquire massive wealth and influence for itself. It is now using the ECB to maintain this power-base, which is a colonial move; yet it is but the final stage in a political and cultural process that began decades ago. Removing this new establishment will indeed have repercussions for international finance. Understanding from the international community as we Irish do this is the central plea of this book.

CHAPTER ONE

THE RECOLONISATION OF IRELAND

1.1 Prologue

> "Once you accept that profit and - practiced on a mass scale create the greatest possible benefits for any society, pretty much any act of personal enrichment can be justified as a contribution to the great creative cauldron of capitalism, generating wealth and spurring economic growth - even if it's only for yourself" (Naomi Klein, 2007, "The shock doctrine" P. 313)

> "Society in general, simply by its effects on men's minds, undoubtedly has all that is required to arouse the sensation of the divine.....The ordinary observer cannot see where the influence of society comes from. It moves along channels that are too obscure and circuitous, and uses psychic mechanisms that are too complex, to be easily traced to its source" (Durkheim, 1995, Pp. 208-211)

Hermann Hesse's "Steppenwolf" has a confusing architecture. When accused of narrative misconduct, Hesse replied that it was in fact the most tightly structured of all his works. It is in fact modelled on concerto structure, with all the themes stated right at the beginning. In order to help the reader navigate through the first attempt to bring early third millennium Ireland into dialogue with modern postcolonial thought, and with this writer lacking the genius of Hesse, this prologue is a modest attempt at orienting the reader. Chapter 7 features a similar effort, based on a set of apparently innocuous broadcasts the author did on national Irish radio in 2006, which resulted in his being banned from the airwaves.

The two quotes above define the extremes of this book's concerns. It is fair to say that, for most of its recorded history, the concept of Ireland has been a moral and indeed spiritual one for its inhabitants, giving rise to acts of great heroism and acts of great institutional abuse as cynics took over the structures established by their heroic precursors. It is also fair to say that, from the mid-1990's, Ireland became one of the more materialistic and crass places in the world. As this book is being read, the result of the bank bail-out of 2008-2010 (and onwards) will still define the Irish socioeconomic landscape. The shards of the attempted coup of 2002-2008, with its monstrous state institutions and equally institutionalized corruption, will still be visible. These grotesque structures are sufficiently entrenched that an orthodox libertarian approach - or, at least, what looks at first glance like libertarianism - may briefly be necessary for their extirpation.

The book issues recommendations that are fundamentally about returning a sense of place to the Irish in Ireland. This is less about "Blood and belonging" than a sense of connection to the land, implemented through appropriate administrative, cultural, and religious structures both within the state and its civil society. Even that has become controversial; part of the narrative sold by the major media in Ireland was multiculturalism, however incoherent. The more ambitious recommendations in this book involve breaking with many of the institutions of globalized corporatism. Indeed, it is proposed that these institutions are fundamentally creatures of the "Washington consensus", and symptoms of an underlying imperial impulse. Of course, all of this has been said before, probably better than I can say it.

This writer is aware that the more controversial recommendations, which include in effect returning many immigrants to their place of origin, and nationalizing many resources, are hateful to many apparently reasonable people. They would require a rare crisis in the body politic even to be considered. Yet such a crisis will reign as practically a permanent state of affairs for the second decade of the 21st century in Ireland. By late 2010, it became likely Ireland would default on its international debt within a year, with access to the international bond markets no longer an option as a means to raise capital. Ireland had effectively lost its economic sovereignty some time before with the ECB (European central bank) the only purchaser of these bond issues before the charade was discontinued in Fall 2010. Ireland ceased pretending to issue bonds, and the ECB ceased pretending to buy them, referring Ireland to accompany Greece at the trough of the European Stabilization fund.

In that case, the failure of the establishment parties (including the ex-Marxist Labour/Democratic left) to anticipate this default has left the country open to radical change. For some period before this change is effected, the tight (if unofficial) censorship of the official Irish media will not be sufficient to prevent the rise of demagogues on the extreme right and left, and of those republicans who will argue that the very creation of a 26-county Irish state is a British plot.

Of course, Ireland may continue the impossible project of deflating out of a recession with micromanagement from the ECB and IMF. The hardship being visited on the populace in this case will need to be justified. To take one specific example, the fact that the amount of Irish taxpayers' money has been used to rescue the cesspool that is the (fully nationalized) Anglo-Irish bank exceeds the total largesse from the EEC/EC/EU received since joining the EEC is rather glaring. The government will need to explain why the taxpayers' money is being spent in this counter-intuitive manner, and why certain anomalies have been allowed to continue. The first is that Anglo-Irish continued to refuse to release critical documents about its fall to the Irish corporate enforcement authorities, to the point of refusing point-blank to issue passwords for encrypted documents. A second is why debtors in the 9-figure range (and higher) still had access to their deposits after the bank was nationalized.

Anglo-Irish is in fact the tip of the iceberg. Here is a prediction; no explanation satisfactory to the Irish citizenry will ever be offered. In its absence, the authority of the state will weaken exponentially – perhaps no bad thing, given its current pervasiveness. The time taken to write this book is in fact a bet that the apparently radical remedies it espouses are in fact moderate compare to the forces about to take the Irish political world by storm.

Therefore, a la maniere de Hesse, what is eventually proposed in this book is a set of recommendations for how the economy, the arts, and technology should be managed. Or not, as the case may be; the state's incursions into the civil society structures that had withstood half a millennium of quite brutal colonialism quickened during the Ahern years, and show no sign of abating. This author's own experience (which features in chapter 8) as a software and music business entrepreneur as a university lecturer, and indeed as a long-serving member of National council of the Green Party, is of a small team of Irish people creating something of excellence, only for the state actually to destroy it, often by allowing criminals on its payroll to steal from the artists (in the music business). Alternatively, the state notices a small, excellent entity (some of the university departments) within its own domain and creates a whole sub-division to administer it, with the initial creators being replaced by incompetents (often foreigners) after being shafted.

Therefore, this book is above all a "J'accuse" directed at the Irish state. Ferriter (2004) points out that the De Valera ideal was a state that governed all aspects of Irish society. That dynamic apotheosized in Ahern; it was misfortune itself that it coincided with roulette substituting for a rational economic world order. As I have documented elsewhere (2004), the state often commits grotesquely criminal acts when encroaching on yet another domain (like music) or, conversely, preparing an attested well-functioning part of itself for privatization.

With perhaps 3.5 million authochtones, and well over a third in the greater Dublin area, a whisper at a cocktail reception, an extra name (in one famous example, that of Ahern's mistress) on a formal reception invite, a police inquiry that doesn't get followed up, all betoken massive power shifts. *In extremis*, of course, there is always the phone – and worse – for more direct types of pressure. Ahern seemed always to see himself as running a club for his friends, rather than anything resembling a country. In fact, when requested to address the houses of congress in 2008, his entourage consisted of a fellow-politician and some businessmen/ "property developers"; no other sector of Irish society was represented. Remarkably, his entourage behaved so badly at their hotel that the Secret Service was called.

At its best, Ireland was a country whose authochtones were capable of responding to global developments in generous and self-disciplined ways to produce a postcolonial culture – as distinct from consuming the most degrading of such global trends. Irish people made good emigrants, because often they had experienced the forces in their new lands in rawer form at home.

Sets of outline solutions are proposed in chapter 8, with many detailed recommendations emerging from the separate preceding chapters. It is clear that in 2009-2010, the ECB provided Ireland with a lifeline by providing liquidity to Ireland's zombie banking system. The national asset management agency (NAMA) was set up to buttress property prices, and provides another undeserved safety-net to the banking sector. NAMA, like Hank Paulson's original TARP, involved "buying" "assets" from the banks – essentially non performing property loans – at a discount. This discount was proposed to be around 30% at a time when bankruptcy cases going through the High Court were yielding an 70-80% discount. The balance was to be paid by the taxpayers, as the Minister of finance explicitly eschewed the simple mechanism, available until September 2010, of turning the bondholders into shareholders - approximately what Germany's Merkel was proposing as of late 2010. Even that massive bank bail-out might have worked, had it not been for the special treatment accorded Anglo-Irish, wherein earlier draft legislation that would require its debtors to access their deposit accounts was laughed out of the legislation. Yet there was a breathing space, as of 2011-2012, wherein things can be returned to normal without any political violence.

It would be very difficult to do worse than the state of play circum 2010. It is also very clear that there was a parcelling-out of various sources of revenue from 2000 or so, quickening with the second Ahern government of 2002. To property developers close to the government went all liquid capital, for the next generation at least, as the NAMA plan demonstrates. Remarkably, in a country which has a large number of non-Irish surnames, practically all the beneficiaries of NAMA – and thus recipients of loans often in the billions of dollars – have Irish surnames (Carroll, Macnamara, Mulryan, Ronan, etc). It can be considered the *reductio ad absurdum* of indigineity as a movement. In fact, these grotesque loans demonstrate, as does the subversion of the other aspects of the Irish state and civil society perfected by Ahern and his cronies for their own enrichment, that they believed that state institutions, including law enforcement, existed only to benefit them.

To forces close to the Minister for Health, Mary Harney, went revenue from health insurance as a USA-type HMO behemoth was created. Another NAMA client, Sean Quinn, believed he owned this – to the point of naming it "Quinn insurance" – until it was publicly taken from him. (Even more than other places, socialized medicine is a moral imperative in Ireland.) The innovation in 2009 was the possibility of the taxpayer having to maintain this feudal system. The midterm elections that year indicated that the taxpayer has no such desire, and e-voting has been called off; therein lies hope.

In Joyce's time, and until 1970, censorship controlled culture; now, stealing from the artists through mechanisms like IMRO and giving the proceeds to anodyne pop "stars", often created from within Ahern's innermost circle (i.e. family) does the same. It will be noted that Ireland's only recent original off- (or even close to) Broadway successes were tiny Rough Magic's "Improbable frequency", a musical tinged with science and espionage, and peopled by such untypical visitors to Ireland as Schroedinger and John Betjeman, both active in their wildly different ways in WW2 Dublin, and the low-budget "Once", a tiny paean to Dublin in its charming cinematographic form. By contrast, the huge budget of

“Grania” succeeded only in acting as life-support in prolonging the run. Has the lode of the “Celtic Twilight” finally been over-mined? Or was the Grania mistake precisely the opposite; that of bringing in the non-Irish writers of Les Miserables?

The epitome of a failed state is a failure by that state to assert its will within its internationally accepted borders. By that token, Ireland still has a functioning police force, and seems not to have failed; yet the grotesque and institutionalized criminality associated intimately with the state since 1997 was not sustainable after 2008. Moreover, the stratospheric costs associated with such essentials as housing, which resulted in the individual's having to compromise with the state merely to survive, decreased rapidly after 2008. (Home-grown food remains the outlier here; it is still very dear).

It is now open to a free Irish citizen(In Gaelic, the word for “citizen is “saoranach”, where “saor” means “free”)to reduce his contact with the terrifying institutions of the Irish state to a minimum while remaining resident in the country – this writer left in 2003 to emigrate to the USA when this was not possible. There will be Schadenfreude as the instruments of repression of her native urges toward freedom and creativity, from Anglo Irish bank onward, become revealed for the putrid carcases that they are. The libertarian's wish for private property and sound contracts will emerge naturally from civil society; the third such desideratum, that of a sound and realistic currency, will emerge after the possible withdrawal from the Euro as costs remain too high to create jobs. The “occupy” movement demonstrated that ownership of public assets needs to be taken seriously; if is ours, we –not you- will occupy it.

There will come massive political and social opportunity as the dead weight of the Ahern state brings down not only its new fetid institutions, but the British one still in existence nearly a century after “national liberation”. Terrence MacSwiney's dream of a liberation both personal and national will be realised.

1.2 The attempted political coup of 2004

There exists a famous cautionary tale about the limited horizons of intellectuals writing in a national framework. Though there are variants in many countries, the Polish version is the most renowned. An editor, appalled at the navel- gazing tendencies of his nationally- obsessed writers, in exasperation commands them to write about elephants. Soon enough, learned treatises come his way about “the elephant and the Polish question”.

One of the central goals in this book is to focus rather more on the elephant, and indeed to attempt to approach many issues of universal import by examining contemporary Ireland. In particular, it contends that Ireland’s main positive role in international affairs should be the provision of an Interlingua (common language) through which the rich north and poor south can find means of communication. Anglophone, yet again increasingly implementing Gaelic- friendly legislation; an ex-colony but seemingly comfortable with some aspects of globalisation; saturated by Anglo- American culture yet adept at preserving folkways under the radar, Ireland can show other traumatised postcolonial states how to heal and repossess themselves.

If the reader wishes to familiarise herself with a more conventional postcolonial discourse, collections like Castle (2001) with contributions like those of Kiberd, Gibbons, and Lloyd are perfectly adequate. Since then, however, the debate has quickened, with calls for new decolonial epistemes, sciences, and absolutely different epistemological and ontological foundations. It is in this context that this book has its origins.

Of course, recent history has witnessed a completely different impulse at work in Ireland from that which would seek to achieve moral leadership in the postcolonial world. The 1997- 2008 administration/Ahern government, the most rightwing government in Irish history, repeatedly attempted to make common cause with the Anglo- Saxon elite in the Iraq adventure. This can be contrasted with the early Irish free State which, almost a century ago, and acting almost alone, supported the first native Canadian land claim at the League of nations. The state that in 2001 was investing least in the EU in social protection has little continuity with the revolution on which it is based and from which it claims legitimacy, the 1916 rising initiated by the socialist theorist James Connolly.

Let us proceed straight to the meat. It is a contention of this book that the Ahern government attempted a political coup, culminating in an attempt to introduce a totally unaccountable form of e-voting in 2004. The vestiges of this coup attempt can still be seen in initiatives that now look like mere political kite-flying in these more civilised times. First of all, privatisations on a massive scale were being proposed. That the disastrous failure of the privatisation of the state telecommunications company resulted eventually in its ownership by "Sir" Tony O'Reilly and George Soros was probably a harbinger of what was really planned.

The outgoing chair of the Higher Education authority, Don Thornhill, argued vociferously during this period for privatisation of the state universities. (There are few such privatisations anywhere in world history; indeed, it is hard to see how the impulse to sell off the granted land and turn the institutions into websites could be argued against. Even in the US, where the landgrant universities receive as little as 7% of their funding from the state in some cases – presumably excluding research funds - the case for privatisation is not being taken seriously). The far-right corporatist (not to mention grossly corpulent) deputy prime minister proceeded to attempt to privatise a perhaps deliberately run-down health service. Plans for the privatisation of the national airline, Aer Lingus, were implemented. That corpus of the accumulated experience of humanity that we call "Celtic music" was privatised, and its current status is still ambiguous, as we see in chapter 7.

In the classic privatisation scenario, corporate enforcement is quickened in the state in order to reassure international investors. Some high-profile soft targets like the ancien regime's Charles Haughey were publicised, but few prosecutions were ever undertaken. (In fact, the Office of the Department of corporate enforcement – ODCE – has failed successfully to prosecute a single case in its first decade of existence). What makes this process suspiciously akin to the function that Greg Palast famously termed "briberization" was this random application of the law, show without substance. While the largely successful attempt at control of the Irish music industry was being implemented (and how many bands can you think of to come out of Ireland between 1997 and now?), companies who supported the government's line (pop bands and U2 only please, we're Irish) were allowed trade flagrantly illegally right under the government's nose. We discuss this in Chapter 7.

Chapter 6 deals with a further aspect of this enclosure of the intellectual commons; the bizarre attempt to centralise all software and digital media development in a Dublin city centre project that featured untenured staff from MIT Medialab as its keystone. The Irish Music Rights Organisation (IMRO), the cornerstone of the music scam, actually appealed for all its activity including the newly-acquired desideratum of the processing of "mechanical" rights (which relate to the physical manufacture of media on which songs are stored), to become part of a "one-stop" shop. To implement this type of centralisation requires a very powerful bureaucracy, and this empowerment comprised the second part of the political coup.

The classic definition of fascism is the unification of labour and business in a corporate structure under the aegis of state. Since 1987, there has been in existence a much-ballyhooed "social partnership" between the unions and business interests, mediated by the state. There existed in 2005, as there is normally, a cabinet post for a minister for Labour. In summer 2005, the Prime Minister (and would-be President for life) announced that a new department for partnership with a staff of over 100 was to be opened under his direct control, unmediated by either Cabinet or parliament (not to mention the electorate). This became known simply and in sinister fashion as the "implementation" body; interestingly, as in 2007, in 2009 the Labour party explicitly rejected going into government with Ahern's party before an election. Ahern' party were in any case too small to form a two-party governing coalition with Labour after the 2011 general election.

The bureaucratization of the country, and incursion of the state into civil society, has continued apace. Grant applications for the arts and sciences are subjected to massive delay as state interest groups extract their pound of flesh. The new class that Ahern created as he massively increased civil servants' salaries is in truth terrifyingly obstructive to anyone trying to make a life for themselves in Ireland.

None of this holds, of course, for transnationals who want to get into Ireland. The way is made extremely clear; as native entrepeneurship shrinks to vanishing point, weighed down by punitive costs and lack of state support, companies like Wyeth and Intel announced expansions almost weekly from 2002 to 2005. The low corporation tax rate approved by the EU (Lord, make them pay normal corporate tax, but not yet), coupled with the effective prevention of strikes in the public sector and acceptance of epidemic levels of workplace bullying, both the result of the "partnership" agreements, promised to turn Ireland into corporate heaven. The inflated wages in the public sector then pushed prices up to the point where private sector employment became prohibitive as costs spiralled. Quite simply, civil servants pushed up the prices of the good housing and other facilities to levels that made them unaffordable to private-sector employees.

Only the crash of 2008 allowed us gain access to another trend of the Ahern years; the allocation of practically all liquidity within the Irish banking system to a set of carefully chosen "property developers". These gentlemen (or at least males) proved to be excitable in the extreme; Sean Mulryan, a friend of Bono, produced a property plan of over $15 billion; Garrett Kelleher paid over $30 million an acre for a 2.2 acre site in Chicago, with the goal of building America's tallest building; Derek Quinlan bought the London Connaught hotel, and – a moment which he and his cronies claim moved them to tears - flew the Irish tricolour over it. And so on; China, India, Britain – Ireland surpassed the USA as the biggest external investor in British property during the aughts – and, bizarrely, the Apthorp building in New York was also in Irish hands.

Toys these boys indeed had; Quinlan's mansion in Cap Ferrat, and the $30 million New York townhouse he would not deign to live in; Mulryan's scores of racehorses; helicopters to the point that onlookers described the scene at the Galway races as the "Ride of the Valkyries" scene in "Apocalypse Now" In Galway, the "developers" came to petition Ahern for even more clemency from the banks (only 25% of the loans transferred to NAMA were found to be paying even interest repayments, let alone principal). The obsession with helicopters is piquant; Ahern's crony Sean Dunne, his companion at the notorious address to the Houses of congress, where the entourage caused a security alert at their hotel, brought a team of architects , visiting Dublin for the first time, straight from the airport to overfly the near-derelict hotels in central Dublin which were to become his masterpiece. Dunne's dream never took flesh; nor did the Treasury holdings fantasy of turning a chimney of Battersea Power station into a one-table restaurant. As for McKillen, his "ownership" of the Franklin building in Boston is compromised somewhat by the fact that Anglo Irish, his funder, is also his tenant and his 2012 English court case v. Quinlan.

Coupled with this destruction of normal commercial life in favour of a self-appointed "elite" was to be the denial of electoral suffrage. As electronic voting almost destroyed democracy in America, and contributed greatly to the climate of fear which existed there from 2001 to 2008, it should not have even been suggested for Ireland, which has a robust history of proportional representation. It is fair to say that, even though the Irish showed little understanding of citizenship, we certainly understood voting even before semi-independence. In 2004 an attempt was made to introduce an utterly egregious e-voting system to Ireland. A panel was appointed under the chairmanship of Justice Smith to investigate it. The firm supplying the software first asked the panel to sign a huge financial indemnification against any leaking of trade secrets. They agreed. When it became clear that the trade secrets were not as valuable as they might have been, in that there was no software ready only 5 weeks before the election in which the system was to be rolled out, the (Dutch) firm in question threatened to sue the panel for libel for its forthcoming report.

When it duly came forth, the report was damning. A typical e-voting system involves about 50,000 lines of code. The author is a Ph.D. in computer science, and can testify that the chances of debugging and testing a bugged program of this length on a security-critical theme in 5 weeks are precisely nil. (Ireland's history of failed computer projects includes E 400 million being wasted in 2005 in the health services on what was essentially a payroll program which had to be abandoned. IBM and Deloitte Touche were the main beneficiaries). We comment about other such lacunae later; the costs of the machines, storage, etc, exceeded E50 million. There is nothing to indicate that this was anything other than an attempt to destroy democracy in Ireland. Ahern's response was to try and force Smith's retirement from the bench. The security for the system was to be handled by a company jointly owned by the British Army and the Carlyle group. All of this information is in the public domain. Only in late 2005 did the Minister in question, moved to another department where he was busily privatising Aer Lingus, confess that e-voting was unlikely for the next general election. Justice Smith will go down in history as an Irish hero, particularly now that the e-voting project has now deservedly reached an ignominious end.

Another innovation was to be Irish involvement in Anglo-Saxon military adventures. While there is evidence that Ireland was originally part of Bush's "coalition of the willing" in the Iraq invasion, and Ahern himself has suggested that Ireland was part of this coalition, we need not focus on this. Ahern later complimented himself publicly on his part in Saddam's downfall, before reversing this after his electoral *annus horribilis* of 2004.While this went on, Ahern broke a pre-election promise in associating Ireland with NATO through the so-called partnership for peace, and allowed Shannon Airport to be used for US soldiers on their way to Iraq as for CIA rendition victims on their way to death by torture God knows where. The fears of a conspiracy theorist will not be assuaged by the news that a tunnel was to be built by a Halliburton subsidiary close to Shannon Airport at a cost of E 372 million to the Irish taxpayer, complementing that firm's projects in Dublin and Cork (and of course the work with BP in the Gulf that ended so well for everybody involved).

While all this was going on, British behaviour has been audacious. Having manoeuvred the Irish into rescinding their land claim on Northern Ireland through the increasingly unworkable Good Friday agreement, they made it clear that they felt free to suspend any provision of the agreement any time they wished, starting with its fulcrum, the democratically elected assembly. Even Ahern's office wrote angrily to Blair, calling this action "precipitate". The British have also quietly been working to write the Irish out of world history, where possible; the move used is a subsumption of Irish history to the encompassing British narrative of an erstwhile world power gallantly and with magnanimity renouncing its white man's burdens.

The final British gesture of contempt was majestic. Having a score years before declared their lack of "selfish" strategic or other military interests in the North-west corner of Ireland, they decided that a centre of espionage away from the British mainland was a good idea. And so an MI5 building was commissioned, and staffed, in "Northern Ireland". To practise, the staff was given the task of intelligence gathering in that locale; the police service were put out to the grunt work. Yet even that is not the punch line; it is, rather, that no holder of an Irish passport could apply for one of these 400 MI5 jobs. At this time of exquisite Anglo Irish union of hearts, no Irish need apply.

1.3 Irish auto-exoticism

No previous knowledge of, or interest in, Ireland is assumed in this book, and it is explicitly a beginner's guide to Ireland. Few countries its size have been written about so extensively. At the extremes, the English occupation is seen as a civilizing force or the most egregious colonisation in human history. Remarkably, the Irish writer Conor O'Brien achieved both perspectives at different times in the course of a long and varied career. The lack of native styles in the classical arts, sciences, and general administrative structures is alternatively interpreted as being due to native dullness or postcolonial hangover (The massive achievements of emigrant Irish in every realm of high human engagement biases this writer to the latter interpretation). Conversely. the relatively unspoiled physical environment may be due either to Irish love of nature or the lack of financial means to ruin it, with recent events like the M3 through Tara/Skryne suggesting the latter.

The term "auto-exoticism" a Hibernian equivalent of Edward Said's "orientalism", was originally coined with reference to Ireland's insistence on attempting to be a mystery to itself. Of course, orientalism is a projection, and auto- exoticism is an introjection. In Joyce's Ulysses, the city described is in many ways a generic contemporary city: the main protagonist is Jewish, perhaps modelled on Joyce's personal friend Italo Svevo, and thus inherently disposed to the cosmopolitan. The stage version of Flann O'Brien's "At Swim two birds", soon to become a film, features a hilarious sequence wherein the players decide that what is unique about them as Irish people is "leppin" (jumping). None of them rise over two feet: Not a bad exemplification of auto-exoticism

Elsewhere (2004, 197-214), I have written about two of the main functions of nation: to protect against genocide and to support those movements of the universal human spirit due to genius loci that we later identify as national culture. The Irish are utterly unique in willing their own ethnic demise. In Armenian communities, the pressure builds to compel Turkey to admit its genocide of at least 45% of the Armenian population. Augusto Espiritu, in "Five Faces of Exile" (Stanford University Press, 2005) speaks of how national longing is heightened by exile. The intellectual class favoured by the Mexican state vets scripts like "Frida" before production is allowed.

By contrast, John Irvin's "The Boys and Girl from Clare" explicitly imposes a blackface minstrel narrative on Irish traditional music, which was becoming a world cultural force. Cubans pride themselves on their social welfare systems, whose efficacy has been admitted by Wolffenssohn of the world Bank; as he left office to be replaced by one of the architects of the Iraq War in 2005, a social welfare officer in Ireland was caught running a male prostitution ring, including a schoolboy, from his workplace. As Ireland is forced to open up to the rest of the world, native Indians in Bolivia's El Alto allow no whites in a population of close to a million.

The Irish have had an immensely proud history in education, health and civil rights (think of Ron Hennessy and the Berrigan brothers, among countless others) both in the US and the poor south. To return to the theme, then, a nation should uphold positive movements of the human psyche and indeed the whole organism. The prostitution of Ireland that we have seen in the past decade has resulted in a decadent, culturally stagnant, and politically suspect entity to replace a country that has been the hope of the world in its finest moments.

It is one of the tenets of this book that, Ahern's political coup now defeated, the impulses, privileges, and responsibilities in themselves that Irish people discern as arising from their Irishness make them fully capable of radical change (if not quite as radical as that from 1997 to 2008). There is no commitment here to any Hegelian notion of nation, although it is perfectly scientifically acceptable to contend that nations have emergent properties unpredictable from their component parts. There is no notion of a "romantic Ireland", which was initially in any case a French concept adopted by the Young Irelanders of the mid 19th century.

The practical steps envisaged here are substantially less radical than saddling the Irish populace with more than E150 billion of additional national debt through NAMA and other mechanisms and involving them in a fascist state which participates in military adventures. It is as well to restate; should the Irish administration of 2011 onwards manage to speak quietly and with respect to its citizenry why the drastic economic steps of 2008-2011 were necessary, all will be well. In its discourse, the establishment will also be able to explain why failed property developers and ex-public "servants" are getting additional billions of public money.

In the absence of this mature discourse, an intense and public attack on corruption will be necessary. This will either be carried on by the state, or the followers of the demagogues who are surely imminent on the Irish scene. Let us be clear; the Irish were perfectly happy to accept a high level of public corruption while their economy apparently boomed. Chang (2008) points out that corruption at this level is, in any case, a relative concept, and that would-be reformers like de Mello in Brazil often end up hoist by their own petard.

Secondly, the single most valuable resource that the Irish have is a feeling for their own country that can indeed be described as love. The neoliberal narrative from 2000-2007 was that Ireland had become great by opening its borders; as Chang's main thesis (2008, 172) goes, the free market is not the correct system for a nation's economic development. In fact, we go a stage further here; economic development is not really what a country is about in the first place. In fact, the first task of a resurgent Irish state is to make official what is now already informally being accepted; what seemed like old shibboleths of culture, particularly landscape (including built heritage), genetics and the arts, are no such thing. They are the real wealth of the country; and given the set of crises that economics is increasingly prone to admit it has, and the palpable end of the Washington consensus, it is economics, not the rest of culture, which looks more evanescent and insecure as foundation material. Indeed, Chang (2008, 217) argues that economists like himself may be precisely the wrong people to plan a country's future.

Some specifics; all energy resources like the Corrib gas field are to be nationalised, and planned privatisations are to be terminated. It is clear, following a government report in 2006, that Ireland's fossil fuel deposits are massive, and their being given away from the 1980's was national suicide. Secondly, a full frontal attack on the problem of personal debt is to be launched. Thirdly, Ireland is to attempt to decrease its per capita energy consumption (100 Giga Joules per person internationally still allows the low infant mortality rates that we have recently been blessed with; a cold, wet island like Ireland will need more). With the attack on personal debt, perhaps through enlightened "fresh start" bankruptcy legislation, will come a freeing of creative energy as people no longer spend all their time and money on repaying banks. The creative status quo of the early 1990's, with a plethora of native tech firms, new creative writers, and technically accomplished artists and athletes, will quickly re-establish itself.

All this is a post-default scenario; or, worst-case, a scenario in which a revolutionary situation has been engineered by ECB/IMF heavy-handedness and the revolution has played itself out. This writer sees Ireland withdrawing from the euro, and protecting the newly nascent (and renascent) native industries catering not just for export, but basic needs like food and clothing. Chang (2008, 214) gives a list of successful such protections, starting with Britain's wool industry. It may be the case that Ireland withdraws completely from the international capital markets, at least temporarily; as of late 2010, it desisted in any case from bond issues, for lack of buyers, and in the face of its old bonds being dumped. On re-emerging, it should do so with a currency that reflects the actual economic productivity of the land and its people. Further recommendations are given throughout this book.

The population of the entire Republic of Ireland is that of a medium- sized capital city. Like other small countries, then, realities can be imposed by bureaucratic fiat and impress themselves first on the state apparatus through government agencies and then on civil society through mechanisms like the social partnership agreements between business and organised Labour. The state broadcaster, RTE, for a long time held a near monopoly on public discourse while also catering to the lowest common denominator. There is no reason for RTE to exist in its current form; a small high-culture station would suffice, with private capital handling popular culture.

An equivalent of the American constitution's first amendment is urgently required in Ireland. It is in fact relatively easy to discern patterns in the development of the Irish state as the official credo changes. The grotesquerie thrown up by the attempt to create a Roman Catholic theocracy from the 1930s onward is paralleled by the attempts that we have noted in the early 21st century to unite labour and business in a corporate structure under the direct control of the political executive. The heady mixture of brutality and arbitrary legal flat in both cases is probably postcolonial in origin as distinct from being the product of native genius.

If Mexico is distressingly far from God and close to the United States. Ireland, at a similar remove from the divine, is but a stone's throw from most of the great imperial powers of the past 500 years. It is also the first port of call for Americans travelling to Europe and Eurasia, the new cockpit of the world. These accidents of geography, which worked against Ireland for the best part of a millennium seemed to deliver unto it spectacular success that has now proved ephemeral.

In macroeconomic terms, the dream became reality, if briefly so; Ireland's economic growth from 1995 to 2007, according to conventional indices like GDP, GNP, national debt as a percentage of national Income, and so on, was spectacular. The low corporation tax regime, it seemed, would ensure massive incoming investment *in perpetuo*. In the apparent paradox we noted, during this period, its strange genius at popular music has failed to manifest itself in any new international success of close to the magnitude of those in the past. A negative moral eschatology, the attempt to become as banal, prurient, and debauched as one can, seemed to have kicked in to national culture.

For example, listeners to RTE, which as we have seen is in state institutional terms Ireland's equivalent to the BBC were likely up to recently to hear lengthy discourses about defecation in the streets, and the necessity for putting Vaseline on one's anus before eating curry. The premature death in 2010 of a major perpetrator of this filth, one Gerry Ryan, resulted in a suspiciously orchestrated national week of mourning as aspects of the control of Irish media threatened to be discussed publicly. When he was found to have died partly as a result of cocaine ingestion, few of us were surprised. The talentlessness of the major Irish broadcasters, particularly on RTE, is striking; their control by a single agency (Noel Kelly) and the trash being played as "music" is unique, with even the Eurovision song contest now culturally above the standard of Irish popular culture.

People traffickers, particularly from Eastern Europe, have brought prostitutes and sex slaves into the country; a land that was pornography free only decade or so ago now has magazine shelves groaning with porn magazines. Finally, even in brute economic terns, the state failed properly to intervene when property prices went up first linearly and then – it seemed – almost exponentially (in parts of Dublin). In conjunction with these trends, the health and social Services were perhaps deliberately being run down. Valuable state land was sold for a song to government supporters.

While the attempts at creating a natural sports stadium and academy of the performing arts sank under their own financial weight, exhaling a miasma of favours and corruption, no attempts were made by the least professionally and academically qualified executive in modern European history to create lasting national institutions that could reflect on the continuity of the present and future with the positive aspects of the past. In impoverished Botswana – to cite just one contrast - the president has made clear amid the Aids epidemic that a country that has lost its history has lost its soul.

So what of the factors that can make Ireland unique, the Soul of Ireland, as it were? Ireland has managed to keep folkways alive; so has Papua New Guinea, where the "bushkanaka" (an equivalent of "paddy" in that Papuans apply it to themselves, but it is a gross insult from anyone else, and can cause the speaker to be deported) bands have synthesised their folk music with Western hymns to produce gems like "Bosavi". Ireland is an ex-colony, a status exemplified by the behaviour of Britain from 1845-

1850: so are exceedingly many other countries. The reels used in "Irish" music and the theme tune from Riverdance are all imports.

No claim is being made here, then, for Irish uniqueness. On the contrary; the project is about the extent to which Ireland manifests a universal object lesson. In its positive impulses, Ireland has shown how a traditional society can successfully confront modernity (that hopeful monster, Flann O'Brien, attempted a leap straight into an often hilarious postmodernity at great cost to himself) It has yet to demonstrate how an ex—colony can eschew derivative political and administrative structures: its leadership has yet to see an international treaty it doesn't like. That this is utterly out of keeping with the impulse behind the creation of the original Irish state will be argued in the next section

1.4 Terrence MacSwiney - Ireland's Fanon - and neocoloniality

It could be argued that the rallying-cry for the decolonial turn (a phrase that will be used here for the active attempt to sunder colonial bonds) in contrast to academic postcolonialism, can be found in the life and work of Terence MacSwiney. MacSwiney will supply the political historical basis for the viewpoint to be outlined in this book, as James Joyce (probably a blood relation) will supply the cultural and existential. Born into Cork's agricultural class, his father a failed and often absent businessman, MacSwiney had risen professionally through a plethora of talents (he was poet, playwright, political scientist, publisher, journalist and accountant) and apparently had everything to live for. There is real pathos in lines from his "Principles of freedom" (which we shall cite from its Gutenberg press edition using chapter and section, occasionally also using his daughter's citations of his work) when he speaks of political martyrs;

> "...not that they despised life or threw it lightly away for none knew better than them its grandeur" (MacSwiney, 2004, XIX-i)

He learned Gaelic, painfully, in adulthood; both his sisters and future wife followed the trend of Cork's "quality" in going to Oxford University to study. Later, as irredentist Irish republicans who did not recognize the Irish state, his monoglot-anglophone sisters ran a private school in Cork and were known as "the republicans with English accents", with all the potential for ridicule that the term implies. It is relevant to mention that his mother was English; many of the republicans of this period were of mixed parentage. Both of the sisters tried hard to learn Irish.

MacSwiney wrote plays, poems, and political tracts; his "Principles of Freedom", which will concern us here, had a lasting effect on the Indian independence movement and indeed throughout Asia, with both the Burmese and Ho Chi Minh paying tribute to him. Ironically, in view of later events, he gave the term "Fianna Fail", roughly speaking "the warriors of Ireland", one of its first public coinages in one of his periodicals. He recruited successfully for the Irish volunteers before the 1916 rising and came bitterly to regret agreeing with the order countermanding Cork's involvement – an order that came with a rash of other mutually contradictory such orders, making him surely blameless. In nay case, his later steadfastness proves that this non-engagement was not due to lack of courage. In 1918, he was elected a Sinn Fein M.P., and two years later replaced his British state-assassinated friend, Tomās MacCurtain, as Mayor of Cork. When later himself arrested by the British, he enunciated (if a trifle grandiosely) the leitmotif of 20th-century national resistance movements:

> "The position is that I am Lord Mayor of Cork and Chief Magistrate of this city and I declare this court illegal and those who take part in it liable to arrest under the laws of the Irish republic." (MacSwiney Brugha, 2006, p. 284)

Presaging Gandhi, he announced that he would attenuate the two-year prison term inflicted on him by embarking on a hunger strike. This tactic of refusing to recognize the validity of the judicial system was used by IRA prisoners arrested in both political jurisdictions in Ireland until recently. The modern use of the hunger strike to death is peculiarly Irish in origin, has roots deep in the culture, and was deployed by the IRA with great success in the early 1980s, leading to the current high electoral standing of Sinn Fein.

MacSwiney died on 25 October, 1920, after fully 74 days on hunger strike. One would shudder at the thoughts that so refined and courageous a man must have had when it became obvious that the British would not back down, were it not for his own testimony that he viewed it as a compensation for his non-action in 1916, and that his hunger strike was the most potent weapon in his comrades' arsenal, and thus had to be continued. He left an infant daughter, whom we shall later hear from, with a beautiful heiress wife whom he knew to be unreliable. His final days were front-page news in France and Italy. La Scala went dark on the night of his death. The US Congress held hearings at which his wife and sister spoke.

Yet these external events, earth-shattering though they undoubtedly are, could well be equaled in impact by his insight into the colonised psyche. Laing (1967) talked about psychotic breakdown as resulting from a failure of self-authentication. In particular, he argued that social pressures can cause a rupture as a "false self" system, identified with the body, is given consensual validation while the “authentic” self becomes increasingly a mental epiphenomenon. In his later work (1990), he develops the theme with the hypothesis that the false self is itself capable of reaching some truth, however distorted.

MacSwiney's variation on this theme is simultaneously Jeffersonian and Laingian:

> "A man facing life is gifted with certain powers of soul and body. It is of vital importance to himself and the community that he be given a full opportunity to develop his powers, and to fill his place worthily. In a free state, he is in the natural environment for full self-development. In an enslaved state, it is the reverse. When one country holds another in subjection, that other suffers materially and morally. It suffers materially, being a prey for plunder. It suffers morally because of the corrupt influences the bigger nation sets at work to maintain its ascendancy." (MacSwiney Brugha, 2006, p. 289).

While many of MacSwiney's public statements are seeped through with Catholic nationalism, by one account this did not stop him from urging the assassination of the pro-British Bishop Cohalan of Cork (suggested in Costello, 2003, pg. 76). We may take it, then, that the self-authentication message of this next quote readily admits of a secular interpretation:

> "We fight for freedom — not for the vanity of the world, nor to have a fine conceit of ourselves, not to be as bad —or if we prefer to put it so, as big as our neighbours. The inspiration is drawn from a deeper element of our being. We stifle for self-development individually and as a notion. If we don't go forward we must go down. It is a matter of life and death; it is our soul's salvation … a majority has no right to annul it, and no power to destroy it. Tyrannies may persecute, slay, or banish those who defend it; the thing itself is indestructible … “ (ibid)

MacSwiney's intellectual breakthrough is the finding of an ontological basis for national struggle. To make explicit the links with the more lucid early Laing (1967), "ontological security" is the state in which the authentic self identifies with the body. Under colonization, the authentic self retreats, and a false self system colonises psyche and organism. The false self system, of course, is not by any means devoid of evidence to support its claim for veridicality: Ireland the theocracy had tens of thousands of massive Catholic churches bedecked with gaudy statues and a standing Vatican army of tens of thousands of Irish celibates. The ideological resources of theocratic Ireland were at least matched in the universal media approval of a permanent bubble economy, the encroachment of the state into all potentially liberating areas of civil society, draconian libel laws with stratospheric legal costs involved in pursuing even the simplest of defences (tiny, broke Ireland had 3 of the biggest 20 law firms in the EU in 2009) and international organs like the EU commission and WTO flattering Ireland for its conforming to their dictates as the Catholic Church flattered its faith in theirs.

“Principles of Freedom” is a book of its time; MacSwiney is innocent of postmodernism. It is above all a revolutionary text. There is little reference to the specifics of the administrative apparatus used to suppress the Irish; the question has been simplified to the search for self-realisation. While “life, liberty, and the pursuit of happiness” is not explicitly mentioned, the sources are ultimately those in the Enlightenment that also produced Thomas Jefferson. Let us be clear; there is no claim here that the Irish are natural rebels, or that what happened is anything but a few steps above the Spanish identification of the guerrilla warrior as quintessentially Spanish (and therefore, in apparent paradox, also an urban bourgeois) a mere few years after Napoleon had defeated their empire. However, it behooves us to listen;

> “A spiritual necessity makes the true significance of our claim to freedom; the material aspect is only a secondary consideration” (I-iii)

The republicanism of his sisters was later dismissed by Fianna Fail, the institutional revolutionary party of Ireland (think of Mexico’s PRI), as too “spiritual” (Ferriter, 2004). Yet MacSwiney is concerned that political violence/armed struggle must have a solid moral grounding:

> “The tyranny must be excessive...intolerable...manifestly no other way...a moral certainty of success” (III-iii)

Let us be clear; the position of this book is that the current Irish state is a colonising force, profoundly criminal, and inimical to the self-realisation of the Irish people individually and as a collective. Yet democratic means still exist for its overthrow; had the removal of such by the introduction of electronic voting been accomplished, political violence against the Irish state would have been morally justifiable. MacSwiney sees the arguments that will be used to counter him and quotes Balmoz:

> "We must overthrow the arguments ... by the advocates of blind submission" (XVII-ii)

One such was his contemporary GB Shaw, who sought to defend empire, and the necessity for keeping Tibet British, by referring to the "sacredness of his own national soil" (IV-iv). On the contrary, says MacSwiney, Shaw "cannot co-operate in the civilising process without practising..cruelty" (ibid.).

While, as already has been said, James Joyce will provide many of the leitmotiven in chapters 2 and 6 for the historical foundations of the existential and cultural suggestions of this book, MacSwiney has an interesting point to make about intellectual freedom:

> "It is the freedom of the individual to follow his star and reach his goal" (X-iii)
>
> Moreover, "a nation's literature is an index to its mind" (X-i)

The use of Celtic revival tropes in the theatrical output of the Early Irish Free State is legendary, in all senses (Ferriter, 2004). (Indeed, the history of the Irish state has been so obviously done to death that Ferriter, still in his 30's, took to writing counterfactual histories. Here we are making no attempt to duplicate this work). Yet again, Ireland simply mimics Garibaldi-era Italy, with the celebration in Verdi; early 19th century Spain, with theatrical references to the expulsion of the Moors and Corsicans; and so on.

It cannot be long before an Irish Milan Kundera emerges to explore the subversion of the relationship between self and other, mind and body, that the ubiquitous Irish state implements quite as successfully as Kundera's communist Czechoslovakia. The totalising dynamic in the Irish state apparatus is one of the many depressing conclusions to be reached from all the multitude of histories (ibid.). Public order acts have limited protest to the mildest of gestures; in any case, as in May 2002, the largely unaccountable Irish police force can be caught on camera breaking protesters' bones in unprovoked attacks and get away almost scot-free. (The Morris tribunal report of 2006 confirmed and indeed amplified the worst fears of many of us about the Irish police.)

The discussion on "consciousness and nation" in Chapter 2 extends our analysis of coloniality, consciousness, and cognition. For the moment, the argument can be anticipated thus: epistemic breakthroughs are subordinate to ontological ones. Specifically, the program outlined by Mignolo (2006) and other decolonial theorists for an epistemic revolution to supercede European totalizing "modernity" is consequent to, and modulated by, an assertion of authentic individuality at that level in the psyche at which the person and nation collide.

1.5 A colony once again

Let us hence to the main theme of this book. In the next few pages, I am going to argue that Ireland is experiencing a modern colonization project. The resources of Irish Roman Catholic nationalism (as distinct from secular republicanism), represented by all three of the Sinn Fein parties (including Fianna Fáil and Fine Gael) are being deployed to represent this project as a continuation of the 1916 independence impulse. Concession to the British claim on Northern Ireland is itself somehow packaged by Gerry Adam's Sinn Fein as part of a nationalist narrative. The resources of the Irish state, purveyors of Roman Catholic theocracy a mere forty years ago, have been recruited to supply whatever infrastructural support and intellectual gloss takeover of Ireland by transnational capitalist interests requires. The trade unions have been domesticated by a set of "social partnership" agreements, and their membership consists mostly of "closed shop" civil servants. Therein, their goal is to prevent strikes, and the emergence of real unions. Academic tenure, and with it a critical societal source of freedom of speech hangs on by a thread after a fortunately botched attempt to destroy it that we discuss later. In the meantime, Victorian standards of industrial relations have led to suicides and stress-related deaths as bullying by employers receives state sanction.

As one would expect in a new colony, alcohol consumption, suicide, and crime have all skyrocketed. Areas in which Ireland once excelled, like the quality end of popular music, have been almost totally destroyed, and not one major Irish act has appeared in the past decade. This we discuss in

Chapter seven. In Chapter six we discuss the simultaneous destruction of the native software industry. While writers like Garvin (2004) would have us believe that Ireland has emerged from a clerical educational miasma into a brave new world of high-tech, the fact is that Irish high-tech has almost died over the past decade. Insane projects like Medialab and (to a lesser extent of insanity but even larger of money) Science Foundation Ireland, state attempts to appropriate technology into its corporate structures, have failed miserably to produce entrepreneurs as the academics involved in them gratefully pocket the additional subvention to their already inflated salaries. The states' own economic research institute confirmed this in 2005.

That worse was planned is now evident from reports on electronic voting in the U.S. Non-paper-trail e-voting will simply never again be used in civilized democracies as the only voting method.; the lesson received by Ireland's prime minister was to try and introduce it in Ireland. Already a corporatist state with contempt for individuals that is most unrepublican, the Irish state has attempted a truly fascist totalitarianism since the proposal of e-voting quickened in 2004.

That we discuss below. First of all, the issue of whether Ireland ever was a colony is discussed in, inter alia, McDonough (2005). Sean Ryder's contribution (166), invoking Joe Cleary's work, adds much-needed clarity:

> "Ireland was a colony because of its position in an emergent Capitalist world system – not just because of its political relationship to Britain" (in McDonough, ed. (2005))

Kinealy's careful analysis of British behaviour during the Great Famine leads her to the same conclusion (63):

> "The responses of the British government during the famine demonstrated that Ireland had not achieved commensurate status with the population of Britain and that the Act of union was colonialism under another disguise"

She is assisted greatly in coming to that conclusion by the census report of 1851 which, referring to "famine, disease, and emigration between 1845 and 1851" adds "demonstrating as they do the general advancement of the country" (ibid.).

Eagleton (2005), in the same collection, points out the many different types of coloniality that exist, with his model of a super-privileged elite bringing in enormous numbers of immigrants close to the model of neoliberal Ireland. He wishes, with this author, to transcend romantic nationalism and to stress enlightenment ideas of autonomy in a new national impulse that in a paradox that we have seen repeatedly starting with MacSwiney, is yet simultaneously existential (332):

> “To be Irish or Tibetan is to be a human being, and thus to be entitled to self-determination on that ground alone....it is people, not peoples, who have a right to self-government”

Let us look at a current discourse on coloniality that fits modern Ireland like a glove. Cheah (2006) follows Mignolo (2006) in indicating the limits of current postcolonial thought, and supercedes him in depicting the new colony. Mignolo (ibid) inveighs against current postcolonial theory for a variety of reasons. Conventional "disembodied" (see below in "consciousness and nation") Marxist theorists, delinkers of political and economical ties as a mode of revolt, he excoriates for their emphasis on political economy to the exclusion of a new episteme. Two comments here: first of all, this book comes down on the side of the notion that the central findings of the physical sciences are not cultural fiats. Secondly, some of Fanon's writings, as distinct from his life of action, are disembodied in this sense.

Mignolo's second target is poststructuralism-influenced postcolonial theorists like Edward Said. These, Mignolo argued, are simply continuing the secular proselytizing work of the major European powers; exalting Europeanism as modernity, preaching racism, and reinforcing the construction of an "other" by a "totalitarian idea of totality" (Cheah, 2006, p. 9)

Mignolo's antidote is disappointing; a two-pronged proposal with frankly anodyne and deeply controversial facets. The former is quite simply intercultural dialogue with a particular emphasis on the global south. As Cheah (2006, 11) remarks, this sounds remarkably like Unesco, which of course does not diminish its truth, but its usefulness – like that of Unesco - remains at issue. The second is a plea for a contextual re-embodiment of thought with new epistemes emerging from the erstwhile colonial’s re-engagement with their land. (We discuss the Cognitive Science implications in Chapter 2.) Yet as Cheah (ibid) remarks, autochthonous “embodied” language is quite as full of hierarchy as that of the colonial powers.

Cheah (ibid) proceeds to an altogether more sophisticated analysis of our contemporary colonial project, one that fits Ireland disturbingly well:

> "Yet, one might argue that exploitative development in contemporary globalization operates not by racist techniques of exclusion and marginalization, but precisely by including, integrating, and assimilating every being into the circuit of the international division of labour. This is done by transforming them into reserve labour power through techniques of what Foucault called biopower," (Cheah, 2006, p.11)

The Irish establishment's concern with racism, as Ireland depopulated countries like Latvia and Estonia of their skilled computer personnel, is above all about introducing reserve labour power in the greatest immigration the island has ever seen. Specifically, there were over 400,000 immigrants into Ireland from 2002 to 2006. Fully 200,000 immigrants and/or potential immigrants acquired Irish social security numbers in 2006 alone. The grand total is now 750k. No blame attached to these immigrants; they are simply pawns in the attempt to story the Irish people as a separate identifiable ethnicity.

In parallel with the people came capital, which was used disproportionately to drive up the cost of real estate. At the start of the Irish boom in 1995, the Irish level of personal debt was €15 billion; 11 years later, it was well over €300 billion. Of course there was an accompanying consumer boon, with regular cheery media reports about just what wonderful little consuming devils the Irish had become. It is a textbook echo of the situation Cheah describes in his analysis of the new coloniality:

> "The different understanding of power as productive as opposed to regressive seems especially important in contemporary globalization where the flow of transnational capital fabricates the economic well-being of nation-states and their individual citizens." (ibid)

Parts of the Irish establishment, like the Irish Times, finally began to recognize this (Brennan, 2006). The state has been preparing for some time in precisely the manner that Cheah outlines by signing every international trade deal submitted to it and attenuating citizenship:

> "First, at the macro-logical level of global political economy, states undertake aggressive policy initiatives to open up their markets and attract foreign capital. Second, at the level of the biopolitical production of the individual and the population, techniques of discipline and government craft the bodies of individuals as bodies capable of work, and create their

> needs and interests as members of a population. Third, at the level of social reproduction, global mass consumer culture also leads to the proliferation of sophisticated consumer needs and desires." (ibid).

Finally, the previously simple logic of coloniality needs to be enriched in this new dispensation;

> "These processes constitute the conditions of the political and economic self-determination and sovereignty of collective subjects and the self-mastery and security of individual subjects. In other words, the current state of power relations is an effect of multiple processes that are dynamic, heterogeneous and unstable, processes that cannot be reduced to a single logic of coloniality, although the latter can emerge as their effect" (ibid).

Ireland was up to recently Cheah's paradigm scenario; at this book's end, we propose an even darker scenario. The colonization is by transnational capital rather than the British who have succeeded by repeated acts of genocide in reducing the Irish population to a minute fraction of their own. All that remains for Britain to do, having neutralized the IRA, is to write the Irish out of world history. In the past, as we shall see, they had to highlight the work of historians like Pocock; as things stand, the Irish state seems happy to fund chairs and seminars to promote its own oblivion – or at least that of the ethnicity that it claims to exemplify and indeed nurture.

MacSwiney's concern about the moral decay of the colonized is not assuaged by the panoply of porn newly arrived in Ireland. Pace Cheah, the "global mass consumer culture" has often led to needs and desires that are less than sophisticated. MacSwiney's great decolonial movement, which produced at least a statelet, was the confluence of many irreproducible trends; the culture of the Celtic twilight at least led to the rediscovery of fragments of Gaelic high culture; Franco-American secular republicanism had yet to be twisted by Roman Catholicism in Ireland. The statelet, as we shall see, was deformed at birth by a civil war. The massive projects it might have embarked on, like the full revival of the Irish language as the main vernacular, were thus deeply compromised; yet it is true that both the language and music are at their strongest for 50 years in the case of the former, and perhaps 500 in the case of the latter, absent the blip of the past decade. Therein lies the hope, as we shall see in the final chapter; use of the notion of an Irish nation for an ontological re-centering.

Let us proceed to discuss the concept of nation. Isaiah Berlin is normally identified as close to the quintessence of liberal anti-nationalism, so let us start with some quotes by him:

> "Nationalism is an inflamed condition of national consciousness which can be, and on occasion has been, tolerant and peaceful." (Berlin, 1991a, p. 245)

> "Nationalism is not consciousness of the reality of national character, nor pride in it. It is a belief in this unique mission of a nation, as being intrinsically superior to the goals or attributes of whatever is outside it." (Berlin, 1991b, pp. 176-177)

> "Nationalism, even in its mildest version, the consciousness of national unity, is surely rooted in a sharp sense of the differences between one human society and another, the uniqueness of particular traditions, languages, customs — of occupation, over a long period, of a particular piece of soil on which intense collective feeling is concentrated." (Berlin, 1996, p. 232)

> "Nationalism — the elevation of the interests of the unity and self-determination of the nation to the status of the supreme value before which all other considerations must, if need be, yield." (Berlin, 1991c, p. 338)

His later (1996) statement credits Immanuel Kant as a father of modern nationalism. While this strikes one immediately as far-fetched, it actually deepens MacSwiney's insight about nationalism and identity. In epistemology, Kant distinguishes between the phenomenal level of appearances and the more real "noumenal" level of "*dingen an sich*", things in themselves. The erstwhile liberal Fichte adapted this distinction to produce a thoroughly terrifying nationalism, a veritable ancestor of Nazism, and one that also advocated expulsion of the Jews from Germany. Fichte argued that our everyday empirical self was sensible only to phenomena; galvanized by a national identification, the now noumenal self gained access to a new kind of *dingen an sich*, the old one having been jettisoned. Napoleon's defeat of the Germans at Jena seemed to be partly causative of Fichte's conversion, as of Hegel's eschatological vision of history. Intriguingly, as we see in Chapter 7, both the post-Cromwell Irish and the conquered North American Indians also sought refuge in eschatology.

The definition of nationalism we use here is that it is simply a synesthesia of one's sense of place through cultural and political mechanisms. This is developed in Chapter 2; for the moment, it suffices to say that I disagree with Chomsky's mentor Rocker that the state inevitably debauches "sense of place", particularly in a country like Ireland which – at least until recently – had a genetically distinct native stock as its primary population (at least until some of these indigenes saw a chance to get one over the rest of us by the coup described above). . As such, nationalism can be a powerful force for good. When used by manipulators as the last refuge of the scoundrels that they are, it is very often violent. It becomes a mechanism to exclude a created Other.

From 2008 on, an outpouring of such miscreants was imminent in Ireland. The situation is tailor-made; there will be a large population of immigrants whose coming, unlike that in Germany, was unplanned; there is a history in Ireland of state involvement in goods provision, and a lack of such goods. Few of the immigrant communities have organised politically. Let us be clear; this writer has no illusions about the immediate future.

That, however, in no way undermines the argument of this book for an ethos which returns the Irish from being the subjects of globalized corporatism that they now are to being at home in their own country. As we see in the next chapter, an appropriate reading of Joyce's oeuvre written during the first truly colossal outpouring of national hostilities gives the key.

Anderson (1991, 101) is often taken as inveighing against nationalism;

> "Here is a fine example of official nationalism – an anticipatory strategy adopted by dominant groups which are threatened with marginalization or exclusion from an emerging nation's imagined community"

Nationalism, he argues, requires the supplanting of a "sacred script" by a vernacular; a removal of autocracy; and, finally, a separation of mundane/secular time from the eternity in which religious truth is experienced, with the consequences that has for religious political authority. Nations are above all imagined communities; they are eternal, limited and sovereign. With respect to the linguistic aspect, he can rely on much documentary evidence.

One strategy of empire is to alienate the locals from their own culture, and, like MacSwiney, Anderson targets Macaulay, exemplified in this comment;

> "No Hindu who has received an English education ever remains sincerely attached to his religion" (91)

Unquestionably, the Berlin/Anderson narrative has cogency. Italian nationalism as formulated by Mazzini has the dual nature of being initially invented by a Piedmontese elite up to 1861, who regarded southerners as Other and treated them worse than before independence, and also in its being a totalising force. In fact, in Carducci, we get a state religion, an interlinking of patria, umanita, and God. Military adventures proceeded apace; the defeat in Ethiopia in 1886 had the paradoxical effect of regalvanising national sentiment, culminating in the creation of Eritrea. The invasion of Libya in 1911 followed lively race discourse. It does not overstretch matters to see a straight path from Mazzini to Mussolini.

Likewise, today's Caucasus is a ferment of would-be nations with Ingushetia and various parts of Ossetia claiming valid historical provenance. While much of the "diversity" can perhaps be traced back to the Bolsheviks in the 1920's fomenting linguistic nationalisms to be administered by its apparat, the Chechen war has yet fully to be resolved with over 35,000 civilians and 7,500 Russian soldiers dead. The spectre of Islamic rule, with the epistemological and power structure Anderson sees as predating nationalism, hangs over this area.

Anderson distinguishes the military, public display and citizen/republican aspects of nationalism. The latter, he argues, is essentially a New World phenomenon. It is uncontroversial to suggest that it is this aspect that has informed Irish revolutionary thought since the late 18th century. Those who claim a partisan agenda in the 1916 proclamation, the culmination of this trend in Ireland, miss the point completely. It is as neutral a citizen republican set of aspirations as can exist. The question of whether Irish men and women were willing to die for them has always since then been answered in the affirmative.

Anderson's schema fails when it comes to Ireland, as he is himself at least tacitly aware; intriguingly, the one paper of his own that he cites identifies him as "Benedict O'Gorman Anderson". He bends over backwards to claim that the paradoxical emergence of the early South American republics is due to their antiquity as administrative entities in "las Espanas". Yet that argument too needs to be informed by the enlightenment of the constitution agreed by newly liberated Spain in 1812, granting 92% of Mexicans the voting Franchise, and Bolivar's history as a slave-owner and autocrat. For Bolivar, a republic was defined by a president for life with the ability to choose his successor.

Ireland is a physical unity, and seems to have had a remarkable cultural unity for a period up to millennia in length. Whether that is the result of inner colonising is an intriguing question; for example, it is a moot point whether "Old Irish" was ever actually spoken, as distinct from written as (*inter alia*) ms. glosses, or whether it was an administrative and/or sacred language in the manner Anderson himself describes. The early third millennium destruction of Tara/Skryne can be contrasted, for example, with the annual Armenian celebration at Mount Arakat, a symbolic substitute for its conquered "sister" Ararat.

Returning to the anti-colonial psyche, find an echo of Fichte in Sekyi-Otu's (2006) Fanonian meditations:

> "Let the alienated self come home, the divided subject retrieve its wholeness, the captive mind attain knowledge of itself."

The decolonial turn is therefore ontological and reflexive. As we are about to spend some time with the Germans, it is worthwhile to note how fragmented their self-concept historically has been. Munster's 1544 Cosmographia, a map of the world including Germany, created a sensation precisely because it gave them a sense of home. Ireland, by contrast, is an island with stable genetic stock for about 10 millennia until the second millennium of the Common Era (In fall 2010, the first full published Irish genome, provisional as it must be, contained 13% of single nucleotide polymorphisms (SNPs) not seen before in Europe, indicating an unexpected genetic isolation – remember Carroll, Mulryan, Ahern, etc) Only in 1604 did the depiction of European countries with lines representing borders begin in earnest; the commentary by the Irish bardic schools in the mid-18th century about the depths of interiority in nation as in self is unprecedented. It was left to thinkers like Humboldt and Herder to conceptualise nation in terms of language (i.e. German) and that notoriously slippery word, "culture".

Berlin is obviously a follower of Herder, who argued successfully against race as a determiner of nation. In fact, he argued, there should be no need for an army. Such thinking would of course have ensured the obliteration of the Irish gene pool, and the loss of Irish culture to the world. In any case, it is to be tested in Canada, which in 2006 found for Quebec as a nation within Canada, hoping against hope that it would not ask for a state.

Unfortunately, Ireland's history shows that extirpation of the culture was as central to the British project as culling of the population to manageable levels. The present-day disparity between the population of the two states is the result of a millennium of social engineering, as is the ease with which Irish professionals fit into England. In 1641, the population of the island had recovered from the Tudor cull to stand at 1,668,000. (Both O'Callaghan, 2000, and Beresford Ellis, 1988, use Petty's British figures). Following the Cromwellian invasion, in 1652 it stood at 1,100,000; 504,000 of the dead were Irish. Following this was deportation of around 50,000 to slavery in the Caribbean. A set of artificial hungers (a famine is a shortage of food, and food was always exported from Ireland) culminated in the gorta mor (great famine) of 1845-1850. The most conservative attested figures for this project a million starving and a further million emigrating. The 18th century had at least one - in proportional terms – even greater famine in Ireland. It is possible that the famed fecundity of the Irish, particularly in the New world, was a response to these culls.

Ferguson (2006, p. 224) laconically points out why the Irish population base is now played out:

> "The demographic transportation of the West has its roots in feminism. Legislation against sex discrimination … At the same time, the ready availability of contraception and abortion gave women an unprecedented control over their own fertility. Europeans, quite simply, have ceased to reproduce themselves".

Remarkably, up to 15 years ago, the other negative trends that Ferguson identifies — "Substitute pornography and NASCAR for orgies and circuses" (ibid) were not to be seen in Ireland. The Irish have colluded in their own genetic dilution on their own island, and in the imposition of a new colonial regime on themselves. What was needed was a generation willing to see home prices triple in a decade, and unwilling to work. The younger generation borrowed their mortgages from the commercial banks, who in turn borrowed such frightening sums from foreign banks that Ireland's banks' credit rating began to collapse along with that of the Irish state itself. The state colluded in this, as did the main opposition parties, and the fantasy of GDP growth replaced that of Catholic heaven. Eventually the ECB "bailed" the Irish out – essentially so that the Irish taxpayer would pay off the debts owed by private Irish investors to foreign banks. Yes, I never tire of saying this.

This can and will happen in every country that becomes a target of the new colonialism. Lacking any tacit or explicit concept of nationhood, the Irish adopted GDP as a cover-all index of development. When, in late 2006, Google introduced "no Irish need apply" in Ireland by stating that only 100 of 500 jobs partly funded by the Irish taxpayer were to go to Irish people, hardly an eyelid was batted. Google later removed all trace of this.

So what is this nation concept? Berlin, we have seen, cannot decide; Pleklanov (2006) identified nationalism simply as preoccupation with the nation state, a preoccupation exemplified by consideration of how the US could pursue its interests vis a vis the EU and Middle East. Herder's cultural nationalism project is now the most appropriate to Ireland. The Irish should consider, *vis a vis* the rest of the world, what exalted human impulses can be served by the activity of the nation-state.(In that context, it is as well to leave the north-eastern corner as a theme park, a demonstration to the rest of the world that sectarian conflicts can be solved, and to remove orange from the national flag in the 26 counties)

The absolutism in Fichte's notorious "Address to the German People" and Rousseau's exhortation to make one's will conform to the nation is a relic of a bygone age. Initially, many nations developed in ignorance of the rest of the world and sought to be self-enclosed epistemes. We can now self-consciously adopt the role sketched above of attempting to reflect on how best we can serve both ourselves and the other 7 billion in the world. We have seen Berlin (1991a and b) oscillate from an ambivalent view of nationalism to viewing it as absolute evil. We can find some kind of synthesis in regarding the issue *vis a vis* holism. Is it the case that all national attributes form an interconnected whole? Can we have the Irish engagement with literature without the Irish postcolonial proclivity for self-pity and criminal abuse of state power? The rest of this discussion assumes that we are cognitively flexible enough to allow for non-holism to happen.

We have left behind essences, noumena, and all those big words that make us so unhappy to adapt Joyce. At a UC Berkeley conference on democracy in India on 15 September, 2006, the following attributes were proposed to characterize Indian nationality: cricket, the Raj infrastructure, Hindi films, the historic imagination of the epics, the geographical location from the

Himalayas to the ocean, and a first-class constitution. A related list for Pakistan encompasses cricket, opium, US aid, bureaucracy, Islam, and the Punjab. A parallel list for Ireland would include the moral imagination of the myths, the island, high Gaelic culture, the culture and political struggle to revive and protect this culture, Gaelic games, Anglo-English literature (apotheosizing in Joyce). the intersection of Europe and the US and that of the colonial and the colonizing worlds, the contemporary use of information technology, and recovering from genocide, with one result of this last being a mainly expatriate population. These diverse aspects all need national institutions, capable of protecting them, independent of dizzying swings in the world's economy.

Caring for its population through prudent social and economic policy is a national project. Tweaking the intersections between the state and the external world so the EU no longer controls our fisheries, and TRIPS our DNA, is a national project. Re-assertion of ownership of national resources regardless of contracts signed by corrupt ministers is similar. Working out how to control the collapse of the banking center so as not to punish the innocent is likewise. In all, breaking through the current colonial miasma into something we can again recognize as Ireland is currently the quintessential national project.

We end this section with recent forays into the miasma of neocolonialism. It may shock readers familiar with his work that the less controversial is that of Chalmers Johnson (2006). He cites Che Guevara in support of the thesis that the modern multinational corporation and chartered company are a fortiori the current vehicles of imperialism (30-31). His next step is that of mapping this colonial impulse onto the growth of the US military, and in this he finds support in General (and President) Eisenhower's famed joust at the military-industrial complex (39). For Johnson, "imperialism and militarism are inseparable" (30). There is yet a third step to be made.

There is no question about what side Johnson is on; Abernethy is castigated for his support of imperialism (29). The almost comically appropriately-named Krauthammer is taken to task for proposing as the moral mission of what he considers the intrinsically superior USA "unapologetic and implacable demonstrations of will" (68). What the Iraq war surely demonstrated to such neocons is that there will always be hard men on the other side equally anxious to be implacable; only when the USA recruited them, the erstwhile mortal enemies of the USA, did anything close to stability begin to re-emerge in Iraq. As we used put it in

Munster rugby (unlike others who use this analogy, I actually have won a Limerick rugby city cup – and as a front row forward) the problem with being a hard man is that somewhere there always is a harder man.

Johnson is, as ever, scathing about the CIA. Its founder, "wild Bill" Donovan, is cited as suggesting that "intelligence analysis as a cover for subversive operations abroad" (10) is a CIA leitmotif. Saddam is outed as a CIA asset (223-224). Indeed, it is pointed out that 8,000 of 11,800 pages dealing with arms sold by the West to Saddam were redacted by the Bush administration in a UN report (224). The CIA, Johnson argues, is a threat to US democracy; the "black budget", used for unaccountable activity, does not require congressional approval (117). As we will see presently in Coll's work, this may have led to the current imbroglio in Afghanistan.

Johnson is scathing about globalized corporatism, which he argues derived from classical economic "liberalism" a la Ricardo and Smith. However, he is willing to go much further in that he argues that it has become a religion of sorts (260-261). The fact that this system, which in his view Clinton pushed even more than Bush, has hindered every poor country that it touched is for him glaring (262); all countries now pushing free trade previously themselves used tariffs (263), as we already saw Chang point out; and the IMF and world Bank are nothing other than surrogates for the US treasury (264). There is yet another move that Johnson wishes to make; we have heard him argue that militarism begets colonialism and that globalized corporatism is the current form of colonialism; what remains is to put the resources of the military under the command of private capital.

It is perhaps fair to say that, for Johnson, such a move is what distinguished the Bush regime from its predecessors, however globalizing in outlook they were. In that vein, the Obama presidency deserves the plaudits it is getting as at least a brake on this process. As GHW Bush's secretary of defense, Cheney introduced the legislation that made it possible to outsource many core military functions to private companies (144). These included Dyncorp, Kellog Root and Brown, and various Halliburton subsidiaries; Cheney's first job in private industry after his demission as secretary of defense was famously CEO of Halliburton. The outsourcing in he Iraq war to the notorious Blackwater (later Xe) is too well-known to be re-rehearsed here; suffice to say that the propaganda was so far-reaching that even Jon Stewart took the side of Blackwater in their assumption of core military functions(he later apologised). Dyncorp, in turn, were involved in the sex slave trade.

It may be as well to remember the terror many of us felt during the middle of the W administration, before Katrina. As Johnson wrote, the US had 474,312 soldiers serving in over 100 countries (156-160) apart from the secret bases (153). The "Echelon" system gathers information from electronic communications all over the world, including neutral Ireland (161-167). It seemed that much of this infrastructure was finding its way into an unaccountable set of private interests; the use of Echelon to reverse-engineer Dragon's speech-processing technology is increasingly accepted as fact. The incompetence and corruption that follows with spying was memorably documented in Robert Lindsay's' "The falcon and the Snowman" (1979), which depicts critical intelligence technology being stolen by drug-addled young men from private installations and sold to the Soviet Union; Lindsay argues that an Australian government fell as a result.

To return to Johnson; his narrative sees 9/11 as a Sepoy mutiny (170-185). The sepoys, trained by the British, mutinied against them in 1857 partly because of egregious cultural insensitivity, with soldiers asked to "bite the bullet" which was coated with pig and cow fat. Coll (2004) extends this aspect of Johnson's thought. He is first keen to clear the ground by stating that "the Cia do not typically work inside the American legal system" (254) as a result of the national security act in 1947. Specifically, "espionage and paramilitary operations abroad are not subject to review by American courts" (ibid.). Coll is prepared to argue that 9/11 was partly caused by a suspiciously incompetent passage in American espionage; hijackers Khalid al-Mihdar and Nawah al-Hazma, despite previous known terrorist activity, had "unrestricted access to the United States" (563) and "neither man had ever been placed on a watchlist" (ibid.) Indeed, "at the FBI, only the New York field office received a request to search for them" (ibid.). The rest, as they say, indeed is history.

Coll's thorough and cautiously-phrased work is above all a sigh of regret that "the opportunities missed by the US on the way to September 2001 extended well beyond the failure to exploit fully (*sic*) an alliance with Massoud" (570). The latter, of course, was Bin-Laden's potential nemesis, the warlord killed just before 9/11 whose "northern alliance' eventually became the vehicle through which Afghanistan was temporarily subdued. The inverted moral universe of the CIA, in which it seems to be the case that it is necessary to create a fake enemy, absent a real one, is a space to be eschewed in Ireland.

Coll's thesis can be boiled down as follows; 9/11 and the current Afghanistan/Pakistan problem is due to the Taliban, which are partly a CIA creation, encouraged initially to fight the Soviets and later seen as valuable in preserving private US corporate oil interests in Afghanistan. Stated baldly, versus worked out over the 700 pages of Coll's book, this is devastating.

Coll is scathing about the current chief of staff in the US military in the lead-up to the events of 1989. Gates, as the CIA's "leading analyst", missed the break-up of the USSR (159):

> "We monitored specific events but too often did not draw back to get a broader perspective"

Let us hope for all our sakes that age has improved him. From the other end of the stick, things looked very strange (160):

> "Gorbachev seemed genuinely stunned to discover that the Americans didn't seem to want to negotiate...they remained devoted to their militaristic jihad"

Yet that is not the main thrust of Coll's narrative. It is above all how the Californian oil company Unocal managed to bend the impetus of US policy in Afghanistan in the direction of securing its pipelines, regardless of the consequences in terms of blowback for US interests. Yet it does seem to be his read of the situation; how Unocal was going to put a pipeline through the physically hostile Afghani terrain remains unasked.

It is an exaggeration to say that there is pathos in the story, but only a slight one (330):

> "It was a tawdry season for American diplomacy....the state department had taken up Unocal's agenda s its own"

The Taliban were to be supported to this end (299-300):

> "The relatively small number of American officials...who followed Afghanistan tended to accept the Taliban's narrative they were a cleansing, transitional force......the state department and the White House believed that for American oil companies too the Taliban could be an important part of a new Afghan solution"

The central US official involved, Robin Raphel, argued at a closed meeting of the UN security council that “it is not in the interest of any of us here that the Taliban be isolated” (335). By 1997, Coll argues, “it was reasonable for the Taliban to believe that Unocal was effectively an arm of the US government” (364). Similarly, for Pakistan the unelected and unaccountable CIA was effectively the US government. When Peter Tomsen - special envoy to the Afghanistan resistance from 1989-1992 - pleaded for a special role for Massoud “The CIA had opposed him, preferring to work with Pakistani intelligence” (557).

Coll's is indeed a bitter vision. Yet it is Pollyanna compared to the Canadian journalist Naomi Klein (2007). This author had much trepidation in bringing any aspect of his extensive neuroscience research to bear on the concerns of this book. Klein, we shall see, has no such qualms. Indeed, so radical is what we are going to hear from her that I will take the opportunity to speculate a little further about the neuroscience of the neo-colony.

It is the contention here that the Irish have gradually, piece by piece, been nudged away from a sense of belonging in their own country. The colonial service officers occupying posts in organizations like the OECD look at countries like Ireland through the filters of neoliberal economization of life. There generally is just about one generation to grow the economy, in which birth rate exceeds the death rate. Of course, immigrants can help greatly, and the provision of draconian legislation prohibiting any criticism of immigration on the grounds of “hate speech” was duly done by the Irish state. The now long-forgotten fecundity of the Irish was replaced by West Africa, with women flying in to Dublin 8.5 months pregnant, and having their newly-minted Irish citizens courtesy of the Irish taxpayer as their refugee claim was being processed.

The Irish people voted overwhelmingly in 2004 to restrict citizenship so that it could no longer be acquired in this way. Yet the Irish Times continued to put immigrants on the cover of the paper, announcing them as Irish. The national news stations were careful to put an admixture of brown, black and yellow skins in any photo of schoolchildren. The self-concept of the Irish in Ireland was nudged gradually away from people of their own ethnicity.

Of even more consequence was the emergence of the "Celtic tiger" narrative, which reached apotheosis in Garvin's (2004) lamentable book. It went something like this;

> "Back in the old days we lived in a priest-ridden miasma, doing research in things like Celtic studies and playing fiddles. Then we hitched ourselves to the neoliberal wagon, and suddenly – as if by magic – enormous financial success came to the country"

Unfortunately, there is another sentence after 2009:

> "Then the world economy collapsed and we were left bereft, not just of our sense of belonging in this country, but of the manufacturing and farming bases that used occupy so many. Unemployment grew to obscene levels, and it became clear that immigration on this scale was a massive mistake"

Garvin has now reversed himself, and now inveighs against the position of his 2004 book.

It is doubtful that Naomi Klein (2007) would have any sympathy even for the nuanced nationalism of this book. Hers is an unabashed "*J'accuse*" hurled at all purveyors of the Washington consensus. I am prepared to grant that there was an ethos of nudging Ireland's indigenous population away from a sense of self that had evolved over millennia. Klein's is a far more radical thesis (127):

> "There was, as Letelier wrote, an inner harmony between the drive to clean sectors of society and the ideology at the heart of the project. The Chicago boys...believed in a form of capitalism that was pure by its very nature"

Chicago is, of course, the home of the Milton Friedman School (69):

> "Though always cloaked in the language of math and science, Friedman's vision coincided precisely with the interest of large multinationals"

Friedman insisted that economics could be a science as precise as physics; what is even more dangerous is that he insisted that life should be economized at a very fundamental level. The result is a claim-jump by economics, such as I described in my 2004 book, and a thoroughgoing procrustean process in all societies to which the process is applied.

This author has worked and published (Freeman et al. 2008) with Walter Freeman III, son of the notorious lobotomist. One way to eliminate dissent was his prefrontal lobotomy; with his son, my work was focussed on ensuring that simulations could take over from real data-gathering in the brain with its attendant risks of abuse. While Freeman II was in his heyday, the CIA was funding unspeakable research in Canada by Cameron, and to a less extent, Donald Hebb (37-38):

> "Cameron on the other hand looked into the same void and saw something else; the blank slate, cleared of bad habits, on which new patters could be written.....Cameron saw shock therapy as a means to blast his patients back into their infancy to regress them completely...shocks..uppers..downers and hallucinogens...barbiturates, sodium amytal and nitrous oxide..laragctil and insulin"

Nor is that all;

> "Cameron further starved his patients' senses in the so-called sleep cure where they were kept in drug-induced reverie for twenty to 22 hours...up to 65 days of continuous sleep..Cameron gave one group curare which induces paralysis" (43)

The idea for Klein is that the "shock doctrine" requires first of all the shock of a visible spectacle like a coup, then the shock of harsh economic "remedies'. It is one of the contentions of this book that Mayday, 2002, was as close as Ireland got to a spectacle designed to intimidate, with young anti-globalizers beaten up in public at a time when Ireland was getting ready to support the US invasion of Iraq.

Donald Hebb is a respected figure in neuroscience and, for the record; he regarded Cameron as an idiot. Yet it is difficult to say where one begins and the other ends:

> "Although he had been in touch with the CIA for years , in 1957 Cameron got his first grant from the CIA...for the investigation of human ecology...the psychiatrists who invented the Page-Russell electroshock machine had recommended...24 individual shocks...Cameron started..a terrifying 360 individual shocks to each patient" (42)

Hebb, by contrast, was pioneering sensory deprivation, with the results clear in the deprivation suits used by the Guantanamo residents and other victims of "special rendition"(40):

> "Within 3 months Hebb had a research grant...to conduct a series of sensory deprivation experiments"

While the Irish have perhaps been nudged away from a sense of how they are, with the figure of Bertie Ahern playing a crucial role in assuring the base that all was still *Erin go Bragh*, Cameron's and Hebb's motives were explicit: (43)

> "two major factors that allow us to maintain a time and space image...to know where we are and who we are...(a) our continued sensory input and (b) our memory" (Cameron, quoted in Klein)

Both of these were to be expunged, to create a blank slate. As a published neuroscientist, it is clear to this writer that Cameron had no idea what he was doing; like Friedmanite economics, it is just gobbledygook designed to justify a course of action already decided on.

Klein goes on to discuss the application of the economic shock doctrine to Chile, Britain and Argentina (161-211); to Poland and China (215-244); to South Africa (245-274); to Russia (275-330); to Asia (332-352); to Iraq (409-453); post-tsunami Asia(485-511); and, finally, Israel (535-557). That there is something sadistic and monstrous at play is without doubt. Whether Ireland will continue with the current "nudge" doctrine of progress to full-fledged shock will be clear very soon. Some portents, like the attacks by paramilitaries and masked, unidentifiable police on locals in Mayo, are not promising. Some of the paramilitaries died trying to assassinate the President of Bolivia; there is no question that evil was very much on the ground in north-west Mayo. The Irish may need frequent reminders of exactly why they have to pay back these debts that they did not themselves accrue…

1.6 Outline of this book

In Chapter 2, we extend the above discussion about consciousness and nation with reference to Hegelianism at one extreme and hypotheses about neural event on the other. We concern ourselves to some extent with the issue of the existence of such a thing as an Irish nation. The existence of two political entities called "Ireland", a mainly Protestant one in the North-east Corner and a mainly Catholic one, the republic of Ireland, occupying the rest of the island, was set in law after a referendum in 1998 seemed to establish the consent of the overwhelming majority of the population of the island.

Within the geographical confines of the republic of Ireland, a dynamic involving a previous dichotomization seemed to have stabilised. We had Gaelic names, played Gaelic sports, were Roman Catholic, preindustrial and then working class, and attained literacy through the rigors of a rather brutal pedagogy. This pedagogy became celebrated, both in guilt and in glory, in the parts of the New World to which it was transferred.

They were comfortably housed while being educated, Protestant, played internationally accredited sports, and found that they were Irish immediately they left the island. Their reaction to this revelation varied, and often did not involve simply attempting to assimilate to Britishness. WB Yeats and his mentor Gregory of Coole Park tried desperately to learn, often from her paying tenants, the native expressions that we have labeled "folkways" here. It will be argued here that a sizeable portion of this culture is a degenerate, orally transmitted fragment of high Gaelic art. A century earlier, Wolfe Tone, Edmund Fitzgerald and other Protestants sought political expression through French and American republicanism, and led the great rebellion of 1798. Some details of Irish history will occupy us in chapter 3.

We were conscious of being oppressed and an underclass rather than Irish: it took them to demonstrate our Irishness to us. Intriguingly, they were influenced by French commentators to stress Ireland's high cultural, particularly musical, past. Now both groups, Gaelic and Anglo- Irish, could work together in an impressive confluence which is Gaelic, Anglo-Irish, European and wide open to American cultural influences: Ireland.

Had the opening of the economy to global forces over the past quarter century been better handled, the resulting country would be much more interesting; thus, we come to the topic of the next chapter. International capitalist organs like the Economist began to praise the Irish for their surrender to market forces just as the Roman Catholic Church had praised their blind faith. The resulting forces were almost millenniar in their intensity as the Irish rushed to buy the dear land. The details of the subsequent economic congeries occupy us in chapters 4 and 5.

The progenitors of the successful war of independence of the 1920's founded Sinn Fein, meaning “ourselves alone”, and the two major parties of the republic, Fianna fail and Fine Gael, emerged from it in due course. The former is in general the slightly more unwashed peasantry, the dramatis personae for the Irish takeover of Tammany hall, who lost the civil war to their slightly more tony opponents and then proceeded to stay in power for most of the State's history, until what looks like a well-deserved demise in 2011. The unnatural marriage between these Catholic nationalists and international capitalism has been the main worrying event of Ireland's so- called economic boom.

Increasingly inept at property deals and realistically cynical about the Anglo-Saxon legal system, technology has proven beyond these characters from William Faulkner, as chapter 6 shows. We then revisit the globalisation/neoliberalism theme in a chapter that takes as leitmotif the reaction of the Gaelic poetic aristocracy to punitive globalizing forces in the seventeenth century in chapter 7.

The issue of a political regime with jurisdiction over the whole island re-engages us again and again. St. Augustine cried "made me whole but not yet" when he realized that leaving his mistress and child for God was, for the moment, beyond him. We examine how the irredentist nationalist impulse for political unity of the island, while being quick to use violence to achieve its aims, has get failed to demonstrate the sincerity of its convictions. Better a wholly Catholic rump than a mixed whole.

The peculiar dearth of new internationally successful Irish artists - particularly musical such - is dealt with time and again. Yet, remarkably, major political challenges of international consequence have been met in Ireland, and these successes are profiled. Finally, the newly secularized state is begetting a plethora of alternative religious movements which I have written about elsewhere (2004).

The chapter concludes with reference to the influence of Irish Home rulers on Burmese independence movements. It is my fervent hope that the defeat of neoconservatism in Ireland will similarly inspire the world, and particularly the United States, where this wholly egregious impulse originated.

Breandan O hEithir correctly described immersion in the workings of the underbelly of the Irish state as “A slow swim in a sewer”. The final chapter begins with one such, taken from the academia in Bertie Ahern's Ireland. We conclude by looking in outline at recommendations for change.

CHAPTER TWO

CONSCIOUSNESS AND NATION

2.1 Hegel or Pavlov?

Discourse about "nation" and "consciousness", taken in isolation, let alone "national consciousness" as a collocation, immediately attracts accusations of naiveté, bigotry, and worse. "Nations" as political realities are often the result of colonial gerrymandering. The very existence of "consciousness" has been denied - at least for methodological purposes - attenuated, or aggrandized, to include everything that occurs in the cosmos, as writers choose (O'Nuallain, 2003).

The controversy surrounding Irishness is so intense that this writer feels compelled to clear the ground by discussing consciousness itself. That there exists of a substrate of consciousness distinct from the contents thereof is a controversial hypothesis. On the most empirical possible level, we can assert the existence of persistent - or at least recurring - thought patterns that can be inculcated by an educational bureaucracy in populace for reasons of state. In that sense, it might be argued that Roman Catholicism has been part of Irish national consciousness since the foundation of the Irish state. There is no necessity to dig any deeper than Pavlovian behavioural conditioning to motivate this assertion.

The symbols and rituals of the Roman Catholic Church were introduced to the great majority of children in the Irish national school systems as numinous and beneficial exactly as a bell was rung to Pavlov's dogs to indicate the presence of food. Absent food, the bell alone could later trigger salivation: likewise, the contents of thought, for which we substitute the word "consciousness" in this account, would include a positive, if fearful, valence for Catholic symbols for Irish people brought up in this system. This is the "minimal commitments" notion of national consciousness: a set of valences imparted for political purposes.

It is totally consistent with the view with which Ellmann (1977, P. 1) opens his book on the consciousness of Joyce:

> "'Consciousness' denotes the movement of mind both in recognizing its own shape and in maintaining that shape in the face of attack and change"

So Ellmann's Joyce encounters "an array of spiritual and secular satraps" (ibid.) and seeks to go his own way "rather than accept the patterns of behaviour they endorsed" (ibid.)

Yet it is this writer's hope that this circumscribed notion of consciousness will soon seem inaccurate, as foreign as circumscription of any belief system was to Joyce. Indeed, Ellmann seems to realise that himself after 63 pages, and to abandon rather than complete the book. But we're getting ahead of the story, and will return to this theme presently.

A few asides before we move on; first, it may be the case that the patent absurdities of Roman Catholicism were useful in the creation of a compliant populace. Someone forced publicly to pretend to believe that a piece of bread was actually a man who walked around Palestine two millennia before, and who must be eaten for the sake of avoiding eternal punishment, would have little difficulty later on pretending to believe that a prime minister notorious for his cupidity and mistresses was a moral paragon, or that a criminal justice system was still intact after another prime minister voluntarily admitted in 2002, during an election campaign, to repeatedly interfering with it. (He was comfortably re-elected.)

Of course, this suspension of disbelief is not unique to Ireland. By a similar account, Britishness defaults to an infantile idealization of the (largely German) royal family. U.S. national sentiment could be seen to default to a legitimisation of the criminal dispossession and genocide of the Native American people and violent oppression of African-Americans by repeated presentation of trivial national symbols throughout an education which is much more explicitly "nationalistic" than its Irish equivalent.

At the least commitments level, then, the issue of Irish national consciousness/identity is an extremely heated row about which contents to inculcate in children, a row which is discussed in the next section. For the moment, let us consider an entirely different take on consciousness and identity, which can potentially subsume the immediately foregoing discussion: that of the philosopher Hegel.

For Hegel:

> "Universal history … shows the development of the consciousness of freedom on the part of Spirit (in German Geist) and the consequent realization of that freedom" (in Leowenberg [ed.], p. 421).

What we experience as reality, then, is an emanation of Geist/Spirit, which comes to know itself in freedom as it manifests itself in different societies, through different modes of knowing. The Aztec, Mayan, Ancient Kingdom Egyptian, and mediaeval monastic Irish civilizations can equally be seen as particular implementations as Spirit seeks to know itself:

> "… Every step in the process, as differing from any other, has its determinate peculiar principle. In history this principle is idiosyncrasy of spirit - particular national genius" (ibid. 422).

In Hegel's schema, then, nations are not simply contingent, a result perhaps of lines drawn on a map by a civil servant in the classic manner of colonial powers. This is exemplified by the division of the Indian subcontinent in 1947 by a London civil servant, leading immediately to a million deaths after Gandhi had refused a healing federal system, and the creation of an Iraq state by unifying three oil wells owned by Kurds, Sunnis and Shiites. Nations have almost a Platonic Ideal reality according to Hegel:

> "It is within the limitations of this idiosyncrasy that the spirit of the nation, concretely manifested, expresses every aspect of its consciousness and will - the whole cycle of its realization. Its religion, its polity, its ethics, its legislation, and even its science, art, and mechanical skill all bear its stamp…. That such or such a specific quality constitutes the particular genius of a people is the element of our inquiry which must be derived from experience, and historically proved". (ibid.)

It is fair to say that most advocates of Irish independence implicitly preferred the Hegelian to the Pavlovian account of national identity. Similarly, it is difficult to imagine anyone willing to sacrifice their life in order that one arbitrarily chosen set of beliefs, rather than another, could be inculcated at school. Hundreds of thousands of Irish people have consciously risked their lives for their vision of Irish freedom, as have hundreds of millions of other peoples for what they saw as the full realization of their nations.

No claims have yet been made here for the superiority, in veridical terms, of the Hegelian over the Pavlovian accounts. Any competent historian will intervene at this point and comment that the nation-state is a quintessentially nineteenth-century construction, and that arbitrary borders are the rule, rather than the exception. By historical irony, Hegel's triumphant Eurocentrism apotheosized in the United States of America, which Hegel saw as the ultimate reflexively self-conscious society; sometimes, not least now in the early third "Christian" millennium, it is hard fully to agree with him.

Let us recap. We are trying to find some principled basis for the use of the term "national consciousness". At one extreme, we have Hegelian essentialism, with Absolute Spirit adapting itself to a physical location to manifest a particular genius loci in a nation. At the other extreme, we have Pavlovian contingency, with arbitrary lines on maps resulting in different systems of indoctrination. For the purposes on this book on Ireland, it matters little whether either, or both, is true. The fact remains that, particularly in a location as isolated and small as Ireland, common characteristics will emerge that we begin to term "national".

Even conservative Anglophilic commentators agree with this. For Landes (1999), both Japan and England are different in that, in an ineluctable historical progression, they produce superior economic systems. Huntingdon (1996) (in)famously insists that, whereas Islam's borders are inevitably bloody, the USA is a quintessentially Anglo-Saxon country where many ethnicities and indeed nationalities can take suck from Britannia's capacious bosom. Perhaps we can after all find a third way between essentialism and contingency.

Let us return to the topic of consciousness itself. A useful distinction may be drawn between groups who contend that only the personal and social substrate on which the activities of commerce and engineering are based is objective (let's call these the "jocks"), and the "arties" who see commerce and engineering as a means to the finer things of life. When they have a substantial say in a society, as in Renaissance Italy, the arties will mobilize its resources to produce beautiful artefacts. Such activity may be difficult to understand for jock groups.

Imposing a distinction that seems to belong to American high-school class factionalism on nations is quite audacious. However, there are several precedents whereby national institutions have bracketed the existence of whole areas of scientific truth. Stalin's support for the biologist Lysenko is the most egregious example: millions of people starved to death due to failed harvests because Lysenko's take on genetic inheritance, though absurd, was seen to be consistent with Soviet theory. Or so Medvedev's (1971) story goes; in fact, Lysenko is undergoing something of a rehabilitation as his views on co-operation in Nature (op cit 167-169), no longer so red in tooth and claw, regain purchase in biology.

The treatment accorded Lysenko's rival Vavilov was undoubtedly unspeakable (op cit 40-76). Medvedev launched a jeremiad against Lysenko's agronomy (153-192); yet there is no knockout punch, and somehow the Soviets, in thrall to this superstition, managed to win a war against one the most fearsome armies in world history. Medvedev is so biased that neo-Lamarckian sentiments put in the mouth of Stalin now seem to humanize the dictator (134) and would have been better to stick with the proscription of Pauli's resonance principle and Einstein's relativity (132) to exemplify the apotheosis of Marxist epistemology.

This tendency is continued in the great and saintly Sakharov (1990) in his rather heated denunciation of Lysenko, and anything that suggests that evolution is anything other than survival of the fittest. Remarkable how reasonable Stalin now seems, and how suspect these Western-leaning soviet scientists! It is worth noting that Sakharov's book, finished before the demise of the Soviet Union, evinces detailed and state-of-the-art knowledge of his subject in a manner that indicates that there was no palpable censorship. In fact, perhaps the fact that Schrödinger could not publish his great insights into molecular biology in Ireland due to the Church's pressure is more egregious than anything in the Soviet Union's science policies. The recent attack on academic freedom in Ireland shows how little has changed since the days of church censorship,a nd will be discussed in chapter 8.

Closer to home, British biologists have closed ranks around a suitably reinterpreted Darwin to inveigh against the French Lamarckian view that characteristics acquired during life can be genetically inherited. Though time is proving the extremes of both sides misguided, and Darwin himself was actually a crypto-Lamarckian, with a wacky genetic theory, the patently incomplete neo-Darwinian synthesis is still a leitmotif in genetics.

In fact. Lysenko (Medvedev, 1971, 74) anticipated many current ideas, popularized in the West by Conrad Waddington, about mutuality of organism and environment.

The Anglo-Saxon intellectual world has been predisposed for close to a century to deny the existence of subjectivity, methodologically and often substantively. The French response in thinkers like Foucault and Bourdieu has been to explore subjectivity in a sophisticated, contextual way. It may be that the impulses that gave rise to Protestant, capitalist Europe and the Latin take on Judaism that we call Roman Catholicism arise from some fundamentally different ways of approaching reality.

Perish the thought, but DNA evidence does confirm a slightly distinct racial provenance for the Irish and English. (See the next section about race and environment; Sykes, 2006, is one of many recent explorations here, but was issued before the first whole Irish genome in 2010 showed massive variance from European "norms") Let us be clear: had England remained Catholic, it is indeed possible that the Irish would have become possessed of a Protestant capitalist work ethic. (As this is being written, Ireland manifests undoubtedly, if temporarily, a failed attempt at a jock state.) As things stand, however, what started off as contingent preferences can get immortalized by national institutions into what seem to be enduring essences, into what effectively comprises national consciousness, the spirit of a nation.

It is a genetic fact that the Irish mature sexually later than the English. It is a cultural fact that first sexual experience occurred earlier in England than Ireland, at least for the first seventy years of the Irish state, and probably for at least a half-century before, as the Great Famine made the Irish terrified of another Malthusian check and/or deliberate genocide. A particularly fantastical interpretation of Roman Catholicism was used to implement sexual ignorance, and a whole literature arising from this fact came into being; Edna O'Brien, John McGahern, and so on.

Therefore, forms of life take root in geographical areas and, through "frozen accidents" of law and history, often become institutionalized in the very fabric of a nation-state. Anglo-Saxon countries seem in general to encourage immigration, at least until the original autochthones are suppressed and the immigrants try and establish themselves on an equal footing; their much-vaunted rule of law is based on common law precedent. (One of the problems in contemporary Iraq has been the insistence on supplanting the more sophisticated Iraqi civil code with Anglo-Saxon common law.)

We do not know enough about cognitive science, consciousness studies, or genetics *a priori* to deny the relevance of the Hegelian account; this chapter ends with some rather less than fully bridled speculation. Were history to be rerun, and Maoris to invade tenth-century England rather than "New Zealand", it is possible that the complete works of Shakespeare would have been written by someone with rather darker skin (so if snow be white, then her breasts would indeed be dun). It is possible that the music of Carolan is genuinely expressive of the land he last saw as a child; certainly, programmatic music like Hamilton's "The Antrim Hills" uses tropes which, echoing similar continental composers, bring the hills into focus in the mind's eye of an educated listener. Conversely, it is possible that the English rugby team would now perform the haka before every game. (Rugby would have been invented in Saxony by Wilhelm Ellsberg as a development of the traditional "Saxon Bulldog").

Let us be clear. The argument here is that national characteristics are a tiny part genetics, a larger part physical environment, and enormously historical and cultural accident. They are nonetheless real, and the attempt to deny them in the Irish case will be treated in the next section.

Recent historiographical accounts of the conquest of the New World, for example by Jared Diamond (1998) focus almost exclusively on the contingent and cultural to explain how the conquest was possible. Europe is full of peninsulas like the Iberian and Italian peninsulas and so is difficult to bring under central control; thus, the centralized government that forbade the far more technologically advanced Chinese sailors to continue their world peregrinations was not possible in Europe. People lived close to their farm and domestic animals, who became exposed to opportunistic viruses and other infections that spread to humans; thus, Europeans had resistance to diseases that laid low the almost equal population of the Americas. Native North Americans had not yet invented steel (though by some accounts, they were close) or gunpowder; and so on.

All this aside, it still makes perfect sense to engage in discourse about national consciousness. To a child growing up in a secure family, or to a German romantic philosopher, frozen accidents of cultural development will be experienced *sub specie aeternitas*, an expression of underlying, unchanging Reality. To a contemporary cognitive anthropologist, the nexus of family, art, law, technology, taboo, religion, and informal social interaction comprising a culture will be seen as a delicate, intricately interconnected organism. To assent to its being damaged is to damage oneself. To deny its existence is purest ignorance.

2.2. Does Ireland exist?

Erasmus Darwin, grandfather of Charles, produced a version of the theory of evolution in verse form. He was excoriated for atheism. Two generations later, his grandson was invited to join the Voyage of the Beagle. Charles was an Oxbridge dropout with little scientific training. The rest, as we say, is history.

Charles Darwin's confused and meandering work lacks any reasonable theory of genetics, which first arose some time later from Mendel's forged data (see my cosmos and history papers in 2008 and 2012). More to the point, the neo-Darwinian synthesis is so egregiously wrong that the whole biotech industry has largely failed on foot of it, often creating genetic pollution as, for example, in the case of organisms which are crosses between tomatoes and fish being let loose on the ecosystem (Charles [2001] describes the failure of the Flavr Savr tomato enterprise; Behe [1996, 2007] adduces evidence, contested with varying degrees of success, contra neo-Darwinism.) Darwin's scientific illiteracy, and immunity to facts, prevented his noticing some remarkable phenomena on the Galapagos Islands. For example, there are two different species of finch called fortis and scandens which occasionally interbreed to produce hybrids. As the finches arrived on the Galapagos 2–3 million years ago, we can take it that they were there for Charles.

Fortis and scandens, obviously biologically close, can easily be distinguished by their song. Yet this song has no genetic component whatsoever! It is transmitted solely by the father between the tenth and thirtieth day after birth. Remarkably, a scandens male brought up in a fortis nest will learn the fortis song. This interrelation of organism and environment, in this case an effective environmental assimilation of what seems at first sight an inevitably genetic characteristic, is well beyond the capacity of neo-Darwinism to explain. (Of course, Wallace deserves much of whatever credit is available for "Darwinism", and Darwin was careful to credit him.)

Charles himself never even reached the foothills of this type of argument, and died a Lamarckian without having a clue about how his theory of evolution could work. Lacking any concept of the discrete gene, he proposed a generic mixing of attributes from both parents such as to ensure that natural selection could not in fact take place. That was repeatedly pointed out to him and his bulldog Thomas Huxley, as the contemporary record shows. Yet Darwin's theory of random changes and survival of the fittest got accepted. Why?

Darwin did not hesitate to draw some inevitable conclusions from his "theory" (if we can dignify it with this name):

> "So again with varieties of sheep: it has been asserted that certain mountain-varieties will starve out other mountain-varieties, so that they cannot be kept together. The same result has followed from keeping together different varieties of the medicinal leech." (Darwin, 1968, 126–127).

Darwin goes on to emphasise the obvious; if a less fit breed of *homo sapiens sapiens* meets a more fit such, the inevitable will happen. Indeed the subtitle of his magnum opus is "The preservation of favoured races in the struggle for life" Prodigious Victorian verbiage went into emphasizing the unfit African ancestry, geographical isolation, and simian physiognomy of the Irish. Hitler was such a doctrinaire Darwinian that he eventually accepted the Russian advance into Germany as proof of the latter's superior evolutionary fitness.

Rifkin (1983) draws the obvious conclusion, in a book excoriated by Gould. Darwin's *Weltanschauung* was proselytized as justification for Empire. Anglo-Saxon superiority could be proven with reference to this secular reconstruction of natural law. Indeed, the action of empire construction, the very sending into battle of submachine guns against bows and arrows, was as much part of the natural order of things as childbirth, or the extermination of the Irish.

For those of us relieved that the Darwinfest of 2009 is over, it is also worth noting that Darwin was utterly wrong about all his central ideas of mechanism;

> "For his part, Darwin was also .guided by long since outdated forms of scientific thought. His lifelong commitment to theories of blending heredity would always have precluded his taking Mendel's rescuers seriously" (Waller, 2002, i56)

In particular, this had the consequence that "any new inheritable modification would soon be diluted and …obliterated" (Ibid 199)

In fact Darwin eventually had given up altogether on the key part of natural selection; the notion of randomness.

Closer to the Galapagos, Pocock (1974) published an obscure paper in an obscure New Zealand journal about Britain and Ireland. Remarkably, in a turn of events that occurs rarely in academic journals who generally like to be first in, the paper got reprinted a year later in the "Journal of Modern History" (both references are given here). The "three kingdom" approach he takes to British history, which is to exclude an explicitly Irish component, is reprised, inter alia, in Asch (1993).

There is nothing unusual about historical revisionism, although the fact that the Irish department of foreign affairs notoriously funded the Center for British Studies at UC Berkeley to take precisely this line is surely *de trop* – as was pointed out in a parliamentary question which ended this activity. What is remarkable is the extent to which the Irish "intelligentsia" is anxious to collude with the negation of the existence of their country, if not themselves. Selling out Ireland has often been a shortcut to a British knighthood. "Sir" Tony O'Reilly, ex-CEO of Heinz and Dublin native, led an egregious campaign against the Good Friday agreement and thus the peace process through his Irish rag, The Sunday Independent, before being granted a knighthood for services to peace.

But what has the brilliant practitioner of the modern historical science novel, and recent winner of the Booker Prize, Wexfordman John Banville, to gain from exposing his ignorance of linguistics in this way? -

> "Irish was essentially lost to us in one decade in an avalanche of change. We took on English and made something new of it because the memory of the older tongue is still there. Irish is full of evasion. You can't, for example, say 'I'm a man' in it. We're still unquiet in our own language. English writing is clear as glass. We love the ambiguities and pile on as many meanings as a sentence will bear." (Banville, cited in Rutten, 2005)

Apart from the internal contradiction, ambiguity in English is good, yet it is clear as glass — there is an obvious value judgement here. Ambiguity is English and good; evasion is Irish and bad. More importantly, the extreme form of linguistic relativism that Banville parades here largely died with

Sapir and Whorf, though there are half-hearted attempts at Stanford to revive it.

To be precise, Irish is a verb-subject-object order language like 19% of the world's languages. Let us take, for example, the dialect of Mixtec spoken in Ixpantapec in the Oaxaca Valley in Mexico. It is worthwhile unpacking this, as many things about Ireland and the Irish are complicated, and riding roughshod over them with a West British accent and attitude does violence to them.

The standard Irish boast is that they learned their Gaelic at the rate of a beating per line. Many beatings were administered for the misuse of the verb "Bí" where the copula "Is" was appropriate. Or, in the famous excoriation of the anti-Catholic provost of Trinity:

> Mahaffy of TCD
> Does not know the verb "to be"

Of course, if the copula in Irish is not in fact a verb, which is the current received wisdom, Mahaffy may remain famous only for his comment that James Joyce showed the danger in educating the wrong sort of people. Standard Irish grammars make the distinction just alluded to of the verb "Bí" and copula "Is". Ixpantec Mixtec (IM), by contrast, seems at first blush to have two copulas; roughly, kuu and ka. Kuu behaves like the Irish "Is" in many contexts:

> *Kuu Juan tata*
> *Is athar é Seán*
> *John is a father*

Ka, on the other hand, initially seems to map onto "Bí"

> *Tá Seán árd*
> *Jiko ka Juan*
> *John is tall*

Yet this is an over-simplification.

> **ka jiko Juan*

is ungrammatical in IM, which like Irish is a VSO language. In fact,

> *jiko Juan*

is grammatical, which leads one to suspect that perhaps something is awry. Can it be the case that ka is not an independent verb, and that the predication structure of the two languages is actually a little more similar than we might have thought? (Pettibon, 2004). I make no apology for this digression, for reasons already given.

O'Nuallain (2004) (pp. 197–214) grimly goes through the morass of revisionist Irish history. Essentially, there are several classic revisionist moves. One is full-frontal assault, exemplified by the British historian and journalist Geoffrey Wheatcroft. For Wheatcroft, the Irish claim on the island of Ireland is less compelling than even the radical Islamists' claim on southern Spain, or Al-Andaluz. So Al Qaeda have more right to Seville than the Irish have to Derry.

Let us call this the Osama version of Irish history. The next is the alien abduction version. There are many people on this planet who claim to have been kidnapped by aliens, or to be aliens. In this vein, the English historian Ellis (1999), whose salary is paid by the Irish taxpayer and while writing in an Irish journal, comments that Ireland was historically full of people who thought of themselves as English, although they lived in Ireland. Well, I am Irish, and live in Berkeley, California. Go figure. I do not make America Ireland – not that I would want to do so!

The next version is the "Irish Nazi" type of revisionism. This sees any expression of Irish national sentiment as morally equivalent to Kristalnacht and Mengele's twin experiments. Hamilton (2003) was quite a find for those people, as he claims to have been brought up in a German-Irish household in south Dublin that forbade conversation in English. His father is a Hitler figure, and humanity enters through his German mother.

Hamilton's domestic upbringing is not of interest to us, but the thesis of the book certainly is. Irish culture = IRA = anti-Semitism = Nazism. Hamilton is a find for revisionists like Roy Foster, as he claims to explore Gaelic culture from within and finds that it doesn't actually exist. The notion of Jews dancing to Irish music is proposed as an exemplification of Irish Nazism; my Israeli Jewish friends rather like doing Irish dancing, and can be found indulging in this perversion of nature on Monday nights in the Starry Plough in Berkeley. (There are up to a hundred dancers each week at this class and dance, which started in the late seventies; often, there is not a single ethnically Irish person among them).

Much more dangerously, Hamilton mocks his father's activity of finding the original Gaelic names for places, and never rises to a description of conversations in Irish beyond the crudest of gossip. Intriguingly, the technical vocabulary in Irish for such matters as information technology is updated just as often as most other non-English languages. The analogy between the authoritarian father and Hitler is drawn out at some length:

> "There was a man called Arnulf, like the story my mother heard about in Germany, and he would not let any of the other puppets speak … So then Kasper had to find a way of killing Arnulf so that all the other puppets could speak again." (Hamilton, 2003, p. 207)

The brutality and bigotry of his fellow students is emphasized. Patriotism is inculcated in the crudest possible way:

> "In school, they teach us to love our own country. They sing a song about the British going home … O ró sé do bheatha "bhaile"….It's a funny song and very polite. It says to the British that we hope they'll keep healthy and have a good trip home." (Hamilton, 2003, 120–121)

Hamilton never leaves this childlike register, even for passages from his teens. What gives Foster and the other revisionist blurb contributors a *frisson* is probably this destruction of Irish from the inside.

The song is very strong melodically, possibly a cognate of "The Drunken Sailor". Due to a set of fortunate musical meetings, my partner Melanie O'Reilly and I have performed it in France with the leader of the Bulgarian folk orchestra and a female Bulgarian choir – it's out there on Youtube - jazz groups in Ireland, the US and France, and have arranged it also for strings. We have also taught it to American schoolchildren, who loved it. It will survive the attack from Hamilton, as well as any damage we accidentally inflict on it.

If he indeed is the native Gaelic speaker he claims to be, Hamilton would be aware that it is often written, O ró sé do bheatha 'Mhaile.'It features verses about Grainne Ni Mhaile, (Grace O'Malley), a familiar of Queen Elizabeth, who failed to provide the naval backing available to her for several Irish uprisings during her lifetime. The title can thus be translated as "Go girl, Grace!". "Grania", based on Grace is the latest (and, given its failure, perhaps the last) production from the Abhann productions, the Riverdance team. The song alludes also to Bonnie Prince Charles:

> Ta Séarlas og ag teacht thar saile
> …
> Is déanfaidh se rince as eircibh.

Charles is coming from abroad, and he will make a dance out of a revolution. This verse is best read as a satire, a very human way of laughing at an intolerable colonial situation. Given the prince's military record, his coming with a couple of soldiers to Ireland as the song announces did not portend a new dawn for the country.

Elsewhere, Hamilton concludes that the word for "green" (glas) and "grey" (liath) in Irish are the same. In fact, Irish has two words for that part of the electromagnetic spectrum that we call "green", with "uaithne" at the other extreme from "glas". He seems not to notice that Irish has a vocative case (p. 27). Finally, his rebel credentials are established by hitting his Irish teacher, the wife of one of the greatest novelists in the language, in the face (p. 70). His mother enthusiastically approves.

Fortunately, we have an altogether more interesting Hiberno-Teutonic story to contrast with Hugo's (MacSwiney Brugha, 2006). Terence MacSwiney sired one child, Maire, whose death in 2012 brought some attention back to this remarkable family; with some prescience, he dictated in his will that care of the child should be divided between his sister, Maire, and wife, Muriel. The child was farmed out to numerous foster parents in France and Germany until she had in fact forgotten English and lived as a German girl. To pre-empt her mother taking her, the child was effectively kidnapped by her aunt and brought back to Ireland, where she had to relearn English and Irish in her teens. There is not a trace of anger against nationalism in the book for her father's death, or accidentally multicultural upbringing; Mrs. MacSwiney Brugha remained a strong nationalist, proud of her country.

Below, we examine the positive cultural existence of Irishness. Right now, let us look at a final revisionist move; the insistence on an absurdly high standard for nationhood by which mediaeval Ireland in particular is judged and found wanting. The conclusion is then drawn that, since mediaeval Ireland did not have all the accoutrements of a modern nation-state, and mediaeval times are the last time that the Irish had unambiguous political control of their island, therefore the island of Ireland is not a natural political entity. Ellis (1999), we have seen, epitomizes this line. Though I have dealt with historical revisionism elsewhere (2004), let us take some time to look at this argument.

Trumpeting their outrage by the carnage in the British-occupied part of the island of Ireland, particularly since 1969, a revisionist school of thought has emerged which places the blame for the violence squarely on irredentist Irish claims to ownership of this land. Writers like the late Conor Cruise O'Brien (1986), erstwhile propagandists for the irredentist Irish cause, began to view even the culmination of the British genocidal impulse of the Great Famine as, at worst, "callous lethargy". (His biographer Akenson has made reference to O'Brien's great feats of alcohol evacuation; bringing matters up to date, one can confirm that, days before the 2004 U.S. election, O'Brien confidently predicted in a national newspaper column that George W. Bush would carry both California and New York, if few other places.)

In the 1980's, O'Brien was (very) briefly editor of the London Observer. His section 31 broadcasting ban, imposed during his controversial and frankly technophobic tenancy as minister for Posts and Telegraphs in the mid-seventies, prohibited republican leaders from having their logical fallacies exposed in the Irish media by a blanket ban on what would be first amendment rights in the U.S. It can perhaps be explained, as can his willingness to allow physical violence on republican prisoners, by an IRA plan to kill him. Other failed campaigns included his attempt to bring the BBC to the great unwashed in Ireland, and his refusal to support Bob Geldof's first publishing venture.

O'Brien is one among very many: Roy Foster, Owen Dudley Edwards, and Jane Ohlmeyer have been encouraged to hold forth on the Irish, *de haut en bas*, from the security of tenured positions in Trinity College, Dublin. Their argument is hydra-headed; ontological (the non-existence of Ireland), ethical (the violent history of Irish republicanism), and aesthetic (the Anglo-Saxons are so much farther advanced in the arts and technology, not to mention *la politesse*).

Very few countries pay a privileged elite with taxpayers' money to question the right of the state to govern the country; indeed, to question the right of the state to exact tax from individuals to pay for these arguments to be enunciated. Let us revisit the thesis that Ireland was never a coherent political state in modern terms. That is undoubtedly and trivially true; for example, the mathematical theory of social insurance on foot of which

Bismarck was able to create his welfare state was not finalized until Condorcet, a mathematical prodigy turned politician, and his colleagues worked on it in the eighteenth century. The Irish occupied their land for upwards of eight millennia before the Saxons came to Britain; yet, the administrative capacities bequeathed by the Norman and Angevin bureaucrats were undoubtedly capable of producing tighter political union than the equally sophisticated, but less political, Irish law. In military terms, the Gaelic uprising of Tudor times undoubtedly failed just as the early twentieth-century war of independence succeeded.

Ireland is a work in progress, and is unquestionably behind the rest of Western Europe in its organic evolution. It increasingly looks as though this is quite simply due to a brutal colonial experience. Intriguingly, it may be the case that whole centuries of exploitation can be negated by people of genius in our age. James Joyce famously imposed on himself the grand task of forging in the smithy of his soul the conscience of his race. One result, *Ulysses* (1986), is a reconstruction of Homer's epic, translated to the prosaic meanderings of a Jewish entrepreneur in Dublin. While Ulysses is replete with and structured by references to Homer, Hamlet, and the Catholic Mass (and equally to the Irish epics like the "Voyage of Bran"), "Finnegan's Wake" is an even more fundamental attempt at advancing human consciousness in every sense.

In Finnegan's Wake (Joyce, 1966), words take on themselves connotations from dozens of other languages (Donoghue, 1986). A rather prosaic story about a Dubliner called HC Earwicker is to apotheosise as he universalizes into Here Comes Everybody. Yet Joyce is after bigger game, an insight into the profound roots of Indo-European culture as seen through the prism of quotidian Dublin experience:

> "The vision of Finnegan's Wake, where the dark hidden father and his Shakti are indeed to come alive again by virtue of the magic of the left-hand way" (Campbell, 1968, p. 262).

In Joyce's Ulysses, Manannan Mac Lir, a Gaelic sea god, adapts the "I am" declaration crucial to Advaita Vedanta in Hinduism to humdrum Irish existence ("I am the dreamery creamery butter").

Joyce's critical and commercial success needs no advertising here: "Ulysses" is repeatedly voted the greatest novel of all time in readers' and critics' polls. Yet his achievement may be greater still: it is possible that he unearthed an ineluctable in the Irish psyche, a universal in the particulars of mythology.

We shall quickly proceed to a very brief history of Ireland; let us anticipate by considering the final, Milesian conquest of Ireland. The notion of the provenance of the hitherto mythological Milesians in Spain has recently been strengthened by DNA evidence that establishes a mitochondrial DNA link between the Irish and Basques. When the Milesians initially land in Ireland, their poet Amergin bursts into a similar theophany:

> "I am the wind
> Scouring the foam
> I am a breaker of the sea
> I am the growl of the ocean
> I am a roaring bull
> …
> I am the god who seized the fire of creation"

Krishna's theophany in the Bhagavad Gita is of a piece with this; many other peoples have similar assertions of the paradoxical universality of "I am".

Joyce, of course, knew his historical antecedents; indeed, his interest in the esoteric was sufficient to impel him to visit "George Gurdjieff's institute for the harmonious development of man" in Fontainebleu. This was very possibly at the request of his first publisher, Margaret Anderson, who moved to Europe and became a Gurdjieff devotee after her obscenity trial in the USA.

There is no attempt here to capture Joyce for radical Irish republicanism; he never understood it, failed utterly to predict its power in gaining some degree of political and economic independence for Ireland, and eviscerated the formidable founder of modern Gaelic games, Michael Cusack, in his portrayal of "the citizen" in Ulysses. Joyce's achievement makes irrelevant such a minor cavil. He managed to advance Irish literature until, incarnated in his oeuvre and that of his follower Samuel Beckett, it led the world. The response of the Irish state was to ban both authors; the banning years over, the Dublin government of 2004 saw as appropriate the celebration of the centenary of Bloomsday, the fictional temporal centre of Ulysses, by the feeding of sausages and bacon to its denizens.

The ban was a better stimulus to great art than sausages; and now we assent to certain radical revisionist critiques of Ireland. Indeed, the country does not yet quite exist; it flails around, lurching blindly from a Jansenist, misogynist Roman Catholicism through wannabe neoconservatism to an oxymoronic, uneasy attempted caring neoliberalism. Joyce's achievement is, in retrospect, metaphysical as much as literary in his universalisation of Irish culture.

Of course, he lived and worked on mainland Europe, and died rather tragically and marginalized. Like Beckett, he revisited Ireland only rarely. Given that his near-contemporary, the pastoral poet Patrick Kavanagh, was interrogated by the Irish equivalent of the FBI who were investigating allegations of obscenity, Joyce's absence was prudent. (Kavanagh's Wildeian response to his unexpected visitors was to make a cup of tea to them and admit to the charge) Though Michael Flatley's work is probably not of the same calibre, we will use it to complete this section.

Flatley's famous "Riverdance" worked from unpromising material. The Irish commitment to dance is legendary; despite the lack of native words for dance, quadrille and other French ballroom styles from the seventeenth century on were eagerly adopted and transformed. However, official Irish state policy declared that a stiff back and still arms were *desiderata*. The reinvention of Ireland in the early twentieth century saw as *echt-Irisch* Munster Irish and Kerry style dancing; the cynics among us marvel that the Prime Minister of the period in question grew up close to this area, after his birth in New York. In the early 1970s, the capacious auditory memories of Irish folk musicians found themselves a new challenge in the tricky metres of Balkan music. Balkan tunes in 7:8, 9:8 and, indeed, 11:8 were incorporated into the Irish canon.

Europe hosts an international version of "American Idol" called the Eurovision Song Contest annually. Ireland, winners in 1981, were compelled to host it in 1982. The composer Bill Whelan worked with Planxty, Ireland's folk band laureate, to produce a suite called "Timedance" that featured Irish and Balkan music and dance.

Nothing whatsoever came of it. In the mid-nineties, the notoriously rigged Eurovision was won several times in a row by Ireland. Flatley choreographed a dance piece in 9:8, an Irish "slip jig", for his fellow American Jean Butler. The show culminated in ensemble dancing to the Balkan "Riverdance" theme.

What happened afterward is the interesting part. As soon as the show grew, it appropriated elements from Russian dance, from African-American tap, and from flamenco to produce a flamboyantly cosmopolitan show. When the inevitable Dublin arguments began, and Flatley had to leave, his response was the same as Joyce's: to dig even deeper into the tropes of Irish mythology in "Lord of the Dance".

Let us be clear: there are strong elements of pure kitsch, brash sexuality, megalomania, historical inaccuracy, and musical plagiarism in both shows. The past that Flatley evokes in "Lord of the Dance" is no more literally real than the Tuatha De Danann, Milesians, or the Battle of Moytura. The existence of these myths, attested over time, is very real. The extraordinary survival of Irish dance, honed to an extremely high standard in emigrant communities like that in which Flatley grew up, as in Ireland itself, is a fact. The eschatological battle between forces of good and evil depicted in "Lord of the Dance" is a universal myth. The universal resonance of both shows is now a critical and commercial fact.

Irish culture at its height is always flamboyantly cosmopolitan. A force gathered within the island itself finds correlates and avenues for expression in its contemporary world. The waves that produced these shows, as well as Joyce and Beckett, have spent themselves. That normally means that another wave is coming.

2.3 The mechanism of colonial alienation

It is time to revisit the phenomenological/existential/cognitive aspects of nationality that we encountered in Chapter 1. Let us start with some simple uncontroversial observations. While the genetic package of Irish people like this writer includes Vitamin D production at the expense of melanin, and an efficient metabolism for dairy products, nature is dwarfed by nurture. We owe our native language, the way we walk, and much else to cultural influences. The overwhelming majority of the Irish population is Anglophone in its native language, with the few native Gaelic speakers now greatly outnumbered by native Chinese, Slav and indeed Uralic speakers. This last point speaks volumes for recent colonial social engineering, as the island's tiny population, Anglophonie, and a large diaspora speaks for a millennium of rather more robust British social engineering.

When we speak of "national consciousness", we really mean specific cognitive items that present themselves repetitively to the individual's consciousness. The state can manufacture such items as propaganda; the Irish state has deftly adjusted its output in recent years from Gaelic Catholic nationalism to neo-liberalism. We are going to briefly hypothesise about the neuroscience of propaganda. Walter Freeman (Freeman, O'Nuallain, and Rodriguez, 2008) has produced decades' worth of EEG evidence that propaganda works by etching trajectories in the attractor landscape of the brain, facilitating the recurrence of the propaganda narrative in the absence of any external stimulus. He refers to William Sargent's (1958) "Battle for the Mind", in which political and religious conversion is described as "abreaction", the creation of a psychic spasm that hard-wires the belief system.

We revisit Freeman's and my work below; for the moment, we need to unpack the notion of "national identity" vis a vis the self who does the identifying. Reviews like Charles Taylor's (1989) "Sources of the Self" describe a self that is embedded in nature and oriented toward the good. At a much finer-grained level, it seems to be the case that the self reflects the operations of data compression that the brain must continually do in order to prevent itself drowning in the myriad irrelevant data that impinge on it from moment to moment(O Nualláin,2010). Moreover, we continually attribute to ourselves the authorship of actions that happened through involuntary neural process. In an extended version of this scenario, in some of Freeman's unpublished work in this author's possession:

> "The contents of conscious states comprise a sparse sample of the wave packets that embody motor commands … and perceptions that we conceive as unconscious … EEG evidence indicates that voluntary actions are initiated about half a second before awareness of the intent to act."

Our core identifications, like gender, profession, and nationality, are less data items than architectural supports to our entire engagement with the world, others, and ourselves. Confronted with arguments undermining them, we will fight, sometimes to the death, to preserve them. Faced with a genocidal foe, the concept of nationality will indeed apotheosize into a Fichtean noumenal entity, as cognitive emergency coincides with national disaster. For the current colonial culture in Ireland, the techniques used by both sides, and the exigent identifications of Irish nationality, will be subtle.

The reader will be forgiven for thinking this an unnecessary digression. It is in fact the core of the basis for the restructuring of the anticolonial psyche that this book envisages. Gandhi (1998, 34-37) locates the beginnings of the colonial subject in the 1619 Cartesian "*Cogito, ergo sum*". The rest of the world outside the cogito becomes the Other, purely subject to one's disincarnate will, and mediated through representations rather than experienced directly. She goes so far (37) as to wonder whether "it is possible, after 10 November 1619, to imagine non-coercive knowledges...to think non-violently". To anticipate a little, Joyce's "Citizen", based on Michael Cusack, is prone to that Cartesian split; specifically, he sees himself as co-extensive with the physical island. He is reprehensible; the anti-colonial narrative in Joyce, begun in Dubliners with the cadging of a sovereign by the miscreant two gallants, is to apotheosize into a nuancing of the distinction between subject and object, into a questioning of time and space themselves.

Gandhi (37-41) presses the attack, calling *inter alia* Heidegger, Foucault and Nietzsche to join her. The disincarnate self is located in a world that immediately becomes disenchanted. Joyce's project is to return the enchantment, suitably contextualised in Gaelic myth as in the classics of other "western" literatures, while displaying a knowledge of advaita vedanta. On a prosaic level, his project is non-violent national liberation:

> "His book examines the servitude of his countrymen to their masters in church and state and offers an ampler vision" (Ellmann, 1977, P. 90)

Joyce's politics included both a moderate cultural nationalism and a rather thoroughgoing socialism:

> "Although he refused to endorse the revival of the Irish language, Joyce was in other ways on the side of the separatist movement" (87)

> "He favoured the Sinn Fein policy ... its effect would be at first only to substitute Irish for English capital....capitalism was a necessary transition to socialism" (Ellmann, 1965, P 246)

He was famously skeptical that any Irish revolutionary movement could survive the phalanx of informers, and did not anticipate the relative success of the Tan war:

> "During the last two years of the Irish fight for independence, the only incident that stirred his imagination was the hunger strike of the lord mayor of Cork, Terrence MacSwiney, possibly a distant relation" (ibid., 547)

In Ulysses, space and time are to be subverted; the identification of Ireland with a place on a map that can be finalized with the colonial ordinance survey is to be undermined. Joyce is after some very big game indeed:

> "Throughout the book, Stephen deals with..philosophical problems...the first is whether the world has an objective existence, as maintained by Aristotle, or whether...nothing exists but subjective state..'there is no self, no external world'" (Ellmann, 1977, 63)

In my research work (O Nualláin, 2010, and forthcoming), I have some empirical evidence that self is, paradoxically, a mechanism for maintaining the operational existence of the external world. In the Advaita Vedanta tradition, with which Joyce is undoubtedly familiar as his Manannan Mac Lir quotes from the Bhagavad Gita in the Circe episode, the true reality is advaita; not two; no distinction between subject and object. Let us note that we have abandoned the notion of consciousness as a set of epistemological dispositions with which Ellmann started his 1977 work, a fact that Ellmann fails to acknowledge as he – correctly – yet lets the evidence speak.

Remarkably, the metaphysical attack also is political;

> "The attack on space and time, then, is elaborately coordinated with an attack on the visible and invisible authorities in Ireland" (ibid. 82)

To be explicit about the Citizen:

> "The dangers of selfhood manifest themselves in the Cyclops episode where the Citizen can see nothing but a nation-wide egoism, and in Circe" (ibid. 63)

Another model for the citizen is Padraig Pearse, who "persuaded...even Joyce to take lessons in Irish" (Ellmann, 1965, P. 62) but "Pearse the instructor found it necessary to exalt Irish by denigrating English (ibid.). Pearse himself was to be "changed utterly", in Yeat's felicitous phrase, by the courage with which the insurgents of 1916 upheld the timeless principles of their proclamation of the republic.

During Circe, Manannan Mac Lir enunciates the "I am" of the theophany in the Bhagavad Gita. Space and time will not be constant again; the body will rest secure, in union with rather than in Cartesian separation from the mind; selves and genders will interpenetrate each other;

> "The first nine chapters of 'Ulysses' concede validity to space and time and the second nine chapters impugn that validity" (Ellmann, 1977, P 94)

Joyce's probable relative Terrence MacSwiney has provided the revolutionary subtext for this book; Joyce himself has presaged its metaphysics. Yet his contribution is greater still, as the reader will hopefully be convinced by the end of this book

That nation is one of our central identifications is due, to some extent, to the brute power of the modern nation-state. That power, if used for the good, can effectively be recruited against the totalizing impulses of global neo-liberalism.

Let us return to neurodynamics. What we mean by a cerebral trajectory is something corresponding to our requirement that a story must have a beginning, middle, and end, that a dominant seventh chord should resolve to the tonic, or its fourth, and that an object cannot be in two places at one time. Quantum mechanics has taught us that the last desideratum, like the other two, is a convention - at least on a certain physical scale. State propaganda, which we all experience as children, attempts to inculcate trajectories that will function at above the relatively slow sampling speed of consciousness, and so can be reflected upon only with difficulty. One such, the notion that the Irish state is benevolent, and a proper promoter of Irishness, is being attacked in this book, and thus hostile reaction to this book's thesis is inevitable.

Modern colonial propaganda does not attempt to attack explicit symbols of nationality. It will be felt initially on the fringe of consciousness, as discomfort, as ontological violation, rather than consciously processed as provocative argument. It will attempt to reframe debates, instead of speaking to the point; it will subtly violate the sense of place on which authentic salutary nationalism depends by disincarnating the country, by referring continually to the political entity "the Republic of Ireland" rather than to that happy coincidence of the political and geographical that we used to call Ireland (and should do so again).

Similarly, the debate about e-voting was reframed as one about whether it will actually save the state one million Euro a year or not. Once dragged into this debate, one is lost. The response of the Chiapas resistors to state complaints about their tardiness in responding to state proposals by using broad consultation was that they did things at the "speed of democracy".

Ireland since 1997 has had political power increasingly centered in a prime minister who refuses to put a coherent narrative together about any of the grave issues that have confronted the twenty-six countries in their health service, vulnerability to political corruption, and so on. The medium is in this case precisely the lack of message, and things are allowed to slide, as Bertie Ahern's assault on the English language (he does not know any other) continued. Ahern's successors, Brian Cowen and Enda Kenny, are little better. An example from the Irish Times on 20 December 2006, when Ahern was asked to explain why he signed blank cheques for his disgraced predecessor:

> "If I ever for a moment had thought that by signing a cheque, which was a practice everybody did in the country, let's be frank and honest about it and not prudish, I would not have signed them."

In 2005, having denied in writing that he would do so, the Irish consul in San Francisco gave a donation to UC Berkeley British studies to put on a lecture series in Irish Studies. There was a golden opportunity to give a moderate nationalist or unionist politician a week in California to enlighten the UC community about techniques, drawn from experience, to end sectarian violence. Alternatively, they could have chosen to fund some of the work on old and modern Irish occurring at UC. They chose instead to bring Jane Ohlmeyer, a revisionist historian, over from Ireland, and the result was posted on the web. The rhetorical device here is subtle; it is to discuss Irish history as if the native Irish themselves did not write any. The response of the Berkeley Irish community has been an annual St Patrick's/vernal equinox lecture, the 2012 "Ireland in Crisis" conference, and – of course! – this book.

Remarkably, as already pointed out, Ohlmeyer's chair is funded by Irish taxpayers, from whom money is extracted by a state that claims charter to do so from a national revolution, the validity of which Ohlmeyer and her ilk question. Surely, in order to be consistent, revisionist historians at Irish State universities should resign.

Since the external symbols of Irish nationality, unlike those of England, are secure, and the national narrative is one of reverence for and military uprising on behalf of universal human values of democracy, tolerance, economic equality and republican citizenship, current neo-colonialism must reframe the debates as we've seen. For "voting is good, as it reflects the democratic will of the people", it surreptitiously replaces "money is good, and e-voting, even if utterly inaccurate, will cost less" and invites one to debate within this frame. Intriguingly, the result has increasingly been the ontological alienation first described by MacSwiney, with the absence of the republican narrative being so fully missed that fully 100,000 people, a huge multiple of previous years, came out on the streets of Dublin for the 90th anniversary of the 1916 rising. Further censorship, however implemented, may produce another, post-al-Qaeda, IRA.

Let us return to Berlin and his prudent caveats about nationalism. The argument here is that nationalism is the most potent force against globalised neo-liberalism, and that when the Irish economy collapses a la Argentina and Thailand, the quickening of national sentiment that will arise must be diverted into creative channels. With respect to the British, it should be emphasized that every word of Irish spoken, of Irish music played, and every moment of every Gaelic Game is a victory over the British, as is every breath of a free self-aware Irish person in a state in which they hold a voting franchise. Revisionist history must be attacked with a force that will provide catharsis to prevent actual physical violence. The aim is intensification of a sense of place, and its diversification through artistic activity and the life of the body.

All of this has much more in common with Herder than with Fichte, and must be undertaken in conjunction with renegotiation in Ireland's favour of its terms of membership in the EU, WTO, and so on as deals are struck to pay back moneys owed (or not, as the case may be when the taxpayer has been put on the hook for items not her business).

Nation, in the positive sense this book promotes, is a fortiori a synesthesia and amplification of one's sense of place through the modalities of art, sport, the intellect, and state politics; through culture. Ireland is uniquely placed in that, as a non-imperial power, it has not debauched its native traditions in imperial ritual; conversely, the great majority of the population can understand the rudiments of the language in which their ancestors named places. While the initial mythologisations are always naïve, it can be argued that few cultural gestures would benefit North

America more than reminding its residents, perhaps through bilingual street signs, of the original names of places. The alienation from the land we sketched in the Tara/Skryne case is amplified by foreign capital making land an artificially expensive commodity.

As the essential political unit, the nation-state can indeed cleave body and mind in the manner Kundera describes. In assenting to colonisation, as it has done in Ireland, it can induce false self systems. If, as has been argued, globalisation is above all the felling of national borders to allow trade, nationalism can effectively fight globalisation. ("Neoloberalism" or "globalized corporatism" are better names for this enemy of human progress). The false self systems in the decade from 1997 are best testified to by the appalling architecture of the building mania, and the dearth of worthwhile artists and thinkers.

Let us pay a final visit to cognitive science. Mignolo (2006) comments on the desirability in the decolonial movement of an emphasis on embodied modes of thought. When contrasted with Marxism, the archetypal disembodied mode, this argument has validity. Marxism is redolent of the fallacy of the solitary thinker; while iron laws of economics can indeed be discerned from the fastnesses of a British Museum reading room, complicated issues about power need the experience of situational, embodied thinking.

As I describe elsewhere (2003), embodied theories of cognition stress that mental acts begin with simple physical interaction with the world and never quite leave this behind. From the physical experience, we learn to abstract certain principles and internalize modes of operation, so an abstract system of thought that is yet firmly grounded in reality emerges. The most famous contemporary expression of this insight of Jean Piaget's stresses that our conceptual thought reveals in its linguistic expression that essentially special metaphorical expressions underlie it. So the US government is "rocked" by scandal, and GW Bush "remained unmoved" about Iraq, though all decent people were and remain "upset".

Since the cultural development of Gaelic Ireland was aborted as the rest of Europe went into the Renaissance, it could allow us a laboratory to see how a culture undergoes the enlightenment and modernism, now that the Irish language is no longer proscribed. We can do a cognitive science analysis of how certain advances in thought force greater mental efficiency. In particular, the contemporary citizen with a car, computer, cell phone and dozens of social roles in a (post) modern environment needs rather greater ontological support than is currently provided by the resources either of religion, psychology, or indeed nationalism.

Pace Berlin, Fichte's goals were ultimately cosmopolitan, and his noumenal nationalism is that of a race and culture facing extinction. No such quickening of the national impulse is being countenanced here. It may be appropriate, however, to look at genuine national differences, A classic article by Cushman (1990) argues that the neo-liberal desideratum is for a citizenry-turned-consumer base that considers itself empty. It might be argued that this is peculiarly American; in the absence of a sense of place, everything intersubjective is regarded as potentially the province of technique. We Europeans often find in America a commodification of what seemed private or unconsciously intersubjective impulses with magazines dedicated to the purpose. Similarly, we find what we term unconscious "social skills" in the intersubjective domain objectified as "rhetorical devices" or, more colloquially, as "hustles".

The equipment with which each nation group attempts the peaks of human achievement will therefore differ. The only danger to Ireland from cosmopolitan culture, as distinct from neo-liberal bullying that attempts to destroy the hierarchy of value, is that we do not engage with its universally valid heights. These heights invariably show self-awareness, complexity and that renunciation of immediate gratification we call "fineness". The apparent paradox is that Ireland's globalised years were the most provincial and under-achieving that any of us can remember.

In the final chapter, we shall consider how the flawed minor leviathan of the Irish state can help. It may be the case that active renunciation on its part, and a delegation of delicate apparati like the music business and high tech may be the way to go.

2.4 Political and Postx thought; theocracy and the self

Let us return to the definition of nationalism used here and revisit the main themes of this section through an encounter with postmodern thought. We define nationalism as a synesthesia and amplification of a sense of place. While the notion of genetic kinship has entered pathological forms of terrorism, particularly when an imperial project is being implemented, the national fervour of those not from the "Ur" genetic stock is attested in many nationalist outbreaks, including the Irish (de Valera, Pearse, Brugha (a liberal rendering of "Burgess"), Childers, Blythe, MacSwiney, and so on). Sense of place is primary; its modulation through cultural means resembles the capacity synesthetes have to "see" perfumes, or to smell colours (Day, 2002). When modulated through politics, we get, on the one extreme, the kind of institutions required to support Herderian cultural nationalism and, on the other extreme, Fichtean or worse types of nationalisms, to be examined below.

Of course, nationalism seems antediluvian, or at best Victorian. The problem for those of us who would like to banish it completely is that sense of place will continue to find political expression, whatever we wish for. Paradoxes abound; the political nationalism of Salazar's regime promoted Portuguese folk arts, which staged a revival only after his demission (Holton, 2005). Ireland's experience too is that delegation of the arts (and indeed science) to civil society enhances them. Politicians' involvement with the arts will almost inevitably create a class of non-productive artistic bureaucrats who smother real artists, and who indeed perhaps resent them. We comment on this in Chapter 7.

Political sectarian nationalism is famously one of the most dangerous forces in the world. It is often kindles by hucksters like Milosevic, who accelerated campaigns against Croatia and Albania, respectively, in the face of protests against his rule and control of the media in 1991 and 1996-1997. A little-known fact is that between 50% and 80% of Serbs went into hiding rather than fight against Croatia. The Serbs in Croatia who protested Milosevic's policies, many of whom were ex-partisans, he began to label Ustashe after the feared Croatian Nazi quislings (who were of course revered in Ireland in its pathological Roman Catholic phase).

Milosevic was helped greatly by his Croatian counterpart, Tudjiman, like him a member of the ancien Communist apparat. On the unpromising foundations of ethnic identity was erected a virtual machine that assessed one's character on the sole issue of blind obedience, or not, to the dictates of those two monsters. Serbian nationalism can always point to the suppression of its identity, even more savagely by the Bulgarians than by the Hapsburgs in the early 20th century. Cui bono, given that Yugoslavia broke up? Actually, the ruse worked perfectly; Milosevic and his peers managed to stay in power for a decade after 1990, and only the implementation of legislation promoting market activity and private property secured regime change. The extreme violence of the 1990s Balkans was due to the low levels of ethnic hatreds there in 1990, with record levels of inter-ethnic marriage, rather than being a boil that had to be lanced through the horrors we all reviled.

Similarly, the Weimar republic had record levels of intermarriage between Jews and Gentiles, and many Nazis knew that their concept of race was absurd. However, it suited their political purposes. The particular range from the spectrum of nationalism being proposed here is explicitly that which conforms with Herderian dictates. The Northern Irish problem pales in urgency at the beginning of the third millennium with the imperatives arising from the influx of global capital, and its possible imminent efflux. In its positive aspects, nationalism is always paradoxically cosmopolitan; at the fundamental level, it is a promotion of human universals of freedom, justice, and decency, and a proposal of how to work them through, taking genius loci into account.

As cognitive systems, we cannot function in the real world in a postmodern, post-structuralist miasma. Ferguson (2006) excoriates atheism, recruiting to his course Chesterton's *Miracle of Moon Crescent:*

> "You all swore you were hard-shelled materialists, and as a matter of fact, you were all balanced on the very edge of belief — of belief in almost anything." (Chesterton, in Ferguson 2006, p. 224)

This, Ferguson argues, is the correct version of "When men stop believing in God, they don't believe in nothing. They believe in anything." (ibid) from the Chesterton apocrypha.

Ferguson's particular target is post-Christendom. Yet Christianity is a highly syncretistic belief system whose survival is something of a mystery. Arnold Toynbee argued that the figure of Christ was a collage of themes from Egyptian mythology, from Roman religious desiderata (like the "Sol Invictus", unconquered sun), and universal requirements for a seed that dies and is reborn.

What is even more intriguing in this context is the story of Christ, as related through all the synoptic gospels. Jesus did not die for our sins, or because he insisted, against state ordinance, on continuing a healing mission. Rather, he came into Jerusalem from the provinces and worked hard at provoking every source of power therein. None of this provocation was done in the service of his healing mission, and it does rather seem that he attempted one of the least successful political coups in history. As

Albert Schweitzer put it, we cannot really see Christ through the distorting lens of the eschatalogical framework in which he worked.

The final irony is that the crucifixion of Christ represents the victorious fusion of the two great loci of power against which he fought: State, qua the Roman Empire, and Church, qua the Jewish religious authorities with their transcendent Semitic desert god. His resurrection yields a considerably attenuated apolitical Jesus, whose ethereality is confirmed by an expeditious ascent into heaven, where he will represent no further threat to earthly powers. So Christianity is a smorgasbord of possible relationships between the individual and political authorities, with St. Paul's letters famously counselling both abased servility and complete rebellion in different places.

The success of Don Brown's Da Vinci Code attests to the strange melange of political power, concepts of the divine right of kings, and esoteric knowledge on which Christianity is based. (Those who lack sufficient masochism to read the book can be assured that the excruciating movie does it justice). Brown juxtaposes, rather than synthesises, just about every gloss on the gospel story he could find, and on at least one occasion spliced text from the web straight into the novel, appealing to "fair use" provisions in copyright law. Essentially, we are asked to believe that the bloodline of Jesus and Mary Magdelene ran in the Meroviagian dynasty, and that Opus Dei sought to expunge it by murdering Audrey Tautou, in perhaps the worst performance by a French actress of all time. Opposing Opus Dei is a line of intellectual descent including Isaac Newton, Leonardo, and many others.

There is, of course, a smidgeon of truth in the sources that Brown uses. The Catholic Church can function better as a pure ideology machine if there is no independent verification, from science or folklore, for its arbitrary fiats. Secondly, like Islam, it depends on suppression of women to maintain a high fertility rate to ensure more members. In Ireland, it created a Victorian establishment independent of autochthonous expression, whose physical locations the Anglicans had taken.

Intriguingly, as I have described elsewhere (2004, p. 193), the Christian Church cannot consistently proclaim its doctrines of parousia, the coming of the kingdom of God on earth, without asserting some jurisdiction over earthly power structures. Constantine's stroke of genius was to recognise the potential of Christianity as a means to prop up his empire. The resulting institutional congeries, as McGraw (2005) argues, endorses the king's right to govern as being concerned with his work with the Church in stopping the people from sinning and getting them to heaven, a far better place than this earth where they toiled dutifully for him. The Church, for its part, upheld the divine right of kings.

There were some troublesome tensions in this cosy relationship between Church and State. First of all, on a hylomorphic level, Jesus was both God and man. No matter that he states, even in gospels, that he is not God, as only God is good; as a person of the Blessed Trinity, he was suitably accredited. Secondly, and much more seriously, he was not only divine but Jewish. In fact, accepting Christianity involved supplanting one's own ethnic myth with those of a desert tribe, and in the Irish case, a revisionism of the national narratives that dwarf in scale the rather feeble attempts by Jane Ohlmeyer,Roy Foster, and their ilk. That there was resistance is a tenable hypothesis; we certainly have a 6th-century text from one of the many lives of St. Patrick that presage the plaints of the dispossessed poets in Cromwellian times, that we will see later in chapter 6:

> "He is coming Adzed-Head, on the wild-headed sea with cloakhollow-headed and curved-headed staff
>
> He will cheat false religion on a bench facing east and his people will answer "Amen, Amen". — (Canon, in Kinsella (ed) 1989, p. 3)

To the pagan Irish, the clerical tonsure seemed performed by an adze.

So political power in Europe was legitimised by the national narrative of a Middle Eastern tribe. There was only one solution: promote the narrative and persecute its owners. The resulting history of pogrom and holocaust remains Europe's darkest nightmare (Carroll, 2001). And, of course, it remains rather worse than a nightmare for the Jews.

McGraw (ibid) credits John Locke with the radical revision of the relationship between the individual, church, and state, that she argues inspired the "Founding Fathers" [sic] of the USA. For Locke, we are free and equal in dignity because God creates us that way. James Madison extended this to argue that conscience is inalienable, because it derives from our relationship with God. In a good society, individuals of conscience were to search for the true and good, while working out how to live together.

The political theology of the US, “America’s sacred ground” (ibid) was to preserve natural “god-given” rights of freedom and dignity through a “civic” public forum, which accredited law enforcement. This forum included the principles of ahimsa/harmlessness, and consistency. It implemented the Golden Rule of morality. The “conscientious” public forum, on the other hand, implemented a dialogue featuring the give and take of conscience. McGraw’s thesis is that pluralism is hard-wired into the American project, and that the real dichotomy in the US is between dominance and liberty.

Neither the religious right nor the secular left has a monopoly on truth; while there is undoubtedly a religious ground to the nation, the founders wanted to exalt conscience as the basis of the nation, not Christianity. It was assumed that freedom of conscience gives rise to good, and that America’s purpose was to make the world a better place.

Let us be clear; this exalted discussion about conscience, and indeed Jeffersonian citizenship, can be at best a half-remembered civics lesson for most citizens. It is nevertheless, McGraw argues, implicit in every moment of their lives, as it frames at the most abstract level their relationship with the state and with each other. Moreover, it is important to note that all forms of Christianity are eschatological; whereas those that ardently await the rapture are explicitly so, both the Book of Daniel and Book of Revelations frame the eschatological battle between good and evil in ways that Christians believe put them alone firmly in the former camp. The result is that a far simpler relationship between self and power, in which Christ bestows a privileged position on oneself as believer, underlies the believing US Christian’s conceptual apparatus.

This boil is lanced by participation in a pluralistic civil society, particularly in its commercial aspect, and the stroke of genius that is the first amendment; the state legislates limits to its own power. Let us note, in passing, that Blanshard studied 1950s Ireland as a test case of how the US could slide into theocracy (Garvin, 2004, p. 282). The problem with America’s sacred ground is that dialogue between individual citizens and a God whose very existence is a controversial topic is not a sound basis for a happy and well-behaved polity. Whereas Thomas Jefferson argued that atheists could be included in this new Parnassus, he seems to have been in a minority. Impulses toward Jeffersonian republics like Ireland aspires to become need a basis other than mental conversation with a fugitive deity. After all, voices in the head still guarantees incarceration in an asylum.

Secondly, we are undoubtedly multiple selves. American Christians seem neatly to be able to fragment themselves into a self who eagerly awaits the imminent end of things on Sunday, and another who does business deals as if the world will go on forever on Monday. It seems to be the case that prolonged control of the psychophysical organism in the context of an animating idea crystallises a self who can drive the organism in the name of that idea (O Nualláin, 2010).

The ideas that drive his contemporary Americans, often to terrifying extremes, are the leitmotif of Jon Krakauer's work (2003). In his exploration of Mormon faith and life (ibid.), he explores the consequences of Joseph Smith's encouraging his followers to have direct visions from God. If these visions result in the brutal murder of a sister-in-law who shows an independent streak, and the continued existence of polygamy and child brides, then so be it (ibid.). Indeed, in a strange variation on Cain and Abel, both brothers assent if one brother receives a divine message to kill the other.

Yet Krakauer's typically robust examination of a frontier experience in American life is trumped in its capacity to disturb by Sharlet (2008). It is the figure of Jesus which initially concerns Sharlet; both god and man, speaking pure eschatology, he allows free rein for extereme political projects to be projecetd on himself, and incidentally sanctified. The next chapter will comment on the religious usefulness of Christianity; let us for the moment look at its political abuses.

Jesus is protean;there is a "Jesus in Miami... who seems to do nothing but wrestle Castro....a Jesus in Manhattan who dresses in drag...a musclebound Jesus in south-Central LA" (Sharlet, 2008, 5). This eventually allows for "an unhindered Christ defined by his muscles, a laissez-faire Jesus" (110). The explicit focus of Sharlet's book, reflected in the title, is "The Family", a catch-all Christian group whose meetings are attended by Hillary Clinton as by the usual rogues' gallery of Republicans and Monsanto lobbyists (276). The transmutation of Jesus is horribly fascinating (ibid):

> "For all the family's talk of Jesus as a person, he remains oddly abstract in the teachings they derive from him, a mixture of 'free market' economics, aggressive American internationalism, and 'leadership' as a fetishized term for power, a good in itself regardless of its ends"

Sharlet (78) is sensitive to the peculiarities of the conversion experience in American fundamentalist Christianity;

> "The two developing ideas of the times...the radical notion that to perceive the divine is to accept divine authority...and the mechanistic understanding of faith as instantaneous for those who want it"

The Family owe their origin to an erstwhile Norwegian travelling preacher called Abram who found his vocation in tending to the lost souls of the rich and the powerful during the Depression-era West Coast docks disputes;

> "They resolved the age-old question of theodicy...this was the birth of Abram's 'positive' Christianity: the censorship of suffering" (93)

In its current incarnation, disturbingly reminiscent of the George W. Bush presidency, Sharlet gets an invitation to the Family's boot camp:

> "You guys are here to learn how to rule the world" (35)

Admiration of the Cadres brought together by Hitler and Stalin in gaining power is frequently expressed. Moreover;

> "Rights, the family thought....are an infringement of god's sovereignty" (43).

The goal is simple:

> "What the family desired was power....with which Christ's kingdom could be built cell by cell" (51)

It is fascinating that these American religious movements can be traced back to Edwards and the Great Awakening (61); what Edwards enunciated was a mystical pantheistic vision, very much in line with what we sense might have been the Celtic view of Edward's Welsh ancestors. . The fact that this almost certainly cannot be gelled with Christianity with its millenniar ethos is what disturbs this writer. As it does Sharlet (367);

> "Our refusal to recognize the theocratic strand running throughout American history is as self-deceiving as fundamentalism's insistence that the US was created a Christian nation"

Fundamentalism's achievements are multifarious (368);

> "Foreign policy on a near-constant footing of Manichean urgency...'free markets' imprinted on the American mind.... a manic-depressive sexuality...democracy as founded on individual rights and yet indebted to a higher authority that trumps personal liberties"

Lacking a God with whom to talk, the modern task is a thoroughgoing analysis of one's behaviour in order to modify it in the context of moral principles that have stood the tests of time, reason, and real engagement in the world. The capacity to do this is rare, and the software hack that press-gangs Americans into a republican egalitarian market in their dealings with each other, notwithstanding tensions inherent in putative sacred grounds, and what counterfactuals they assent to in their religious rituals on Fridays, Saturdays, or Sundays, is probably what has prevented religious wars in the USA. Such prevention was indeed a primary goal of the "Founding Fathers."

Ferguson (ibid) dreams of a return to happier theories in his exegesis of Chesterton:

> "Evidence to support his point is now abundantly available in post-Christian Europe, where all kinds of New Age cults and irrational beliefs flourish…They delude themselves that attendance at a concert will reduce poverty in Africa…Drawn to conspiracy theories as the ancients were to superstitious, some Europeans blame the U.S. government for rising sea levels."

This author does not have Ferguson's Oxbridge background or imperfectly implemented propensity to mask a Scottish burr underneath Blairish purr, but believes that the appropriate Anglo response to this rant is "Quite."

The forces impinging on each individual today are so radical and diverse that engaging intellectually with them is very difficult. The most common response, inevitably, is fragmentation into multiple selves in the manner outlined above. Neither the law, nor any but our most intimate friends demand any but the most coarse-grained consistency of thought and behaviour from us. To work for Lockheed during the week and pray on Sunday to Jesus, the Prince of Peace, is perfectly feasible. SUVs with Sierra Club bumper stickers are hardly extinct. The neo-spiritual path of finding a self-consistent approach to the myriad forces impinging on us is one chosen by few. Disintegration is a perfectly feasible alternative, though authentic engagement in the disparate domains may produce the gift of authentic reflection on oneself, and with it a truly engaged citizenship.

With this in mind, let us examine postmodernism and post structuralism (to be lumped together as postx). It is worthwhile first to point out that all the French postx thinkers were civil servants, and that several served in what was in effect a colonial army, with Pierre Bourdieu participating in the Algerian war. For the civil servant, the state provides another layer of social contract, job and financial security for life in exchange for a further surrender of autonomy than that required under the Lockean dispensation. While academic tenure provides a liberating freedom of expression, it is hard to believe that the French state would continue to fund these postx thinkers if they really threatened it. In that, they did not let their employer down.

The French revolution was doomed to be domesticated by the state, initially in Napoleonic imperialism and currently in bureaucratic excess, by an ignorance of civil society. While there is a trend to identify civil society solely with NGOs, the thrust of the term has far more potential than that. For example, Costello (2003) describes the genesis of the republican courts during the Irish war of independence, systems of justice arising independently of state participation. Consider its potential: instead of the tripartite separation of powers implemented by the fiat of the US constitution, until their civil war the Irish had the jewel beyond price of a consensual system of justice originated outside state control. The return to the current bewigged farce, with appointment of judges by political parties, is perhaps the single most destructive result of the Civil War. Civil society is distinct from community as from the state; the more nimble constitutions on earth honour it, as they should, in the breach rather than the observance.

Let us continue with the job done by postx thinkers as propagandists for their contemporary power relations. Derrida famously introduced deconstruction, the disassembling of false dichotomies to yield true interpretation. Yet to posit a false dichotomy between X and not X is itself a proposition Y, just as Hume's related inability to find within a constant self is the report of a self who did the investigation armed with the logical principle of excluded middle that Derrida deplores. As Washburn (2005) implies, their immersion in postx thinking by university English departments has resulted in the understandable reaction by university regents that if those people don't think they have a discipline, why should we? This is particularly the case as many postx faculty are ex-sixties "radicals" looking for the new trend.

A single successful, self-aware political activist is worth an infinity of academics. Bourdieu, to his credit, inspired Lois Waquant's "Carnal sociology," and remained vehemently engaged in order to unearth the "Doxa," the unthought structures that underlay the public's and politicians' actions. However, Bruno Latour's analysis of fetishism in science and nihilistic posturings need to be read in the context of his Roman Catholicism. Lyotard's inveighing against grand narratives needs to be asserted as a grand narrative. Derrida's interpretation of Foucault as "nihilistic" needs to be juxtaposed with his petitioning, among with many other postx thinkers, for pederasty to be legalised in France, if the minor "gave consent." A minor cannot give consent in any meaningful way, as we note below.

Lyotard, to be fair, argued that postmodernism with its fragmentation of grand narratives is - paradoxically - a perennial idea. It is not just perennial, but will quicken in intensity as technology changes the nature of the items with which our cognitive systems engage to ever more informationally rich, diverse (consider the web), and physically powerful (consider household appliances, and the car) items. What postmodernism could help us with is ridding ourselves of precisely the kind of solipsistic, academically cosseted engagement that postx thinkers exemplify.

Thus, Foucault's equation of democracy with totalitarianism is the rant of an attention-seeking bureaucrat. Like Hume, and indeed Descartes, he asserts the ontological insecurity of the self through (implicitly) positing an imperial self. His views on language are essentially structuralist, an apotheosis of the French provincialism and self-importance he shares with Kristeva, rightly mocked by Sokal et al (1998). Pierre Bourdieu's attempt to break out of subject/object duality through positing habitus, a subject's disposition, versus the field or consensually-validated world and the notion of practice as a mediation restates the subjectivism of Kant's theory of categories.

Above all, in their approach to social change, postx thinkers mirror the error made by their employer in vesting all authority, including that in the "Droits de l'homme," in "La loi." The notion that much precious human development occurs in family, community, and civil society structures, which paradoxically need to be protected by the state from the state/law, is one that they, being bureaucrats and a part of the power structure, are innocent of. Let us again be clear; as technology changes our nature, bringing us into contact with a bewilderingly diverse range of human experience through travel and increasingly human-centred information technology interfaces, grand narratives will indeed fragment. One first begins to explore one's nation after having been exposed through mass and personal media to myriad others, and national narratives like MacSwiney's were fully aware of this even before modern communications

The basic structure with which a state works with is still the same; distinct spheres of private space implemented normally through family, then in turn community, civil society, and the public sphere that the state controls, financially and intellectually. Modern identity includes the capacity to cathect integral self-systems in technologically-sustained virtual spaces, and thus to postpone almost indefinitely authentic reflection on oneself. The public sphere includes artefacts of technology and capitalism driving whole human organisms, little bits of people blown up to be the whole in Somerset Maugham's description, rather like Guth's scenario for an inflationary universe starting from a tiny subset. The possibilities for domination, for destruction of innocence in the ebb and flow of projection and introjection, are almost endless, and the state should do everything it can through systems of representation and pre-emptive legislation to protect us. Directly to confront one move of Derrida et al, a child cannot give informed consent to sex with an adult any more than an under-nine rugby team can agree to take on an adult one, and for more or less the same reasons.

Walter Benjamin stressed that socialism was not at all radical: in fact, it is a brake on the far more radical ethos of capitalism. The latter will always declare a year zero, unprecedented technological advance, and seek to appropriate all private and public property in the name of the resultant new ethic. The job of state-funded intellectuals is to fight these forces with every fibre of their being, rather than engaging in shadow-boxing with the hand that feeds them. While Jeffersonian citizenship is an abstraction, the process of engagement with the brute realities of money, technology, and political power will hone certain listening and comprehending skills in the adult populace. It is the job of the public intellectual to explain complicated issues such as neo-colonialism to this audience. Criticising "the state," necessary as it is at times, is simple by contrast.

Moral and aesthetic relativisms are less intellectual positions than symptoms of a structural malaise. Integrity of one's moral being, a dynamic balance between care for self and others, between the expression and suppression of desire, should perhaps be described as "moral health." The postx problem seems to be that the French legal system is also a taboo system. A documentary called "Dig" was made about the early days of the 1990's bands "the Brian Jonestown Massacre" and "The Dandy Warhols." Both were busted for drugs on camera, the former clinically and consequentially in the U.S. (There is a truly dark moment when singer and bandleader Anton Newcombe allows the cops search the vehicle by waiving his privacy rights, fully knowing that his band will get criminal records like the one that he himself already had). The latter had it patiently explained to them in broken English by French customs officials that, while they were being let off this time, the next time the (trivial) fine would be doubled. One was reminded of the Monty Python sketch wherein, bereft of their normal tools, Torquemada and his colleagues were forced to inculcate orthodoxy with a (drying) rack.

It seems rather the case that the ubiquitous French State nationalises aspects of morality by exploiting a taboo system on top of legal sanction. Continuing the tribal anthropology of France, one might argue that "les philosophes" occupy a role similar to "an file" in mediaeval Irish society, a figure whose curse could sentence to death as a thaumaturgic consequence. Returning to morality, we can bound the subject with two contrasting tales. NBC's "Dateline" ran a series of stings in 2006 in which internet predators were lured into a studio where they expected to meet an under-age prospective sexual partner. In the set-up in Petaluma, California, as elsewhere, a disproportionate amount of the predators were foreign. They mistook the abundance of sexually explicit material used in advertising in the U.S. for actual sexual promiscuity in its WASP population.

Conversely, tens of thousands of Irish men (vanishingly few in percentage terms, and less than the population at large, have been convicted) were effectively told at 18 or younger as they entered clerical life that they would never experience sexuality. The impossibility of this move manifested itself in sexual cathexes on the young boys and girls in their care. The rest of course is history of an extremely dark nature. As with sexuality, so with financial greed, abuse of power, and other appetites; we need to strike a balance. Just as too much exercise cripples the immune system, and too much immune activity a la auto-immune diseases destroys the organism, too much "morality" destroys itself.

The complex situational nature of moral development is echoed by, and intertwined with, the recruitment of psychic resource in fruitive work. One must choose a professional activity that resonates with one's skills, facilitates providing for a family in a changing technological and economic climate, and seems meaningful in view of what one has experienced about the world. The preservation and amplification of this complex of impulses through civil society and corporate enforcement is what binds many people to the USA. The self emerging from this complex of imperatives is the addressee of citizenship urgings. Ireland currently interferes with this impulse, and debauches morality, through compulsory membership in its public sector state "unions."

The leaps of faith by dint of which one solidifies moral stability in the power, financial, and sexual realms are determinants of one's moral power. To come through a confrontation with an unjust ruling system without bitterness, having bettered the lot of others, and with one's skills intact is a strengthening process utterly foreign to postx "thinkers." Likewise, to restrict one's aesthetic experience to art forms that show a sophisticated interplay of indulgence and delay of gratification, self-awareness manifested in humour as in violation of expectation, and complexity is to acquire aesthetic refinement.

Again, it is the task of state intellectuals to form judgements in this sphere in ways that are situationally dependent. The core unit in society, the potential citizen, is pretty much as Jefferson described her, with the layers added by technology subservient to the continuing need to engage with structures of community, state, and finance. Remarkably, people have always had the sense to reject postx as higher influences of a moral and aesthetic nature enter their lives. It is up to the state to do what it can to navigate between world economic trends, global political structures, and disruptive technologies to provide an environment for human self-realisation. Currently, what Ireland does is merely to borrow money and relax moral stricture.

Many self-evident moral truths emerge from this analysis. The golden rule needs to be enriched with prescriptions about means and ends; will the action you embark on achieve the goals you require, and are these in themselves valid? One of the many problems about Marxism is its over-simplicity; markets work for certain processes because they map well onto fruitive efforts that people are willing to make.

Therefore, instead of Marxist revolution, we ask what is a fair price, and fair regulatory system, for non-essential systems. In classical social democratic fashion, it is appropriate to erect institutions to cater for the basics of food, health and shelter. The important insight is that the moral dimension of life is as real, and psychologically more immediate, than any other comparable dimension. Just as we risk our health to add piquancy to our life, so do we responsibly take moral risks. The production of a system identifying these and the corresponding aesthetic considerations we leave to the Guardians, to use a Platonic analogy. Just as the republic is an extended metaphor for mind, so is the citizen a state in microcosm. We assent also to classical anarchist thought in the insistence that, whereas some surrender to the state has to be made in order to implement the rule of law, the extent of this surrender should be minimised and the state's will implemented through concentric circles of committees, and that will should be regarded as irrelevant in a burgeoning civil society.

For postx thought to have had any ecological validity, reference in the real world, its proponents would have had to experience radical alienation through bullying by the forces of state and commerce sufficient to induce alienation for themselves. Postx thought reflects the mind-set of French enarques as surely and uselessly for our purposes as the Bible does that of Neolithic desert tribes.

We wish, then, fully to engage with the highest achievements of the human mind and spirit, with Albert Schweitzer and Jean Moulin as with Albert Einstein, Ludwig van Beethoven, Frank Lloyd Wright, and Keith Jarrett, in the context of a national ethos that does not obstruct this engagement, and at its best increases its intensity. The nation state has the most potential to counteract the negative effects of globalised neoliberalism. The assertion of universals in human development is a cosmopolitan affair; their implementation in a particular location is a national one. Instead of talking only to students with a pseudo-radical debauchery of the intellect, the job of a state-funded intellectual is to raise the understanding of a mature citizen of the important impacts of technology, money, and political change. As mutual understandings increase, a vocabulary will solidify around them.

The context for the faux radicalism of the postxers is at least scores of millennia of cultural and political development in France culminating in a thermonuclear-standard revolution. Yet, despite its universalist ethos, the revolution was intrinsically French; the reluctance of the Alsaciens to accept it was explained as due to their non-Frenchness. Apart from their role as fili, and the taboo system around la loi, the posturings of the postxers were implemented in a republican revolutionary state which had impressed on them perhaps the most sophisticated cognitive development in the world. The fundamental contextual psychic movements, Frenchness itself which yet nursed a universal credo, is the ocean on which les philosophes are froth.

Foucault's attempts to be trendy involved excoriating the humanitarian psychiatrist Pinel for substituting mental imprisonment for the physical imprisonment and abuse Foucault seems to have found more salutary. The apotheosis of this type of French nihilism is possibly Francis Lucille, a military enarque turned tourism chief turned vedantin sage. Vedanta preaches the unreality of the world, and the sole existence of the self. Will and action of any sort is an illusion; the task of life is to identify oneself solely as passive, receptive, consciousness which — and here's the rub — is reality itself. Gesture without motion, and so on (see francislucille.com).

So we leave this section asserting contra the postxers the reality of the moral and aesthetic dimensions. To say otherwise compares to denying the existence of the air we breathe, or an opponent on the other side of the net on a tennis court who wants to beat us. The search for moral and aesthetic excellence in one's life, and in the life of a nation, is fully as real and infinitely more fulfilling than the search for riches. It must often proceed without signposts, like all exciting exploration; we can erect them retrospectively both for ourselves and our followers.

Instead of looking for Catholic Church-type rules, try to cultivate moral health and aesthetic activity; written rules will follow as a consequence. With respect to our relation to the state, we need thus to secularise Locke as being about the cultivation of a secular political morality. Our conscience leads us to moral health in a dynamic way, and one that is capable of irony through self-awareness. If we cannot believe in a God that rewards and punishes, we can rest assured that moral transgression without restitution is its own punishment, just as virtue is its own reward. The nation-state can assist by inculcating "doxa" in the process of formation. These unconscious impositions provide the ground for future risks and achievements in the moral sphere.

It bears repetition that postxers give us no tools to use against the negative aspects of globalisation, or any other forms of exploitative capitalism. For such capitalists, there is no abiding problem of subject/object relations; there are simply human subjects to be exploited.

To recap this section, we are arguing that, as a result of its historical jurisdiction rather than any Platonic existence, the nation-state has the potential to counteract the negative effects of globalisation. The individual, as Plato knew, begins less as a republic than as an unruly psychic mob whose numbers and vociferousness are daily being increased by the creation of new needs and "selves" by the market and technology. In the course of most individuals' development, a coalition of selves emerges with some tentative control over the others, and this coalition can participate in civil society and the state as a worker and citizen. One of the paradoxes of postx thought is that it implicitly demands a punctual imperial self, a neo-Cartesianism. The sacred duty of the state, which it implements if necessary by setting limits to its own power a la the first amendment, is to facilitate the development and unification of the individual in all realms of life. Failure to do this by the state, as in contemporary Ireland, induces self-alienation, the development of false self systems, and eventually - one fears - mass psychosis.

CHAPTER THREE

THE HISTORY AND MYTH OF IRELAND

3.1 The quiet land

The idea of the physical island of Ireland as itself a goad to spiritual achievement is perennial. Ireland arose from the collision and fusion of the ancient continents of Laurentia and Avalonia. (I need to issue an alert here; the following few paragraphs may be redolent of History channel's "ancient aliens" to some readers and yet is all correct, as far as I can tell). The trauma of this collision can best be seen around Clogherhead in Co Louth, where "European" fossils are to be found just south, and "American" fossils just north.

Ireland was historically divided into "Leath Conn" and "Leath morga" (respectively, Conn's and Morga's halves) corresponding almost precisely into the Laurentian and Avalonian components. In medieval times, after Brian Boru's death, it is attested that this division was incarnated as a political gerrymander. I would never have believed the following contention, had I not checked the math; the estimate for the geographical center of Ireland along the north-south axis, as given by ancient sources, is more accurate than the current ordinance survey estimate. East-west, the same very possible holds once the land mass of the country is taken into account.

Therein lies a tale, told with great passion by Dames (1992) in his Thames and Hudson (London) book "Mythic Ireland". Let us start from the middle; to be precise, from the hill of Uisneach (196);

> "Mide, the notional centre of Ireland, was conceived of as a point where an umbilical cord attached the body to the womb of the Gods, who endlessly created and sustained its existence from above and below. Yet Mide was a real place, namely the hill of... Uisneach"

Uisneach is not only the notional centre, but is very close to the actual center; taking the latitudes of the north-south extremes of Ireland at Mizen and Malin heads (respectively 51'27" and 55'23" and finding their average, Uisneach at 53'29"is closer to the center of Ireland than the official ordinance survey estimate at 53'30". It is also directly on the Lipetus fault that divides Laurentia and Avalonia.

This division Dames (198) finds was already salient when Giraldus wrote his screed in the 12th century;

> "Their bounds met a at a stone called...the Umbilicus Hiberniae...in the middle of the country"

Uisneach divides the five provinces in this way. It is not difficult to find in Dames' writing a nature mysticism, an environmental cri-de-coeur that he sees as based in the Irish scriptures (211);

> "The Uisneach view of Ireland as the living divinity Erin"

Indeed, Dames, like James Joyce, is attempting to re-root ourselves in our land in a way that makes this move one of towering mystical experience. Whether we do so physically at Uisneach or on the other side f the globe will not matter if the native Irish manage to root themselves once more in their own land.

3.2 The Gaelic period and its echoes

This book makes no commitment to a Platonic Ideal of Irish identity; on the contrary, nothing is presumed beyond a relatively genetically stable population who sank roots on the island of Ireland beginning between seven and twelve thousand years ago. The spectacular success of their neighbouring Anglo-Saxons (of course, the English are a more complex racial mixture than this) within a millennium of arriving in the same archipelago connotes a certain underachieving ethos in the Irish, at least in their tendency for *lebensraum*. One might argue that following the fall of the Roman empire, Ireland was for a few hundred years the closest thing to a neighbourhood superpower and the official Scottish line is that they are the result of an Irish invasion dating about 500 A.D. /common era.

The author of "the confessions of Saint Patrick" may have been taken to Ireland as a slave as early as 350 AD, according to Dan Melia of UC Berkeley; what is certain is that the expansionist ethos of his contemporary Irish society, which begat colonies in Scotland, England, and Wales, died shortly after Ireland's conversion to Christianity. What succeeded it was a missionary zeal to convert and educate Europe. In this writer's lifetime, the historical reality of that zealousness was invoked to motivate prodigious Irish medical and educational work in the parts of the globe where such work was most needed. (An intriguing spin-off is the Live Aid and Live 8 concerts; Bob Geldof is an alumnus of Blackrock College in Dublin, run by the missionary Holy Ghost fathers! It is fair to say that Bono's rather more morally ambiguous work arose from careful study of Geldof; neither is from native Irish stock).

The historian Arnold Toynbee described early Christian Ireland as a society with the potential to become a great civilization. To Huntingdon's (1996) controversial categorizations involving Sinic, Indian, Islamic, and Western could possibly have been added one more. It has often been observed that early Christian Ireland was founded on a past that must already have seemed great. The builders of Newgrange, Knowth, and Dowth in County Meath, once arguably the oldest sophisticated buildings in the world, seem to have had detailed astronomical knowledge as they aligned passage graves to the solstices (de Paor, 1986). Echoes of their spiral designs and celestial alignments have been found, inter alia in Malta and in Chaco canyon; moreover, as we learn more about the past, Newgrange, like the pyramids, may turn out to be a relative newcomer as ever older buildings are found.

This writer argues that there is sufficient material in the undoubted high achievements of Irish culture dating back at least 5,000 years to root the Irish back on their land, and to do so with a sense that none of the higher reaches of human achievement are alien to us. Indeed, one of the paradoxical benefits of the famine has been that people of 100% Irish genetic stock climbed every scientific, artistic and political mountain, including the presidency, available in the USA at the time it was the most powerful nation ever seen on earth.

Thomas (1988), perhaps at times fancifully, interprets the carvings of the Boyne Valley. He argues (32-34) that Neolithic Irish astronomers and mathematicians solved the vexing problem of having a denary system given us by nature with a year of 365.25 days by producing a calendar with 16 months each of 22-23 days. He offers an account of the Newgrange roof stone, east chamber that specifies a period of religious ceremony (55) – yet his acceptance of a multiple invasion hypothesis does him no favours. . This he continues with a detailed analysis of the visual language at Loughcrew and Knowth. What seemed perhaps fanciful in the extreme in 1988 seems less so now, partly because of our more detailed knowledge of the great achievements of indigenous cultures, and partly because the use of icons of this kind has spread into engineering disciplines like visual programming languages and – more recently – synthetic biology, at Stanford.

There is no evidence to suggest that this Neolithic work is of people other than the original gene pool of approx. 10,000 years ago, with obvious cultural parallels in neighbouring islands suggesting a healthy openness. The lack of evidence for any kind of Celtic invasion, and the paradoxical flourishing of a Celtic language and mythic substrate in the country , is tackled in Raftery (1994).It may indeed be the case that the Bronze/Iron age Celtic culture was mathematically inferior to its predecessor. Raftery (200-228) inveighs against the invasion hypothesis, arguing instead that such massive works as the 148BC Corlea road and the first century BC Navan Temple, coupled with the development of the southern hillforts, suggests that inter-tribal instability may have resulted in an elite adopting a foreign culture, which thereafter spread.

To some extent, this tendency for an abrupt change in culture has been observed twice within living memory. The initial republican ethos of the state was supplanted with a suffocating Roman Catholicism between 1925 and 1950, only to find itself again being usurped by neoliberalism after 1995. In each case, the state's resources were dedicated to imposing a slavish dedication to a clearly flawed belief system, on behalf of an elite who clearly believed not only that their positions as administrators of this new pantheon placed them above the law, but that they were perfectly entitled to exact tribute from the great unwashed populace

Can it be the case that the impetus in NAMA to force the people to pay for the bad investments and stellar lifestyle of a vanishingly small set of property "developers", all of whom have Irish names, is actually an atavism? Remarkably, several of the aforesaid – McKillen, Quinlan, and Mulryan – actually used some of their money to pave their way to eternity, surely in a similar state of unearned privilege, by donating to a Vatican chapel, where their names still are inscribed for the benefit of St Peter, surely, for the day he comes to assess their celestial prospects. Let us remember that one interpretation of the Irish gene pool suggests a scenario where a very few men controlled many women.

The emotional tenor of pre-Christian Ireland “Celtic” Ireland is perhaps captured in the epic Tain Bo Cuailinge. While devoid of anything approaching Christian redemption, the set-piece battle descriptions and intimate details of the Achilles-like hero Cú Chulainn’s “warp-spasms” (riastraidh) of anger are unforgettable.

Gaelic (which we will refer to here also as Irish) is, as we have seen, a VSO language, and may have been many more millennia in Ireland than the mere 2.5 normally predicated of it (Titley, 2000). One stark incident emphasises its continuity:

> "And sometimes a poet like Padraig O hEigeartaigh, an exile from South Kerry writing of his son’s death in Boston in the first decade of the twentieth century, can marry his grief to traditional professional expertise in something of the manner of the distant masters." (O Tuama et al, 1981, xxv)

The Tain, remarkably, is mainly a prose opus. Despite later depredations, there are still about 5,000 pages of text from the early Christian period available to us:

> "… Myths and sagas, biblical glosses, laws, lives and martyrdoms of saints, names of persons and places, poetry, hymns and politic-religious propaganda. The laws alone have been edited in six fat volumes amounting to 2,353 pages or more than a million words." (Titley, 2000, p. 27)

It rather seems as though the rule of law predated Anglo-Saxon conquest:

> "We have specific legal texts dealing with contracts, robbery, marriage, property, the professions, the obligations of judges, and others which all seem very modern." (ibid.)

In 1907, the founder of Sinn Fein, Arthur Griffith, called for Republican courts to replace the state ones. Their recognition by the populace during the subsequent War of Independence hastened British withdrawal. This writer dares to repeat throughout this book that few developments would be as salutary as their reinstatement to supplant the wig-ridden absurd legal carnival that scleroses contemporary Ireland. Anglo-Saxon common law has recently proven spectacularly inappropriate in Iraq, the origin of the rather more ancient code of Hammurabi.

Irish pre-Christian religion lacked a formal pantheon, and two competing most High Gods can be identified. Lu seems cognate with Varuna and

Mercury; while most famously seen dancing at Lughnasa (August) with Meryl Streep in recent times, he inspired the names of Lugdunum, Leyden, and perhaps London. He seems to have been a cultural being; music, poetry, history and magic were his métiers. Fighting he shared with his Jungian shadow, Dagda, the other CEO, a king of druidism. We shall explore these and other characters in the final section of this chapter, in the context of the links with classical Indo-European thought-patterns.

Irish started to decline as a language of court and business in the seventeenth century. O'Faoláin (1962) brilliantly and imaginatively reconstructs the Tudor Wars against Ireland that led to its first complete conquest. Part of the thesis of this book is that we Irish have to return back this far to heal and continue to be a vital force for good in world affairs. This period is given a chapter of its own here.

O'Faoláin's extraordinary prose ability has perhaps obscured the sophistication of his geopolitical thinking. He comments that the Irish rebels:

> "Fitzmaurice and Desmond and Sanders had thus opposed to the idea of a Nation welded by patriotic fervour the idea of the People informed by something midway between religious idealism and an intellectual idea. It was their tragedy that their idea came too late … There had intervened something on which the Roman vinculum broke into pieces - but which strengthened centralization. The event occurred when Columbus stepped ashore in what is prophetically called the New World. At that moment modern international commerce was born." (O'Faoláin, 1942, p. 86)

And so we take a full chapter later on to examine globalization and the Irish poetic response thereto.

The activity by English soldiers in Ireland was indeed callous, but far from lethargic, to adapt O'Brien:

> "Then by March 1580 … Elizabeth at last agreed to spend some more money on Ireland … and the horror began - a slaughter which remains in the Irish memory with a sense of dread and rage exceeded only by that associated with the name of Cromwell." (ibid., p. 78)

This, rather than the later O'Neill uprisings, was effectively the end of the Gaelic order. Shortly afterward, the author of the "Faerie Queene" began calmly to propose the genocide of the Irish from his Irish estate.

In the 1630s, there were seven thousand Irish in the army of Flanders. The dream of bringing Irish with military experience home to do battle became a reality shortly after, as it did subsequent to the Irish participation in the American Civil War (Wilson, 1998). O ro se do bheatha alludes to the return of the military diaspora.

One cannot but be astonished at the persistence of the Irish desire for independence for the 400 years following the Tudor conquest. In 1798, many Cromwellian planter families fought on the Irish side in an uprising inspired by the French and American revolutions that took 30,000 lives. In 1848 the Young Ireland movement implemented an ultimately abortive uprising; yet the caliber of the persons involved is attested by their brilliant careers in later exile.

In 1858 a secret society was exposed in West Cork; its al-Qaeda-type cell structure prevented further arrests. The coordinator, James Stephens, may eventually join Michael Collins and others in the pantheon of Irish guerrilla chiefs. The major manpower was to be supplied by Irish members of British garrisons in Ireland. The revolution, when it came in 1867, failed. Many of the Irish captured were deported to the Antipodes to face the horrors described in Hughes (1986)

Yet the Irish had risen in his generation, as Stephens had wanted them to do. The same impulse impelled the initially quixotic 1916 uprising, realized by the socialist theoretician and British army veteran James Connolly, some of the consequences of which I have described elsewhere (O Nuallain, 2004). Remarkably, it led to partial independence by late 1921.

The IRA campaign of 1969–1997 is also described in (ibid.) and below. One comment should be made as data about the IRA become more public. They desire the political unity of the island and may eventually achieve it. They oscillate between an utterly ruthless war mode, and a compromising peace mode, when they attempt war by other means through politics. Had they had the political nous to enter peace mode in 1981, when they could have held the political balance of power in the Irish republic, the history of the past quarter-century would have been much more advantageous to them. Had they continued in war mode past the 1992 Canary Wharf bombing, when it finally dawned on them that hitting commercial targets in Britain without civilian casualties was an effective strategy, likewise they would now be in a stronger position. As I write, they choose the al-

Qaeda 7/7 London bombings finally to demobilize, which is appropriate strategic thinking.

Lest obvious allegations ensue, the writer is aware that many Irish openly colluded with their colonists during the periods briefly sketched above. Yet the template of a people striving to achieve full national expression in a politically united island can be discerned at all times. Let us very briefly review Irish history from the middle ages; the reader does not lack for other sources written by authoritative historians should she wish to read a much fuller account.

3.3 Irish history from the middle ages in brief

While the sin of auto-exoticism has rightly been condemned, and Joyce's radical move in making his archetype for a Dublin Ulysses a Jew and therefore a cosmopolite by definition rightly praised, it is yet not difficult to find ways in which the development of Irish society differed from its contemporary European ones. Nicholls (2003, pp. 3-4) comments that the relatively slight incursion by the Church into social life resembled Ethiopia rather than Europe. This we will find echoed below in Quinn's speculations, somewhat less than fully bridled though they are on occasion. Nicholls continued that the political unit was the *fine* or *sliocht* and that lineage resembled modes in Asia or Africa, rather than Europe.

The stability of the Gaelic order over perhaps millennia is deeply impressive. It does rather seem as though Ireland was in a position to play the same role in the "dark ages" for the preservation of Latin, and classical learning, that Tibet played in the preservation of Sanskrit Buddhist texts after the Muslim sack of India. Like the Tibetans, the Irish included text in their own language. Southeast Asia contains further parallels with Ireland in that both Thailand and Cambodia occupy territory that was essentially monastic grange until the advent of the Thai and Cambodian gene stock. The former country, like Ireland, recovered from its occupancy (in the Thais' case by Burma) initially by de-emphasising economic activity. Finally, some of the ms. discovered in Tibet, for example Nagarjuna's refutation of Isvara as Creator God, are as consequential as anything from Ireland.

There is no doubt that the Catholic Church had too much influence in Ireland until recently, and Nicholl's research on the Abyssinian-type church-state relations is fascinating. By contrast, Islamic states started as theocracies and lack the rupture of Church and State exemplified by the dispute between Pope Gregory VII and Henry IV of Germany. Sharia jurists hesitate to implement the legislation dealing with personal morality, which blunts the edge of their jurisdiction.

Irish missionary activity undoubtedly had a role in preserving classical culture. Its innovations included the breaking up of text into different words, as distinct from classical Roman letter strings, the use of enlarged letters to start texts, and perhaps the first secular literature in Europe, which is preserved in these manuscripts. Wax tablets were the pocket notebook of antiquity; the Irish climate does not encourage preservation through papyrus.

We have reasonably good sources of information for the studies required to become an Irish "master". Biblical studies and grammar might be expected; however required also was the "computus", the ability to calculate the date of Easter. In 664, as described in Wallis (1999), the old system used by the Irish was deemed heretical. Intriguingly, we have found preserved in Switzerland an Irish computus dating from 663. We might argue that the lament for Saint Colm Chille, reliably dated to 597, is the oldest vernacular literature in Western Europe.

In 1183, Gerald de Barri visited Ireland to write a revisionist history for his Norman peers. He had just spent an extended period in Paris, where the cutting-edge of polyphony was said to reside. His hatred of and contempt for the Irish rings down the ages, yet he argued that the polyphonic achievements of the Irish harpists exceeded anything that he had experienced in France. Then, in a pattern to be repeated through the ages, he comments that the Scots and Welsh had outstripped their erstwhile Irish masters. We return to this in Chapter 7.

Ireland thus had great expertise in many aspects of culture; one need only look at "dark age" constructions like the round tower at Scattery Island in the Shannon estuary to add architecture to the list of achievements. We have seen Titley commenting on the scope of the Brehon laws; by mediaeval times, according to some sources, they were essentially just aphorisms, with the standard European ius commune (common law) being used (Nicholls, p. 50). No English judges were appointed post-1400 as the pyrrhic defeat of the Bruces in 1316 had effectively sown the seeds of Norman retreat.

The Irish legal system did not include any separate notion of criminal law, and financial restitution, rather than the death penalty, was the norm for criminal acts (ibid, 59). It has proven immensely difficult for the modern Irish state fully to implement a white-collar criminal jurisdiction. Nor is it out of keeping with today that a transgressor unclaimed by his family became the sport of his "victim". Finally Galway/Gaillimh, the city of the foreigners, uniquely had Roman law during this period.

It is worth noting that the Brehon Law society of Ireland does not agree with Nicholls' account that common law was in place at these dates, instead focussing on the 1608 decision on “Tanistry” (from which the word “Tanaiste” for deputy PM in Ireland) i.e. inheritance of chiefdom, which has reverberated through all the English colonies, as being the touchstone for the supercession of the early Irish law. Indeed current Irish Supreme court judge Susan Denham reportedly has expressed a willingness to countenance Brehon law in her courtroom. In fact, a debate in the Irish senate in 1998 specifically addressed this topic;

“Brehon law was practiced in Ireland for over 1,000 years, maturing by the eighth century. After the 12th century it co-existed with the common law system of England, but was extinguished as an operating system in the early seventeenth century, by the Case of Tanistry, Dav. 29, 80 Eng. Rep. 516 (K.B. 1608). Yet, miraculously, the native Irish laws have survived in various ways. Most importantly, the vellum manuscripts provide us with a mass of primary material, which we are trying to access through use of technology and breakthroughs in language studies. But there are other scattered legacies all around us, including case law, parliamentary debate and the Revolutionary Dáil Courts (1919-1923) were an example of the importance of the legal tradition to many of our great statesmen.”

The old saw that the Irish had no towns until the Viking invasions is of course nonsense; monastic settlements like Clonmacnoise, Scattery Island, Glendalough, and up to hundreds more each included up to thousands of inhabitants in their vicinity. That they were plundered by Vikings who were, by comparison with them, barbarians, is a historic fact. The erstwhile urban myth that Vikings took Irish women with them to Iceland from their raids on Ireland has now acquired a genetic basis, however ill-founded (Sykes, 2006).

The distinction of this culture is attested not only by the few manuscripts, mainly stored in continental Europe, that have survived but the missionary efforts in Europe that were popularised in Thomas Cahill's book (1996). Fergal (aka Virgil) of Salzburg constructed a church there that lasted almost a millennium up to Renaissance times (Dopsch et al, 1984); his scientific speculations included the proposal that ensouled humans existed on the southern hemisphere of a round earth (ibid). This great civilization, potentially as ineluctable in its expression on the planet as the French, Italian or Spanish, met political defeat at the Synod of Whitby (Wallis 1999) in 664.

The issue was the date of Easter. The Irish were accused by the Anglo-Saxon Church of using a heretical method in their computus to calculate it. In recent years, the computus einsidlensis, a contemporary Irish computus, was found in a Benedictine monastery in Switzerland. Dáibhí Ó Cróinín has found that it establishes an 84 year cycle for Easter echoing that of the third century Anatolius of Laodicea. One and a half millennia after Whitby, the Irish have been vindicated; it is hard to imagine that an Irish Catholic Church would have been any worse than the Roman Catholic one, particularly given Ireland's non-imperial history. We owe an immense amount to the Celtic scholars at which Garvin (2004) sneers. Let us make it clear; no claim is made here for the mid-European "Celtic' genetic inheritance of the Irish. It does seem to be the case that there is a trove of cultural material preserved in Ireland, and to a lesser extent those parts of Britain to which the Saxons pushed the Britons.

By mediaeval times, Ireland was essentially a feudal system; as Nicholls remarks (op. cit. pp. 78-79), the peonage was not a political one, but a social and economic one. James' Connolly's notion that socialism is intrinsic to the Irish project is hardly borne out by the facts. Yet the ancient professions were still held in sufficient esteem for their holders to qualify as "erenaghs" who did not have to pay rent. Families transmitted these franchises; the Breslins were jurists, the Cassidys were doctors, the McGraths and O'Dalys poets and historians. The Ollamh (currently translated as "professor") was the head of his profession. The file (op. cit. pp. 93-94) seems to have been an atavism; part philosophe, part shaman, with a capacity to curse others to death with his word. The bard, who lacked this capacity for action at a distance, was his assistant; the surname Ward derives from this. We can unpack meanings from Irish surnames that indicate professions and distinctions; McEntee is the son of the wise, McInerney administers for ecclesiasticals, and so on.

Quinn (2005) is, by his own admission, not a scholar or musician, but his attention to visual media often yields surprising and possibly valid results. While the interpretation of texts always leaves room for controversy, the facts are that the statue of the Celtic nature-God Cernunnus that comprises part of the Viking raid on Ireland we call the Osberg haul does feature him in lotus meditation position; the left side of the north cross of the Celtic bible crosses in Castledermot, County Kildare, does feature the ecumenical gesture of depicting a burial in the pagan fetal position of the time, and so on. Quinn's first venture into the area was, however, auditory rather then visual; he examined the Sean-nos (old-style) singing of the West of Irelend and declared it identical with muezzin and several central Asian styles. Let us be clear; sean-nos, which is unaccompanied and uses intricate knowledge of what is, in effect, intervals between semitones, is a distinct stream from Irish classical music (Danny Boy) and dance music (some of Riverdance).

Microtonality is sometimes exploited by singers like the great Nancy Wilson to add piquancy to their interpretation of standards. Psyche Louie, in work done at UC Berkeley, adduced evidence that listeners can induce microtonal grammars and determine if chords in a microtonal system are consonant or dissonant. So Quinn might have had more faith in himself when he weakened his hypothesis on being told that the main body of the melody, the non-microtonal part, was pentatonic (Quinn, 2005, p. 156). It was explained to him that therefore, it was inevitable that the tonal melodies would sound similar, as the space of possible pentatonic tunes is a limited one. Quinn's hypothesis had the Swedish Vikings exploring the Volga and Dnieper waterways from Central Asia to Ireland, and should not be discounted. We should therefore argue that Kazan also has sean-nos.

Quinn is on even stronger ground in myth and iconography. In Arabic mythology, Hubal loses an arm in battle to have it replaced with a gold one. So does the Irish Nuada. That the shamrock is of non-European origin is now attested fact (op. cit., p. 191). Again, there is no doubt that Irish illuminated manuscripts feature reds, purples, and mauves from Mediterranean plants and insects. Shampoo planet; the recent study of the ritually-executed Irish Neolithic "bogmen" showed that one was using hair care products of Mediterranean provenance. Slightly more controversially, Quinn points out similarities between the Irish Book of Durrow and the Abbazid Koran.

Quinn's final concern is to solidify the link with the Coptic Church that Nicholls hints at. The Nile Fellucca does indeed have a sailing rig similar to the Connemara pucan; it does rather seem that "Aran" sweaters have Coptic patterns (217-219), even taking into account their recent re-invention. Finally, the Tau Cross is pre-Christian, like the ankh it resembles, and of Ethiopian origin. Quinn points out several examples of the Tau Cross in Ireland. That the cenobitic ideal of the desert fathers was echoed by Irish monks in such fastnesses as the Skelligs is not controversial, nor is it controversial that Irish hermits explicitly sought a desert in the ocean, often at least as far away as Iceland.

By contrast, Quinn argues (2005, p. 247) that Ireland is today a trading post, a place for interesting economic experiments. That is too kind; there is nothing in the slightest interesting about borrowing - at a conservative estimate - €70 billion from foreign banks from 2003 to 2006 chiefly in order to keep house prices rising. This was followed, of course, by borrowing further €tens of billions to rescue the banks whose idiocy in keeping these process rising had bankrupted the country – the NAMA scheme.

Nor is the media fascination with GDP figures interesting; it betokens, rather, a vacuum in those activities that make life worth living that we term culture. In fact, Ireland is behaving exactly as one would expect from a neo-colony; at Christmas 2006, the prime minister was in a position to say that he cared not a whit about whether his new coalition partner was to be the crony capitalist PD's, Greens, or the ex-communists in Labour.

Borrowed foreign capital has set the political and cultural agenda with disastrous results; the task of the government is somehow to convince the public that this is continuous with the past, a necessary and organic modernity. Fortunately, personal debt is so high that the EU is both unwilling and unable to prop the 2011 Irish government up as effectively as they did Reynolds in 1992. There seems to be an eternal dynamic in Ireland of a cultural vanguard open to the world being replaced by insular Bertie Ahern types for the benefit of globalised furies, at the expense of a world cultural jewel, and in the name of a totalising "modernity".

The demographic asymmetry between Britain and Ireland established through genocide, what remains to do is to write the Irish out of world history. That the culture destroyed in turn by Vikings, Normans and English was one of the most exquisite spiritual and cultural refinement is attested by O'Duinn (2000). By “spiritual”, we do not mean that alacrity to repeat blatant absurdities for which the Roman Catholic Church, aided and abetted by the British and then the Irish states, praised us “for having the faith”. It is rather a renunciation of carnal appetite and facile identification of the self with ideology for indwelling on some reality mediating psyche, organism, and cosmos. While this mediation has been expressed in Christian terms in Ireland for some time, it does not seem a stretch to posit a continuity both with pre-Christian and post-Christian ways of conceiving the infinite. The final chapter here outlines, with appropriate tentativeness and irony, what such a system of integration with the cosmos might look like.

O'Duinn (2000), a Benedictine monk, goes to pains to express the possibility of process pantheism in the Irish mind:

> "While safeguarding the transcendence of God, the Gaelic-speaking peoples laid great stress on the immanence of God."

This is a hard trick to achieve; in Hindu thought, it is implemented by noting that Isvara/Paramesvara, the Creator-God who maps most closely onto the Christian God, is God in relation to this world and thus in a relative sense. In the absolute sense, Brahman, the ultimate reality, is identical with Atman, the authentic realisation of selfhood. The discernable world is an illusion; in the cinematic metaphors that vedantins often use to explain their thought, reality and our authentic identity is the cinema screen, and the fleeting world of experience the images projected onto it. Sri Ramanashram (1972)- in truly impersonal tradition, the closest one can get to an author credit on the book is the name of the ashram - features an extended such analogy (27-28).

Once one has achieved enlightenment, the narrative of union of Brahman and Atman is to acquire psychological urgency as immediate as the conventional tenet that the external world does in fact have external reality. (If one is reminded on les philosophes, and their apotheosis in the wife-murdering Louis Althusser denying that Stalin’s atrocities really happened using a particularly psychotic ontological three-card monte, check out Francis Lucille, the convergence of two types of world deniers, once again.) Once we unenlightened types attempt to achieve spiritual understanding, we are to begin with the reality of ourselves, the world, and Isvara, a Creator-God.

O Duinn is concerned to maintain some kind of Christian orthodoxy while honouring the pantheistic tendency of the Irish. The Christian narrative features a transcendent God, whom the Old Testament portrays as seriously bipolar, and whom Joseph Campbell insisted was a projection of the desired social order. O Duinn (2000, p. 8) is going to have his work cut out:

> "Native texts in Irish rather than in Latin tend to stress the immanence of God - God-ri-na-ndul - the God of the elements."

So we might get a sense of what was really bothering Bede as he set about framing his Irish neighbours, whose scholarship and hospitality he otherwise admired, with trumped-up charges about the date of Easter:

> "Celtic Christianity expressed the immanence or nearness of God ... present everywhere ... in the trees ...in the rivers ... in people ... " (87)

Indeed, the spiritual path advocated was, according to O Duinn, both environmentally and socially salutary:

> " ... advancement in holiness ... the Celtic way ... an effort to develop an awareness of the presence of God in everything and everybody" (ibid)

We can call this sli na firinne, and, its Christian influence removed, it may indeed be a valid spiritual path.

The attempts to fit Christianity with its Semitic God into the Irish conceptual structure quite simply did not work. We outline later a possible scenario for a contemporary devotional system that celebrates the mysteries of selfhood, consciousness, the existence of order in this cosmos explained (away) by the anthropic principle, and the strange necessity for continual struggle for social justice in Sli na Firinne, the way of truth. To return to O Duinn, the joins are beginning to show between a "pagan" pantheism and Judeo-Christianity. While the Tain bo Cuailgne expresses

> "... the association between an unjust war and the destruction of world order" (op. cit., p. 82)

The hero Setanta, prone to "warp-spasm" rages against his enemies in "riastradh" (pronounced, roughly, reestra), is hardly a Christ-like figure as the Church and State needed Christ to be understood. The solution chosen in general was for the Church to Christianise Irish myths; given the predominance of the enraged hero in Irish epic, Christ undertakes an argainn Ifrinn, a plundering of hell (129) to put him on the warriors' dias with Setanta et al.

The concept of neart, the immanent power of cosmic order, can be rescued intact from the first articulation of Irish thought (84-86). We can be more specific:

> "The showing forth of God in nature was a vital element in the Gaelic way to the world of the divine" (173).

Yet the paradoxes surrounding an omnipotent and omni-benevolent God stumped the Irish, particularly as they were experiencing the horrors of Cromwellian genocide. All that one can do is moan to this God, in the manner of the dispossessed 17th-century poet Sean Ó Conaill in Tuireamh na hÉireann:

> "You formed the moon and stars … are you deaf or where are you looking?" (42)

We are in standard theodical mode, of course, a symbolic response to injustice that replaced the heroic Setanta riastradh with another tribe's conceptual regalia. As usual, qua the book of job, the complaint is withdrawn and replaced by a Te Deum:

> " … forgive all our sins … restore their religion and their rights to the Irish … " (ibid)

Remarkably, this religion that he wants restored itself usurped the native pantheism that seems natural to the Irish mind, and which we will find echoed in the great Irish mediaeval philosopher Eriugena.

O'Duinn is clear about the links between the Irish Bealtaine, with its burning-man type feast, and Easter (140). The reader does not need to be reminded about the Irish commemorating of the winter solstice, incarnated in the passage graves at Newgrange and surrounding areas that are possibly the oldest sophisticated buildings in the world, and its usurpation by Christmas.

O' Duinn (1990, 172; translations by current author) is even more radical in his Gaelic work, perhaps because the threat of being labelled a heretic is decreased as the censors in Rome, like most "Irish studies" academics, could not be bothered learning the language;

> "as a result of the important resemblances between Celtic and Indian texts ...perhaps the nature and ubiquity imprecations are part of old Indo-European heritage ...still (alive) today in Hinduism, that got spliced into Irish Christianity"

Indeed, he goes as far as to assert that the famous "breastplate" of St Patrick may well be an adaptation of the *Chhandogya Upanishad*:

> "The Infinite is below, above, behind, before, to the right, to the left. I am all this. This Infinite is the Self. The Self is below, above, behind, before, to the right, to the left." (ibid. 14)

The conceptual violence that the Irish visited on themselves in accepting Christianity can perhaps be explained in terms of what seemed at the time its syncretistic brilliance. O'Duinn hints that the missionary expedition we personalize as "Patrick" may have deliberately stressed the immanence of God in order to placate the "druids" or whoever were the custodians of the ancient religion (170). Indeed, he argues, Eriugena's neoplatonism was an extension of this fundamental insight (103-104).

It may indeed be an opportune moment to revisit our roots in Indo-European thought and culture. Attempts to resurrect Christianity as a mystical path fall short. Needleman (1980) produced his most incoherent work in this attempt. Smoley (2001) produces a more readable version of a similar failure. Smoley (2006) and Kinney (2004) search among the shards of the Gnostic midden for something coherent, having previously combined forces (Smoley et al, 999) with in this writer's opinion an equal lack of success. One of the highlights of Smith (2001) is his fearless attack on scientism; then he comments on his debate with some Brits (229):

> "Oxford English makes me feel inferior before ideas even enter"

Yet Smith feels confident enough to assert the end-point of his search for ultimate religious experience (265);

> "Consciousness proper – pure consciousness, consciousness with no images in it – is the common property of us all, when we detect pure consciousness..what I experience is identical with what you experience in that state. And identical with what God experiences. Not in degree but in kind"

It is perhaps in our capacity as Irish people to produce a historically accredited religious path that does justice to this experience of consciousness and has less of an inferiority complex.

The military violence that followed in the absence of a single unifying political idea to oppose it is perhaps the darkest chapter in that bizarre phenomenon, the British Empire. The brute figures we have seen already; the cull of a third of the Irish population was the standard British aim of that period (Ellis, 1988, p.9). Let us not forget that the Cromwellian campaign was above all about paying his soldiers for their English campaign:

> "The war became a gigantic capitalist speculation with Ireland as the prize." (ibid, p. 9).

Cromwell himself had a certain propensity for revisionist history and addressed the Irish thus:

> "You broke the union. You, unprovoked, put the English to the most unheard of and most barbarous massacre without respect of sex and age that ever the sun beheld." (Quoted in Ellis, 1988, p.20)

Hold it, you say. We have resolved all these differences, and the world is full of little people with grudges about historical incidents that they never personally experienced. However, it is extraordinary to see how the English urge to project onto the Irish is still in place. Wheatcroft (2006) relays a rugby incident, and it should be noted that the Englishman Neil Back's action is as rare as a defence in the NFL getting away with taking the ball from the opposing quarterback before play begins, and redolent of referee inspiration from above:

> "In the 2002 Heineken Cup final, Munster lost to Leicester. The Irish side might have scored in the dying minutes but for Neil Back using his hand to knock down the ball being fed by the Munster scrum-half."

Most of us go through our rugby careers without seeing anyone in Back's position attempting this, let alone getting away with it. One would think it would make Wheatcroft ashamed to be English, and the Irish furious. On the contrary, Wheatcroft is concerned to excoriate Ireland's Anthony Foley, who was on a self-blame trip:

> "We've never blamed the result on Neil Back. Fair play to him." (ibid).

This gives Wheatcroft charter to home in on his preferred target:

> "With his perfectly ludicrous use of the Irishism … Foley summed up the spirit of the age." (ibid).

Lest we forget, it was Back, not Foley, who cheated. Wheatcroft's rant might be read in the context of his similarly ill-informed attacks on Irish republicanism. After Cromwell, a year zero was declared in Ireland, and an Orwellian process began:

> "An act was quickly passed in the English Parliament in 1652, quaintly called the Act of Good Affection." (O' Callaghan, 2000, p. 44).

Great generosity was to be expected, as exampled in the Successor Act for the settling of Ireland:

> "It is not the intention of Parliament to extirpate that whole nation." (in Ellis, p. 50).

Eventually, the one-third cull was considered insufficient, and a policy of transportation of some of the Irish to the new world and transplantation of all others west of the Shannon was embarked on. From the state papers, we find:

> " ... proposed unto his Highness ... the yearly transportation of some fit number of Irish children into England." (ibid, p. 113).

Even the arch-revisionist historian Roy Foster estimates a number of 12,000 for the English transported to a life of slavery in the new world. The next step was to be the use of Irish women as sex slaves for British soldiers:

> "Thurloe had immediately written to Henry suggesting that 1,500 soldiers be sent to Barbados as colonists with 1,000 'Irish wenches'" (ibid.)

Henry (Cromwell) wrote back as follows:

> "Concerning the young women, although we must use force in taking them up, yet it being so much for their own good and likely to be of so great advantage to the public that it is not in the least doubted that you may have such a number of them as you shall think fit to make use of upon this account ... Henry also added that 1,500 to 2,000 young Irish boys of twelve to fourteen years could also be sent." (ibid, p. 149)

The late Sean O'Callaghan was an ex-Irish army officer and Fleet Street journalist who published several books about the international slave trade, including the sex slave trade. He is alert to the rather less than habeas corpus legislation in force:

> "The ethnic cleansing of Ireland may be said to have begun on 24 August 1652. On that date … a proclamation was issued that gave ultimate power to the Commissioners of Ireland to seize and transport anybody of whatever rank who was judged dangerous to the Commonwealth." (O' Callaghan, 2000, p. 77).

He also claims that, in the midst of frequent uprisings (123) that eventually dissuaded the British merchants from the Irish slave trade, human stud farms were established:

> "A worse fate awaited some of the girls and women … there are records in the public archives of Barbados of stud farms being set up" (115).

O'Callaghan had unprecedented access to the files of the Barbados Museum and historical society, and describes the slave markets:

> "Then came the turn of the young Irish girls. These aroused the greatest interest, as the planters wanted them mainly as concubines or sexual playthings … The children, boys and girls, came last … pedophiles frequented these auctions." (ibid, p. 113).

Remarkably, Irish scholarship continued during this period, if on the continent, including MacColgan's work:

> "His study was on the 9th-century Irish philosopher, John Scotus or Eriugena … his ambition was to show the world that, in spite of English propaganda, Irishmen were citizens of no mean country, a country with a rich and superb native literature … Father Mason, in claiming him for England, was merely exercising the English prejudice of the day." (Ellis, p. 138).

The so-called "Great Famine" of the nineteenth century was a population cull in the same vein as similar British imperialist efforts in Bengal and Kenya. Public records show enormous export of food from Ireland during this period.

Revisionist historians continually look for a fascist subtext in the 1916 proclamation of independence, but to no avail. They are completely missing the point; the 1916 proclamation is an impeccable document and the rising was entirely about showing its moral force through the courage of its participants. Fortunately for Ireland and the world, the 1916 proclamation with its universal suffrage, feminist principles, and social egalitarian ethos is the one by which Ireland got its independence:

> "The first Dail had, of course, attached itself formally to the Republic proclaimed by Connolly and Pearse during Easter week." (Costello, 2003, p. 154)

Again fortunately, the notion of a republic refused to die;

> "With the election of de Valera over Griffith as President of Sinn Féin, the official policy of the organization moved from the dual monarchist pro-Grattan Parliament restoration that had been its trademark to the 'securing of the international recognition of Ireland as a sovereign republic.'" (ibid, p. 26)

The republic had been declared fifty years before by the secretive, mainly American-based IRB (Irish Republican Brotherhood). That Arthur Griffith had outstanding qualities is not in doubt. His account of "the resurrection of Hungary" focused on the desiderata of economic independence and non-colonial courts.

While it did not initially recognize the Irish republic, the role of America was crucial. A contemporary Congress commission report states boldly that

> "British 'justice' has become a discredited thing. The Black and Tans in Ireland compete for dishonor of Anglo-Saxon civilization with our unofficial lynch mobs." (Costello, p. 106)

Griffith's strategic thinking was as follows:

> "For Griffith, the establishment of independent courts was part of the process of peaceful refusal to participate in the institutions of the British government …The Prestige, the dignity, the strength such a national legal system would confer upon a movement for national independence is obvious…but in addition, it would deprive the corrupt Bar of Ireland of much of its incentives to corruption, save the pockets of our people." (Costello, p. 186)

With respect to today's Bar, it is a case of plus ça change. Costello (pp. 186-204) describes the functioning of the republican courts, which the Irish state urgently needs to reinstate in some form, perhaps initially as rights commission extensions into civil law. This too we discuss presently.

Let us recall that America's stance was ambivalent. While the British cabinet was concerned that America might intervene (ibid, p. 118), one of

Woodrow Wilson's concerns was to seek British support for the League of Nations (p. 49).

It was Griffith, above all, who was given the invidious task of formalizing the reduction of the aspiration from a whole-island republic to a twenty-six county statelet. His main independence concerns were economic; with respect to political association, a dual monarchy was acceptable to him, as we have seen. Let us be clear; the notion of a whole-island republic has been abused by hucksters and cynics since it was proclaimed; arguably, the kleptocracy that comprises one of the main strands of Fianna Fail remained in power only by judicious raising of the temperature on the "national issue" when all else failed, as in the mid-1980's. With the rise of Sinn Fein and the sacrosanct nature of the "peace process", that door is no longer open.

However, to surrender to the notion of a republic is to surrender several of the key aspirations of republicanism, including the link between freedom of the individual and of the colony, enunciated in the American Declaration of Independence:

> "We hold these truths to be self-evident, that all men (sic) are created equal, that they are endowed by their creator with certain unalienable rights, that among these are Life, Liberty and the pursuit of happiness…that whenever any Form of government becomes destructive of these ends, it is the Right of the People to alter or to abolish it, and to institute new government."

Griffith's economic nationalism is of course utterly irrelevant today in an Ireland that accepts EU law and indeed specific directives about state investment, and a further superstructure of the WTO, Unesco, and so on.

To surrender the notion of a whole-island republic was, in turn, to trade sense of place for the arbitrary fiat of a twenty-six county state, and to lose the psychologically potent link between liberation of the individual and the nation. If nationalism is a synesthesia of the sense of place, we are now categorically in its political modality. To continue, it is argued here that an engagement with a place, initially through its geography and its history as encoded in the "Doxa" of the culture, will inevitably produce the kind of sublime symbolic expressions we witness in the creative works of free humans always and everywhere.

It may have been a mistake for the Griffith-Collins delegation to agree to the Anglo-Irish treaty, one that immediately cost Ireland a civil war with 4,000 dead, a further 25 years of Civil war from 1969 with an equivalent death toll, and a bizarre political dynamics in which two conservative civil war parties vied for power with random policies. The ultimatum given the Irish delegation of war within three days (Costello, 2003, p. 269), even if acted upon, was unlikely to produce a more destructive result. Indeed, one of the reasons for the Civil War was that the IRA's membership had trebled during the ceasefire and it did not want to hold a vote under Churchill's threat. Contemporary reports by the American consul comment on the increased discipline and effectiveness of the IRA.

General Macready's report to the British Cabinet in May 1921, pre-ceasefire, warns:

> "There is a risk that a position of virtual stalemate may continue throughout the summer and that winter will be a time of decisive advantage to the rebels." (In Costello, p. 104)

The history of republican compromise has continued with the Good Friday Agreement (GFA) of 1998. Up to then, the 1937 Irish Constitution effectively rescinded the Anglo-Irish treaty by claiming the extent of the Irish State as the whole island of Ireland. The GFA rescinded this in turn, substituting aspirational language with the requirement of a majority vote, ending the idea that a united Ireland could be achieved by Parliamentary means alone. The citizens of the republic of Ireland voted for this with the most overwhelming majority ever seen in a referendum in the state. Only later did it emerge that the British are free to rescind any of the provisions of the agreement as they wish (Costello, 2003). In particular, the assembly was unilaterally suspended twice, once by Blair's confidant, Peter Mandelson, for spurious reasons, and later for the manufactured spy incident we review below. Like the Anglo-Irish treaty, it was entered into in a power asymmetry that would condemn it as a legal document. The position I take here as in (O Nuallain, 2004) is that it has at least provided peace, and that in any case the main opportunity was lost long ago, and may not come around again. Let us look from the IRA's perspective.

Under the threat of "immediate and terrible war," as distinct from what one was assumedly meant to conclude were the tender mercies shown by the Black and Tans, the Collins/Griffith team brought a peace treaty that they had signed in London back to the Irish parliament, Dail Eireann. Until then, the Irish people had voted overwhelmingly and repeatedly for a united Ireland whether this initiative was presented to them as Home Rule or a Republic. While the Collins/Griffith delegation had been given plenipotentiary powers by the Dail, they mysteriously failed to consult with Dublin when the final document was thrust at them with a heretofore hidden, private agreement with the British signed by Griffith (Costello, p. 269). It included two bridges too far; acceptance of the partition of the island, which the British had made a fait accompli by the prior creation and recognition of a northern Irish state, and an Oath of allegiance to be sworn by members of parliament. Whereas the anti-treatyites were prepared to countenance partition, which then as now was regarded as rescindable by southern economic success (ibid, p. 294) and judicious guerrilla destabilization of the Northern state, the issue of the Oath was seized upon as an abomination - at least until in 1927 it looked safe to De Valera to accept both it and seats in parliament!

It is fair to say that the second Dail, which voted narrowly for the treaty, was not dissolved properly, and that the IRA had some justification in claiming charter from this constitutional vacuum to proclaim themselves the true inheritors of the republican flame. The second Dail voted narrowly in favour of Collins/Griffith, and de Valera's famous rejection of the expressed will of the people set the scene for a violent civil war, and a loss of confidence by the populace in the institutions of state that has never really been recovered.

The IRA, then, have historically claimed to be the legitimate government of Ireland through its Army Council, and Sinn Fein's GFA acquiescence to partition has been seen by republican dissidents like the 32-county sovereignty movement/Real IRA as betrayal. It can consistently be maintained that IRA campaigns have been encouraged, and on occasion, as we see below, partly run, by the British. Once the "provisional," IRA was founded with a policy of non-engagement with southern security forces, the 26-county republic of Ireland was effectively off the hook with respect to an attack on its legitimacy.

The British, for their part, were happy to have a training ground for their army on the doorstop. The IRA political leadership, exemplified by Gerry Adams, has been anxious for a quarter of a century to divert the movement through exegesis of republican theology and force of bureaucracy into a solely constitutional movement. There has been an agreement in the pipeline for 30 years; it was only when British commercial interests became seriously threatened through the City of London and Canary

Wharf bombings that the movement toward it quickened. The unionist population in Ireland were put there as a nuisance, and ironically the current dispensation neutralizes that role, so is to be welcomed. The true opponents of Irishness reside in the bureaucracy of the Irish State, transnational capital, and the criminal element surrounding Fianna Fail in particular.

Moloney's (2002, p. 84)"Secret history of the IRA" makes the point through an IRA member that the PIRA initially gained its impetus from a desire to reform the NI state, and only British provocation like the introduction of internment quickened the impulse to national reunification. Gerry Adams began as a socialist but, in classical Free State tradition, later moved to the right (p. 197) despite the role of the labour movement in winning independence. Exploiting his mastery of republican theology, Adams continued to insist to Army council that British military withdrawal was necessary while in fact secretly conceding that political neutrality was all that he desired from the British (pp. 394, 413). He memoed the irredentists into submission, and the result is a peace that will probably last all our lifetimes, for which we must be glad. That is quite a different proposition from accepting British narratives about Ireland, Ireland's current colonial state, and so on. Most of all, the IRA was riddled with informers, and effective active service units like those in Tyrone were betrayed from high to the SAS, with deadly consequences, as was Qaddafi's ultimate largesse, the arsenal on the Eksund that was intended for a "Tet offensive," irrevocably claiming parts of NI.

South Armagh was ungovernable during most of the IRA campaign. Toby Harnden (2004), a correspondent from the right-wing British Daily Telegraph, relates many testimonies from British soldiers lost in admiration at their erstwhile enemy there. Indeed, they were happy to stand for the Irish national anthem there (2004, p. 55). The SAS are quoted;

> "It really was the IRA's domain. They'd become so sophisticated they had mobile communications…the sniper dominated the area and could take his time." (ibid, p. 397)

Eventually, of course, the British began to see the republicans as allies in building a liberal democratic consensus in NI (p. 462).

Underneath the surface of car bombs was a far more interesting technology war. The British cryptography system had been broken by the mid-1980's, and algorithms for doing so on low-specification PC's of the time were available — to British universities — from a University computing department in Ireland. Radio-controlled detonation was another issue as the ex-IRA man Eamon Collins (p. 364) explained;

> "There's a cat and mouse game that goes on between the IRA and the British army. It's a war of technology…the Army had broken the code of the radio-controlled devices…"

Richard Clark Johnson, who had worked on the voyager and space Shuttle projects in the USA and had no Irish ancestry, came up with a solution:

> "He had come up with the ingenious idea of using the Weather Alert Radio frequency to trigger IRA bombs … activated by satellite … Its frequency of 162/55 MHz was not in use in Europe and was therefore a clear channel for the IRA." (p. 356)

The IRA's Martin Quigley was studying computer science at Lehigh University and was finally apprehended with Johnson in an FBI sting (p. 366).

Harnden also relates the tale of Robert Nairac, perhaps the most fantastically inept undercover operative in history. The viewpoint taken here is that NI was essentially never more than a pinprick on the British behemoth, and its role in providing an active service environment for the British army prolonged the conflict. Were it possible militarily to expel the British, it would be right and proper to do so; apart from an outside chance in 1921, that has not ever been the case. Whatever energy and passion went into the military struggle should now be recruited to retrieve some vestige of sovereignty in Ireland.

Nairac (pp. 293-312) attempted to teach himself Irish republican songs, and repeatedly sang on stage using the alias of Danny McErlaine, and ex "official" IRA member. That in itself was a disastrous choice: few Southern Englishmen can say the "r" in McErlaine. On the night he died, he sang republican ballads on stage at the highly dangerous "three steps" bar: few southern Irishmen would drink there. He was abducted on the grounds of grossly suspicious behaviour and beaten before being shot. In the IRA paper An Phoblacht.

> "The officer was portrayed as an upper-class buffoon in a stirring tale fall of action, adventure and the gross stupidities of the Brits. An example of

> his attempts to mimic an Irish accent was: 'Hoots mon, would you ever be giving me a pint of bitter, begorrah, the noo?" (pp. 309-310) (Translation: A pint of ale, now).

Many such mistakes were made as the British experimented in NI. Teague (2006, p. 53) wishes us to believe that it will eventually lead to successful infiltration of Al-Qaeda:

> "British spies subverted the IRA from within, leaving it in military ruin, and Irish republicans...have largely shifted their weight to Sinn Féin (sic) and its peaceable, political efforts."

The relation between Sinn Féin and the IRA was never clearly that between peaceful political and military impulses like the above. Teague (p. 56) follows the career of Freddie Scappaticci from IRA activist to head of the IRA's internal security squad and paid British informer;

> "Scappaticci's history as an IRA sharpshooter gave him an advantage as an agent, and he quickly made his way to the top of the Nutting squad ... The position gave him access to the IRA's innermost secrets; missions completed and upcoming; arms storage sites; travel and security details."

From the early 1980s, the British were in a position to call the shots everywhere except perhaps south Armagh, which was largely autonomous (Harnden, 2000, p. 250). While being party to the IRA's secrets seems already an embarrassment of riches, the British had another highly placed source:

> "In Belfast I met with Denis Donaldson, a Sinn Féin party leader and an IRA veteran alleged to have run the IRA's intelligence wing. He's a folk hero who led hunger strikes." ... (Teague, 57)

Teague mentioned Scappaticci and his fellow spy Fulton to Donaldson, who replied "I still can't believe it" (ibid). Within months, Donaldson outed himself as an informer, and revealed that the "spy ring" unearthed by the British as a pretext to collapse the NI institutions in 2002 was a fantasy by the British. Weeks later, he was shot to death.

It is nonsense to suggest there are any lessons to be learned about handling Al-Qaeda. The NI violence was a grotesque farce, with the moneyed classes being spared, and the IRA leadership being led by Adams down the current path since the 1970's, regardless of the success or failure of the military campaign. George W Bush's special envoy to NI, Mitchell Reiss, declared ex cathedra at a seminar in UC Berkeley in spring, 2012, that the

British had spared Gerry Adams to the point of helping loyalist terrorist elimin ate his rivals. The 1990's bombing of Britain by the south Armagh IRA were the most successful operations ever, and one would have thought the IRA leadership should have intensified the war; in fact, it called two ceasefires). The nationalist impulse must channel itself into peaceful modalities with an intensity that is currently noticeably lacking.

McPhilemy (1998, 379-381) famously identified an "Ulster loyalist Central co-ordinating committee", and their associates, including the Nobel Peace laureate David Trimble, which controlled the "Loyalist death squads" (379) which murdered at least 58 republicans and Catholics, named in Pp 382-385. McPhilemy, Irish and resident in Britain, seems to have been forced to become a full-time litigant to restore his reputation through libel suits; at the time of writing, he has won every single suit, bolstering the credibility of his (difficult to obtain) book. Let us make it clear that the war, such as it was is over; Langewiesche (2007) points out the perils of the brave new world of terrorism unleashed by Pakistan's AQ Khan and his nuclear bazaar. The rule of law is sufficiently established on the island of Ireland that the naïve techniques proposed by Kurlansky (2007) in his book on non-violence may well work. (Essentially, he calls it non-violence only if it succeeds).

The alternative will be to have Ireland written out of world history. Welsh (2002, p. 34) is willing to accept that pre-conquest "Irish society was homogeneous, with a common language, law, and culture." Yet the Norman invasion of 1169 was not that of a country;

> "The land was little more than a geographical expression…the idea of an Irish nation, enthusiastically propounded centuries later by nationalist historians is to say the least, questionable." (p. 163)

The charter given by the English pope, Nicholas Breakspear, to Henry II to acquire Ireland was edited by the latter; significantly, and correctly, Ian Paisley admonished the Irish about Catholicism and the English when textual scholarship revealed the adjustments in 2006. Welsh hails the "ingenious persecutions" of Cromwell and comments that the Irish Diaspora intensified after 1690 with hundreds of thousands of young Catholics leaving the island, often to lives of great distinction (p. 217). By Welsh's admission, at home the Irish were "barred from political life, from the legal professions…from bearing guns, denied a university education." (ibid).

So the further assimilation to Great Britain is justified on the grounds that "the definition of the inhabitants as a nation" is doubtful, as there were two communities (p. 289). In this vein, Duddy (2002) regales us with a history of Irish thought that is replete with Anglo names; Ussher, Wheeler, Wisdom, Boyle, and so on. Eriugena, who lacks a surname, is credited with an emananationist panentheism, an organic continuation of the trends O Duinn suggests.

By contrast, Mac Craimhin (1966) far more interestingly, appropriates the Anglo-Irish scientist to the Hibernian cause, in a book written in Gaelic. Not only do Richard Boyle, Hamilton, Tyndall and so on appear with Gaelic forms of their names, but so do O Callainn, O hUiginn, the author's own namesake Mac Cnaimhin , and the mathematician Robert Murphy. The bias toward the non-scientific manifest in Duddy is combined in revisionism with refusal to engage with Irishness as manifest in language, science and the arts in Contemporary Irish studies. As currently practiced, academic Irish studies often abets the elimination of the uniquely Irish contribution to civilisation.

3.4 A Myth of our own?

Duddy conforms to the humanities bias that exists in Irish studies. In this final section of chapter 3, we will attempt to weave together a narrative that conforms to mythic archetype and scientific basis in fact. The notion of a new world-saving religion of any sort is, to a large extent, an absurdity; science will constrain the discourse in any putative new worldview. This we shall explore in the final section here; the litany of sex abuse cases involving Irish religious is approaching Gothic proportions, and a restructuring of what religion is, and where it fits in Ireland, is urgently important. First, let us dig into the worldview of our ancestors.

Rees et al. (1961) are keen to impose an Indo-European, rather than Semitic, structure on the thought-patterns of the Irish and Welsh. Following that book, we will call them the "Celts", while remaining fully aware that there is no racial connection to Central Europe. The positing of a cultural one, in which influences from the Indian heartland were transmitted, is the central thesis of the Rees' book. They are careful to provide a justification in this scientific age for their study and promulgation of myth:

> "A poem, likewise, is a synchronization and synthesis of many things... there are ideas, there is rhythm which may bear no relation to the syntax....there is rhyme which ties together in near-puns words which do not otherwise belong together, and there is alliteration or assonance which establishes further connections where reason would find none...From a mythological standpoint, such correspondences are neither accidents nor inventions. They are discoveries, their validity grounded in the inexhaustible analogical riches of the universe." (351)

So far, so good; in fact the Rees may be giving away too much to their implicit scientistic opponents. Elsewhere (2004, 113-123), I have assented to the age-old argument that scientific theories are, to a large extent, also stories. While not going as far as Joseph Campbell's positing of epistemological equality between myth and scientific theory (Segal, 1990, 265), in that such theories are often based on at least a restricted set of cogent observations, this writer's opinion is that narrative structure underpins both genres. Moreover, as we're going to see at the end of this section, the attempt to create an "eliminative materialism", one that does away completely with the mental predicates of narrative, is doomed before it starts.

Where the Rees may be seen as going too far is in their version of the *mysterium tremiendum et fascinans* that Campbell (Segal, 1990) is always proposing as the *eschaton* of the mythic endeavour:

> "..their magic has delighted and supported the spirit of man throughout the ages, for it has the power to breach the constraining boundaries of the finite so that the light of eternity may transubstantiate what is commonplace and fill it with mystery" (Rees et al, ibid.)

It is this search for the infinite which religion will always dominate, in that it uses materials from everyday life more immediate than the austere apparatus of good science, and messengers more affable than the crabby loners that many of us scientists become. There will be (a) religion(s) in Ireland to follow Roman Catholicism, recommended patterns of thought and behavior that exploit the extremes of our moral sense and search for the cosmic. On that, more later; let us look at the Rees and their insistence on the Indo-European roots of Celtic culture.

Rees et al (1961) regard many of the connections between the two as elementary; it is not my intention to argue against them. So, for example, the "Sovereignty" whom Joyce incarnates as Molly Bloom is identified as

Sri Lakshmi (73-76). Medb is another cognate; both are interrelated to the soma, whose consumption prefigures the creation of Indo-European culture (ibid.). Elsewhere (2004, 122) I have commented on the clear references to the Bhagavad Gita in Joyce's Ulysses; "I am the dreamery creamery butter" is analogical to "I am the ritual, I am the act of worship, I am the food to be offered in Bhagavad Gita 9:16 (ibid.).

Yet that is only the beginning. Rees et al (98) give an abridged version of the Amergin poem that we have already seen;

> "I am wind on sea
> I am ocean wave
> I am roar of sea
> I am bull of seven fights..."

This is continued by Robert Graves:

> "I am a stag: of seven tines,
> I am a flood: across a plain,
> I am a wind: on a deep lake,
> I am a tear: the Sun lets fall,
> I am a hawk: above the cliff,
> I am a thorn: beneath the nail,
> I am a wonder: among flowers,
> I am a wizard: who but I
> Sets the cool head aflame with smoke?
>
> I am a spear: that roars for blood,
> I am a salmon: in a pool,
> I am a lure: from paradise,
> I am a hill: where poets walk,
> I am a boar: ruthless and red,
> I am a breaker: threatening doom,
> I am a tide: that drags to death,
> I am an infant: who but I
> Peeps from the unhewn dolmen, arch?
>
> I am the womb: of every holt,
> I am the blaze: on every hill,
> I am the queen: of every hive,
> I am the shield: for every head,
> I am the tomb: of every hope."

Each "I am" is an invocation, bringing its predicate into existence. Similarly, Australian aboriginal culture posits such a sequence of "I ams' as the beginning of its land. As I described elsewhere, (2004, 126) it is possible that Christ, if indeed he existed, may have attempted to reintroduce these thought patterns into Judaism, where they perhaps had been forgotten.

Rees et al (ibid.) move on from the metaphysical to a concern with how social order was created in these societies. They follow Dumezil in arguing that the connection between Indo-European and Celtic culture is more direct than that between the Indo-European and Roman pantheons (143-144):

> "...whereas these five deities do not figure as a group in roman religion, and the Roman Mercury is not described as the inventor of all arts, the five leaders of the Tuatha who confer before the second battle of Mag Tuired do correspond to them as regards function"

Specifically, to take four of them; Dagda is the god of druidism, Ogma is a champion, Dian Cecht is the god of Health, and Goibniu is the artisan. (142). Dumezil argues (111-112) that the three basic free classes in Celtic society; the sacerdotal (Brahmin/druid or file), the warrior/royal (Ksatriya/flaith) and farmer (vaisya/bo-aire) are parallel between the two cultures.

Let us be clear; the Brahmin class, perhaps 1/55 of the Indian population, has no financial privilege. In this account, the notion of moral power has been lost in Irish society in the past generation, and the ascent of flaith and bo-aire to the ramparts is one of the trends that has all but destroyed it. There is an element of truth here, in this writer's opinion, however slight it is; that is particularly the case as the ascent of a new near-billionaire (and sometimes actual billionaire) business class through mechanisms like Anglo-Irish bank was ultimately a national and thus implicitly a moral project, not one based on conventional business mechanisms like actually selling something in a free market. Forcing the price of land up through coercion of a young, burgeoning generation and the importation of immigrants, many of whose children will end in affirmative action programs, are not free market mechanisms.

Moling in the battle of Mag Tuired corresponds remarkably closely to Vishnu in the Ramayana (78): both are cenobites, have contests with evil, take three steps and three leaps after which they are named, and have a weapon. Moreover, the predicament of the Gods that initiates and underpins the Ramayana corresponds to the plight of the Tuatha de Danann before Mag Tuired 2. Near-precise parallels continue (53):

> "The vedic goddess Danu...is paralleled by that of Danann in Irish tradition" (53).

The five Gaelic peoples correspond to the Indian five kindreds (107), and the eight sons of Mil map to "the eight supreme Hindu Gods known as Adityas" (107). Donn sacrifices himself like Vivasvat (ibid): Eremon even sounds like Aryaman (108).

The analogies continue. The fire at Tara, possibly a Christian rewriting of a battle that Druids won against demons, corresponds to the third fire in Hindu tradition(53) The Dessi expelled from Munster correspond to the demonic Indian dasas (127). The sequence of peoples arriving in Ireland in the Book of Invasions corresponds very closely to the Indian Caste system (116-117). For example, the sudras, untouchables, correspond to Partholon (116).

Yet the parallels go deeper still. Nera, like many figures in the Celtic myths, emerges in various guises in various stories. In "The adventures of Nera", he runs into a man who has already been hung and is dead (298). After failing at an ambitious task for which he volunteers, he must retreat to the fairy-fort, the sidh, until the end of time (299-300). The story is told as an object lesson in how to deal with visitations from the other world, and massive political changes are effected in the society around as a result of Nera's actions. So is the Indian "25 stories of the scepter in the corpse" , with the king who cuts down the hanged man instructed by him on how to outwit the occult forces that seek to dethrone him (300).

The macabre element of this story, celebrated in the gothic turn in Irish writing in the English language from Le Fanu to Stoker, apotheosizes in Hallowe'en ritual:

> " .. a period of disorder in between the old year and the new in many lands...the elimination of boundaries between the dead and the living...all symbolize the return of chaos" (91)

So much for these parallels; they are perhaps ineluctable at this point. Campbell (Segal, 1990) was always, in this writer's view, a little precipitous in identifying the Occidental myths with the male and Oriental ones with the female. Likewise, his bald assertion that Semitic Gods reflect projections of the social order, unlike Indo-European ones, while intriguing, remains unprovable. There indeed remain the possibility that Yahweh began as a tribal god assimilated by the returnees from Egypt who found that a social revolution had taken place in Palestine, and later invented the character of Joshua and others to find a military narrative for what was an unplanned societal collapse.

Yet Campbell's reading of Joyce, as I have described elsewhere(2004, ibid.) strikes me as reasoned. Campbell is a metaphysical radical in his reading of Joyce as in his notions about the function of myth itself (Segal, 1990, 62):

> "... by contrast to Campbell, Jung never denies the existence of the everyday world and so of ego consciousness"

It is worth quoting Campbell from his own famous "Hero with a thousand faces" (1949, 217):

> ""the values and distinctions that in normal life disappear with the terrifying assimilation of the self into what formerly was…otherness"

Joyce, in Campbell's reading, is similarly an advaitin, a non-dualist in the Hindu tradition. This theme is going to recur throughout this book; it is interesting that Campbell in early 20th century America went through a Catholic education that resembled Joyce's, and against which both rebelled. Where Joyce differs is in his detailed celebration of place, with Ulysses a dindseanchas, and this is explored elsewhere in this book.

Joyce was on solid ground with respect to his Celtic antecedents. Place is celebrated, indeed revered; while Tara is a common hill name in Ireland, the current pushing of the M3 through the Tara/Skryne valley is being done for little more reason than enrichment of a privileged set close to political power. Place also held a sociopolitical role; while Meath, the "province" in which Tara is located, is "the middle "province, a distribution of roles is posited by Rees et al (1961, 123) with the West being concerned with learning, the north with battle, the east with prosperity, and the south with music. In this schema, the Tain is about an attempt by the learned class to usurp those in the North, an attempt which ends disastrously. Like the narrative about the Battle of Allen, those who break the law end up defeated, with the social order in tatters.

So much for myth. We do, I believe, see a strong Indian influence in Celtic thought. Moreover, it is being hypothesized that the concept of "neart" and the metaphysics of subject-object oneness achieved through myth may correspond to patterns deeply encoded in the Irish psyche. Let us take some time out to look at what a modern "Irish" religion (of course, all religion is 'Irish' to the scientistic perspective!) might look like.

3.5 Religion, the academy, and civil society

Religion has lost every battle in which it has engaged with science qua reason, and this will -for the most part – continue, and for the most part that is a desirable outcome. Much of the forthcoming discussion is context for the argument in my 2012 paper on this topic. There will be successful rearguard actions on the part of religion, when the enemy is not science but dogma like Darwinism as conceived of in the early 21st century USA.

However, there are many more fundamental points to be made about religion. The first is, of course, whether it should exist given what we now know about the power of reason and experiment to investigate and successfully manipulate physical reality, including our own brains. The second is whether, given its history of pogrom and fatwa, whether religion has a right to exist. The second is the easier question and was successfully answered, in this writer's opinion, by the authors of the first amendment to the US constitution; religion is to be tolerated as a part of civil society, and a theocracy is preventable by forbidding the establishment of any religion as the state religion. The move here is a subtle and powerful one; by protecting all potentially non-established religions from the state's act in establishing one of them, the state also protects itself from the truth claims of all religions.

Yet this seeming exile from state structure to civil society has actually produced in the USA perhaps the greatest diversity of religious expression in the world. That this expression includes millenniar sects that would overthrow the state at the first opportunity strengthens the hypothesis that the authors of the first amendment got it exactly right. Absent any real chance of a millenniar state, forms of Christian worship that explicitly promote that aspiration thrive in the USA. They thrive side by side with atheism, Hinduism, Buddhism, Islam, scientism, and many other faiths that contradict each others' founding propositions as radically as is possible.

Now we have a new context for the first question about science and religion. Absent a chance to implement its truth claims in state structures, religion thrives regardless as part of civil society. The challenge from science is mild by comparison. It can be asserted with confidence that our early 21st century molecular biology and neuroscience will look primitive indeed in a century. In fact, by that point there may be a consensus that science should not infringe on areas of human experience currently catered to by the arts – to give just one example – because its grain is too fine, and it has nothing to say to the layperson. Indeed, anything it has to say to the specialist in these areas that might bear on psychology is currently the subject of massive dispute, and may in fact always remain so.

What are the areas of human experience currently catered to by religion in an authentic fashion? Essentially, this writer argues, they combine a sense of cosmic origins and mystery with the recruitment of the moral sense to protect a set of practices that heighten the experience of that mystery. In the past, religion has seen fit to privilege cosmogonic and other narratives to the point of torturing and killing anyone positing alternatives to them; likewise, its truth claims for these narratives have led it to the creation of theocracies.

The beginning of a new religious sense is the recruitment of the moral sense against precisely that aspect of theocratic religion. The search for truth, as rational and presuppositionless as is humanly possible, must itself be privileged. This search, it should be made clear, is itself conducted in the epistemological context of cosmic truth and socially within civil society. Yet this is not to cave in to scientism, and the current business-military-university complex. The assertion of truly free inquiry is increasingly threatened in the state and other corporate structures charged with such assertion, and a "Church of Truth" (to use a hackneyed expression due to, among others, Flannery O'Connor) could indeed establish a righteous basis.

Such a Church would be cosmopolitan, as indeed is the ideal of science, and removed from any specific culture. Yet there are practices that it can insist on without any claim jumps. For example, it can insist on a list of scientific and epistemological questions that continue to be asked, and a curriculum that a neophyte must master. It can insist that the arts and humanities practised should have the universal aspects of complexity, self-awareness, and a dialectic between expression and sublimation of emotion that characterise great art. This is also non-trivial; it puts the practitioners at odds with the ethos of the arts in an age of digital replication that titillation is the goal.

What of the truth claims? The aim of the good life in classical liberalism as advanced initially by Spinoza underlies this project. We can remain agnostic about even his God and yet assert that perhaps there is some sense in which we can experience our lives, if briefly, as being continuous and consistent with the unfolding of the cosmos. A more substantial claim is made about the structure of consciousness, and the degree to which science can penetrate it, and this writer has written extensively on the subject. Briefly, it is asserted that good art, and good science – even on a low budget – can bring us to truth realisations of greater veridicality than those coming from corporatist institutions not informed by a real search for truth.

What of the other practices? Again, the author has written on this (2006), and comments on Feldenkrais in a spiritual context, and exercise in a thermodynamic one(2008, 2010; et al, 2011), . The notion of "self" as a contingent entity he has looked at in a scientific context that allows for the idea that the self may be dissolved in meditation. He has left the door open for a scientifically-defensible panpsychism/emanationism wherein the person can come to know through being influenced by a "field" of consciousness-knowledge-bliss that pervades the cosmos. The mathematics or other formalisation that encodes the knowledge is the gift of particularly talented individuals; however, the basic insight is open to many. Finally, he has written why good medicine is socialized medicine (2008); and here the moral sense awakens in a social context.

While a part of civil society, within that the "religion" envisaged in protean. It may be a commune, a college, or just a small group meeting for coffee once a month. However, the kind of attempt to establish non-democratic states we have seen in the early 21st century by such devices as e-voting coupled with massive financialization of the economic systems are political trends to be fought. Conversely, individual rights, representational structures for citizens being picked on by a corporatist state, environmental protection that yet respects individual autonomy, and freedom of expression are to be subsumed under the moral sense.

A casualty of this is YHWH and his various cognates. The moment of meditation, whether achieved through "just sitting", cosmic awe, aesthesis, or an act of self-giving, is instead to be valued. The unfolding of the human individual in her social context is conversely to be revered as the highest expression of nature. Given a social context of western liberalism, many of the psychic forces that conventional religious disciplines attempt to trap are mediated through the individual's relationship with the state and civil society. The creative challenge is to manage the recursive competence of western technique in a context which has quietist overtones, AS I outline in the 2012 paper; yet those who have grown up in the West in Vedanta-influenced religions can show us the way here.

3.5.1 The academy and the world

It is perhaps an exaggeration to say that ours is the first era in which scientific concepts of the brain have challenged our common sense experience; this goes back at least as far as Burton, Le Cat and others from the 17th century. However, the pace of this challenge will quicken. There seems to this writer to be limitations beyond formal Goedelian ones concerning the brain processing its own output.

Scientific concepts of the brain are normally uttered in an academic context, where they are subject to rigorous challenge. As this is being written, it is clear that much of the recent claims of social neuroscience can be accused in this forum of premature closure – to put it gently. These claims –much of which recent statistical analysis have proven spurious - have involved, for example, locating feelings of "awe" in particular locations in the cortex (again, see my 2012 paper). Even the few such findings that will stand the test of time are relatively trivial; to predict behaviour we need, at the very least, to know several million state transitions into which the brain enters over time. For example, we may indeed find something in the brain's stereotypical state transitions that explains why we always want a story to have a beginning, middle, and end. Likewise, there may be a factor in the geometry of the brain's interactions that explains why we always assent to modus ponens. The path to finding these processes and structures will be long indeed, and we are still at a trivial stage compared to claims countenanced by eliminative materialism (EM), which would claim to reduce all our experience to equations.

When these claims are enunciated in a non-academic context ("public space" - PS), a separate set of considerations kick in. In PS, people are looking for guidelines to action, often of a very consequential sort. Were a killer conclusion to be arrived at about neural stem cells, ageing, and distractability, many would all queue up for surgery. It is when claims are made from Neuroscience about being able to tell when someone's lying, as is happening even now, that major issues arrive.

First of all, most of our common sense – not any eliminative materialist (EM)system - will turn out to be the most economical and veridical compression of data to provide guidelines for action in the PS context. To get people to accept EM descriptions in public space, with their almost intractable justification, would require political coercion. Such coercion would far more likely use a much easier message like nationalism to get its way. EM will never enter the public arena, and in PS we will stick with common sense and its long, painful history to handle the daily issues of expression and delay in gratification of desire, administering our lives through the calls of family, finance, race, age, gender, technology, and so on. Those that can give articulate, accurate and economical expression to our subjective lives using often workaday resources like musical instruments, canvas, paint, pen, and theater we call artists. Those that can make sense of our lives and motivate us to action we call activists and politicians.

On an explicitly political level, EM is a threat to freedom of conscience and its attendant notion of privacy. A quick reductio of this threat can be found if it is insisted that freedom of conscience is in fact a political prescription, not a psychological hypothesis. It refers to a renunciation by the state of thought control, which mediaeval Christendom as modern totalitarianisms have proven quite feasible. The state can indeed still control vast regions of our psyche by the modern equivalents of bread and circuses; but that is not the point. Were the individuals in modern states to renounce their sense of free will (as distinct from realty thereof, an entirely different category) to the state, it would be either the result of a coup or a long, excruciating set of court processes and expert testimony with the "experts' initially being rightly assailed by lawyers for their statistical assumptions and logical non sequiturs. Even a coup would beget a heretic like Spinoza within a generation as subjectivity proved resilient to the impositions of state-sponsored "science".

In fact, it is the academic ethos in which EM can thrive which is in danger. EM is an attack on discussion of ideas more than on other political processes. The provision of academies within society in which ideas can be tested – whether they are originally conceived there or not – is vital to society. To put it in the language of neural dynamics, the whole state space arising from the cortical perturbation caused by a new idea can be explored in an academy; in PS, the perturbation might fatally lead to action after vicious action. The self-identification into which one slips at the advent of some new dogma can be coolly observed in an academy, while in PS the new self may wish to "save face" by upping the intensity of its engagement with the world that is filtered through the new ideology. The primary social purpose of the academy, apart from but related to education, is the analysis of ideas. As they are currently discussed in academies and intelligent lay discourse, ideas form a much better compression of the underlying realities than anything likely to come out of EM for at least a hundred years.

So now we have a new take on religion; its location is civil society, not the political apparatus; its domain is the set of human activities that can recruit both the cosmic and moral senses; and it must not claim any purchase on the supernatural. That frees the state simply to provide the physical, political and moral infrastructure for human lives in which freedom for self-discovery is the paramount value, subject to the requirement that the state must reflect the will of the people through a democratic electoral process. That obviously leaves vast room for maneuver on what the division of civil society and the state is for any given country, what representational structures should exist from the borough up to the superstate level, and so on.

Consideration of EM leads us to the final set of considerations about the role of the academy and the artist. It is argued that one result of political freedom in the classic liberal thought espoused by this writer is that the individual's autonomy will always trump any EM description. To say otherwise is to give the academy a role in PS that does great damage to both. The role of the artist, the politician, and the activist is secure as that the academic in this dispensation. Finally, the establishment clause in the US constitution's first amendment simultaneously liberates the individual and the institutions of religion to full self-expression.

Therefore, we can summarize as follows;

1. Religion recruits the moral and cosmic senses to provide prescriptions for behaviour and interpretation of experience
2. It is part of civil society. Any attempt at state takeover ultimately destroys it; conversely, it can exist only in societies that have achieved advanced political freedom.

3. Historically, religions have proposed cosmologies, psychologies and political prescriptions that we can now see are manifestly incorrect.
4. These have led to clashes with established scientific knowledge, and – more seriously – hard-won societal freedoms. When religion has also claimed purchase on state power, this has led to horrors like the inquisition.
5. What religion should do today – as well as its long-established protection of peace and harmony -is protect advanced modes of thinking and creating, including in established western idioms that may not seem threatened, but actually are in grave danger. These include sophisticated and emotionally refined music, genuinely truth-seeking science (as distinct from commercially instrumental science and music). At an existential level, there should be sufficient resources to protect the dignity of the individual, and the advances in development we as humans make from infancy, from the ravages of intrusive states.
6. It can lay claim to an area of human experience that is not immediately evident. That is the subjectivity that precedes our experience of selfhood.
7. Techniques like Feldenkrais, yoga, and above all skilled self-observation amplify this experience
8. This experience, in turn, points to our oneness with the cosmos. That is the great universal of human religious experience
9. Any "new" religion should be able to embrace genuine scientific advance. Its description of experience should be of a precision, immediacy and yet degree of abstraction that removes it from danger of contradiction
10. The intensity of the personal urgency that sparks its acceptance should be of sufficient controlled nature that one can still respect it in the morning!

In the final chapter, we shall outline what the bare bones set of spiritual experience underlying an Irish "religion" could look like. The provision of ritual and forms of everyday life will depend on the emergence of some religious genius in the country. We also look at what sophisticated scientific thought-forms might be preserved by religious activity.

CHAPTER FOUR

HOW THE IRISH BECAME BORING: FROM THE CREATION OF THE FREE STATE TO THE CELTIC HOUSING BUBBLE

4.1 Alternative Narratives of the Genesis and Development of the Irish State

We are about to enter a fractious area, and it is a relief to recount some facts. In 1921 the 26 counties of Ireland that currently together compromise the republic of Ireland achieved partial independence from Britain. A border commission was put in place to establish the precise borders of the statelet in the north-eastern part of the island. A civil war broke out in the nascent free state wherein the supporters of the treaty with the British defeated their erstwhile comrades in arms, often with the utmost brutality. The brutality was not forgotten by the vanquished, who came to power as Fianna Fáil in 1932. In 1937, their leader Eamon deValera succeeded in getting a constitution accepted by popular vote. The constitution was highly programmatic, establishing a special place for the Catholic Church and another one for women (the home). The ethos of a sectarian constitution has been imitated elsewhere, not least South Africa. Ireland remained neutral in World War II, and, logically if disgracefully, deValera signed the book of condolences on Hitler's death.

It is worth pointing out two things immediately. The first is not contentious; de Valera went further in his expression of sympathy than even his peer neutral countries like fascist Spain and Portugal, let alone Switzerland, which was actively helping the Nazi regime financially. The second is one of the ancillary arguments of this book; the state's foundational vacuum makes it behave with sociopathic lack of concern for moral stricture, and with a legal casuistry that would do the Jesuits proud. In Fianna Fáil's case, matters are in fact much worse. De Valera's deputy, Sean Lemass, was echoing party policies a mere score of years before in issuing encoded communiqués as minister of defence of the alternative government (Mahon et al, 2008, 45); he went from "Minister of defence" of the alternative state to an ordinary parliamentarian in 1927, less than two years after his "demission" from the Ministry

The contempt for the structures of the official state apotheosised in Ahern's administration, when it became feasible that these miscreants could end up owning a great deal of the national heritage through privatizations, corruption and bank scams. Ahern followed de Valera's leadership in the state's incursions into civil society – the goal being a country with all activity micromanaged by the state – and a single will at the helm (Ferriter, 2004).

For a small country, the scale of the corruption is cosmic; paradoxically, the corruption is aided by the tiny scale of the country, and over-centralized bureaucracy (to a dizzying extent, government is implemented in a square mile in Dublin's south city). A provisional list of the recent corruption would include the 400 million wasted in a payroll program for the health service, NAMA, the fact that many of the bankers who caused the crash are still in place, bonuses largely intact, the government employment training scheme (FAS), the MRSA rampant in the filthy hospitals, the lack of any real corporate enforcement, incinerator executives (from Indaver) appointed to the EPA, Microsoft executives of the health executive(why??), Medialab, children going to school in rat-infested condemned buildings (with 50 million being spent on prefabs), and the destruction of 3 areas of island excellence we will witness in the concluding chapters of this book ; software, music, and public university education.

Ireland is intrinsically neither more nor less corrupt than any other ex-colony. There are a few confounding factors that make getting rid of Ireland's corruption the number one priority. One is that the judiciary is appointed, rather than elected. Far more important is the small size alluded to above. A third is that isolation from the development of post-mediaeval thought has allowed a cancerous reliance on law as instrument to achieve often unethical goals; in fact, tiny Ireland often has three in the annual European list of the biggest 20 law firms. The dizzying powers available to the political executive must make the rest of the world's would-be dictators envious.

To continue the history; De Valera's constitution had explicitly laid claim to the whole island of Ireland. Had he actively, rather than covertly, participated in World War 2, it is probable that the British would have given it to him. It is probably the greatest missed opportunity in Irish history. A contemporary American diplomat explained De Valera's decision as being simply politics; a united Ireland with a fully enfranchised unionist populace was unlikely to vote him in as prime minister. Since he had convinced himself, GW Bush-like, that his mission was to save his country, he did not participate in one of the few wars in history in which there was a discernible moral imbalance (Coogan, 2000). Irish men have fought, effectively as mercenaries in the absence of a country of their own, on both sides of many wars of the past five hundred years.

In 1969, violence broke out in the North-East of the island. A group of irredentist Irish republicans chose to launch a violent campaign for the re-unification of the country. The issue was finally resolved with much American help in the Good Friday agreement of 1998, in which British sovereignty of the North-East was accepted until a majority in that region vote otherwise. On foot of that and other developments, GDP continued to grow at record levels in the republic of Ireland, until it was by 2005 the second-richest country on earth.

In 2008, the economy collapsed, and fully four years of belt-tightening has failed to wreak any positive results (as predicted in Krugman, 2010). Ireland is perhaps the exemplification of the adage that deflating out of recession is akin to contracepting into pregnancy. Indeed, the main argument for the contraction seems to be that international currency speculators like it (Krugman, 2009).The multifarious origins of the Irish crash are parsed in Ross (2009) and Cooper (2009). Neither has any clue about how to proceed; indeed, the latter finds hope in the scenario that the over-leveraged property "developers" who partly caused the crash might be helped to rise again, courtesy of the taxpayer. The viewpoint of this book is different. It suggests at the extreme – if the EU does not reason with us – a period of default, followed by relative economic isolation and protectionism, including withdrawal from the euro, as the Irish people begin to find their feet again. This is to be accompanied by a quickening of the emphasis on the national culture, and a reaching-out to the Diaspora, both genetic and generally ethnic. Indeed, the ghost estates might be offered at a rebate to the Diaspora, who are far more likely to find an estate in co. Leitrim charming than a Dublin city-dweller looking for a holiday home. .

There are two main interpretations of Irish history. One, following Pocock's (1975) schema, as we saw, refuses to distinguish an Irish history distinct from contemporary North Atlantic events. O'Brien (1986) points out that the Irish supported various pretenders to the English throne, and had to be chastised.

Litton (1998), p. 122) concludes her little popular book on Irish rebellions with the plaintive:

> "Were any of the rebellions really worth all the suffering they caused? Would Ireland have been worse off without them?"

The revisionist answer is clear: absolutely not. Home rule was going to be granted in any case, and the 1916 rebellion simply pre-empted it with great consequent suffering. The partition of the island was necessary, both to safeguard industry, in Co. Antrim in particular, and also to protect protestants from sectarianism. Wisely, in this narrative, the Dublin government has finally had the maturity to agree.

The narrative would continue that indeed the Irish have progressed from being priest and nun-ridden to a tech-savvy, sexually liberal (not to mention permissive) society. So much the better! The disastrous isolationist policies of the de Valera governments led to economic backwardness and massive emigration. During bad decades like the 1950's fully half the available adults failed to find work in Ireland. The situation reached crisis point in the 1980s, and following the earlier example of the Netherlands, a set of agreements between the unions and management was convened in 1987 under the aegis of the state. Since the, there has been remarkable industrial harmony and economic growth, with the numbers at work almost doubling until the crash in 2008.

Emigration is not unique to Ireland; however, the low number of returnees is unique, as is the scale over two centuries. Between 1951 and 1961, 412,000 emigrated (Ferriter, 2004, 465). Even in 1951, there were 523,000 Irish-born in Britain (Ferriter, 2004, 473). Before then, the figures are equally shocking; 700, 000 emigrated, never to return, from 1870-1920 (Ferriter, 2004, 475). The same source (455) puts the Irish-born in the USA in 1920 as a cool 1 million. English (1984) depicts the often criminal subworld the Irish entered, and their response in creating what often turned into local government.

It is fair to say that the welcome many of them received in the USA was less than warm; occasionally, as in Shilts (1982), the antagonism is renewed. The hagiography of Harvey Milk takes repeated shots at Irish cops (53, 89-91). Milk's redefinition of gender roles allowed for the "clone" look in promiscuous gay men, with the female being handled by drag queens, leading to his rejection by moderate gay opinion and serial defeats at the poll booth (70, 276). Milk's strange se life, with its attested preference for very young males, is glossed over (206-207), and the suicides of several of his long-term partners gets little attention (230-234). Indeed, the takeover of the Castro from the Irish, who had to sell under gay pressure, increasingly looks like a property scam (84).

The alternative narrative risks "blood and soil" nationalism interpretation, and for that reason alone is suspect. It shares with the Hegelian viewpoint on nation genesis we saw above, at the very least, a notion that there is a considerable intensity of engagement with one's native place, an engagement which is then exploited to become a nation when lines get drawn on maps. (Of course, the neo-Hegelian Marx would comment that nationalism is simply another opiate of the people, pushed especially in times of economic recession).

This view sees the Irish nation as continually attempting to create objectifications for its sense of its genius loci:

> "In the Hegelian conception the spirit, Geist is itself alienated in its works; it constructs intellectual and social edifies and projects itself so to speak, outside itself." (Aron, 1965, p. 147–8)

The goal is total self-awareness:

> "At the end … mind will find itself once again in possession of the whole of its works and of its historical past and will be aware of possessing this whole." (ibid)

The national search for self-expression in this scenario is also the universal search of mind/spirit to know itself through specific accidents of history and location in this description. The search is obviously political, cultural and historical but, less obviously, also cognitive (it is a search for knowledge) and metaphysical (the boundaries of subject and object are redrawn throughout the historical process).

Images of young men following the paths of the Teutonic Knights eastward may be coming to mind; however that is perhaps disingenuous. The fact remains that Irish culture has yet to realise itself in many critical ways. Titley (2000, p. 108) comments in a mixture of pride and exasperation:

> "Gaelic culture and the Irish language are both very real and very symbolic … and the symbol is the compliment that the actual pays to the ideal. At a very deep level the country knows where it has come from. The shoddiest workshop, the most wonderful fleadh cheoil … the epenthetic vowel, the most skilful hurling match between Cork and Offaly, ogham pennants, Aran sweaters … the formalisation of informality, mediaeval banquets, and whatever long list makes Ireland distinctive all owe something to the Gaelic tradition. It is not just the ghost at the feast but the very shape of the room we live in."

Hamilton (2003), we have seen, sneers at this leprechaunism. Let us unpack one item of this list, the hurling match. Hurling, for the uninitiated, rather resembles three-dimensional field hockey with full body contact. Sticks called camáns (hurlies) propel cork balls called sliotars in blows called pucks (and thus came the name for the "ball" in ice hockey). Players wear minimal or no padding; up to recently, even the wearing of protective headgear was considered rather over self-protective. The game was brought to great heights of skill a very long time ago; unlike rugby union, to take one example, TV film from the 1960s and before shows a game played at levels of skill and fitness very similar to today. (Rugby players from that period look lethargic and anorexic compared to today's terminator types.)

Gaelic football is nowhere near as attractive to watch for a neophyte; the two games were perfected in different parts of the island. Hurling does seem to cluster in places where the land is good and a local magnate could afford to foster its development; Kilkenny is the most frequent winner of the all-Ireland competition. Gaelic football, won most often by Kerry, is by contrast, the specialty of Mountainy men. King (1998) gives a history of hurling, starting in the second millennium BC and proposing links with ancient Greece.

In 2005, Cork won the all-Ireland hurling competition. The cup was lifted by their captain, Sēan Ōg Ō hAilpín (John Halpin junior) who gave his oration in Gaelic, his first language. Sēan, as might be expected, is tall and athletic. Whatever, you might say; however, he is also half Filipino. As non-Irish readers are much more likely to come across Hamilton than Hailpin, this writer cannot point to a more concrete example of the likely new hopeful face of Ireland as it increasingly, and against the electorally expressed wish of its citizens, becomes an immigrant country. The Dublin footballer Jason Sherlock is also of mixed race.

So let us view an alternative narrative; priests and nuns created alternative educational and medical systems for the nation. After the attempted genocide of the Great Famine, the Catholic Church provided a social focus for the huddled masses of Irish in America and other parts of the New World. The Irish adherence to Roman Catholicism had little to do with literal belief in virgin births, resurrections and other miracles, none of which supernatural ethos was ever involved in their politics and practical life. It was recognised, however that the Church was the means through which certain institutions critical to the sheer biological survival of the Irish was implemented. Unlike Tibet, Ireland did not have a history of theocracy.

The nascent Irish state, which yet did not involve any anti-protestant discrimination, was inevitably going to have some Catholic themes,. The excesses that happened due to idiosyncratic interpretation of Catholic teaching were terrible enough without any official state *imprimatur;* for example, during the 1940s and 1950s women were denied caesarean sections, and the pelvic bone was sectioned instead to facilitate childbirth, as some Dublin doctors had decided that caesareans were not compatible with church teaching. Women who endured the truly gothic resulting operation, the symphiosectomy, got public attention only in the first decades of the new millennium. Many were unable even to walk. Edna O'Brien (1984) has famously depicted female subjectivity in the gothic scenario of what may have been Ireland's only historically attested theocracy.

The sacrifice of many middle-class Irish men and women in joining elite teaching orders like the Jesuits and Loreto nuns allowed the emergence of elite schools both in the young free state, and the Irish diaspora. James Joyce, Bob Geldof, Tony O'Reilly and indeed mother Teresa of Calcutta come from precisely this background (Mother Teresa's alma mater was

Loreto Abbey, Rathfarnam, Dublin). It is impossible to explain the motivation of these brilliant, globally aware, altruistic, and successful educators, many of whom sacrificed a comfortable life in the top echelons of Irish society to teach and heal non-blood relative children, without being tempted to fall into explanations involving a national spirit. The education system for the *petite bourgeoisie* and lower was handled, often brutally if effectively, by Christian Brothers, Sisters of Mercy, and so on. Many individuals from many races in many countries owe their high levels of literacy and numeracy to these vowed individuals; in the rush to distance themselves from the roman church, the social capital generated has been forgotten.

Of course, there was sexual and physical abuse (at a rate lower in each case than in the population at large), and conspiracy by the imperial Roman Catholic Church to hide their effects. Like symphiosectomy, this is unforgivable for the victims; the Irish state is finally going some of the way to compensate them. We are left, however with the tempting possibility that the "Irish people" does have whole, emergent properties; indeed, an entire 5% of the adult population might be involved at a particular time, celibate and chaste, in caring for others' children.

Ireland has an attested intellectual history going back at least 5,000 years, with the solar alignments at Newgrange predating the pyramids. Time will tell whether other of the 150,000 or so Neolithic monuments contain more such mathematical gems; the "Dingle diamond " and "Stone of the seven suns" likely do, with the latter apparently referring to its contemporary Pleiades. While we have some preliminary indication that a Vedic religion was one of the cross-currents in "druidism", the failure to create a native religious expression (with ceremony, community and so on) has been a massive loss. Conversely, the absence of a proselytising imperialist movement like Japan's Nicherene missionary sect has been a massive plus; Irish missionaries have taught and healed, if perhaps unfortunately in the name of Christ and other Judaic sects.

The view of this book sees current Irish "culture" as simply State-sponsored assent and amplification of the worst movements in the Irish psyche. While "culture" is notoriously one of the most difficult words in any language, it is fair to say that what has happened due to the so-called Celtic tiger is the replacement of discourse about the normal human activities that comprise a full life-art, music, the personal genuinely becoming political and vice versa — with discourse centred on a minor part of the means to support a society, the how of money. In their new role as artist, the money people become deluded. What is $500 billion debt but a metaphor? Sadly, in this case a rose is a rose.

And so, adapting Ignatiev (1996), the Irish have become boring. Ignatiev traced the decline of the US Irish from abolitionist followers of their own religious liberators, Daniel O'Connell, to racist as they began to sense the privileges their skin colour brought. The thesis is tendentious, and fails fully to explain, inter alia, why the San Patricio brigade fought with Brown Mexicans against white Anglo-Saxons. That Irish have become boring is less controversial; not a single quality popular music artist has emerged for over a decade from the country that, in times of deepest recession and Catholic stranglehold, brought forth Rory Gallagher, Van Morrison, Sinead O'Connor, and so on. Likewise, it is hard to think of a major Irish writer from the Celtic tiger period.

The thesis here, then, is that the current configuration of Irish society from 1997 to the present is pathological, the result of a succumbing to global capital, and is inherently unstable. The relationship between the state and the people is feudal; having failed to protect the people from the vagaries of the money markets, the state now serves them up to be leeched from. Every time an Irish person buys an unnecessary car, the bureaucracy gains over 20% through VAT. House purchases net around 30% in stamp duty and other taxes to the state. The bureaucrats can then preen themselves on their next trip to their EU counterparts, as the public finances and GDP growth seem to be "on the right track to re-enter the bond markets".. Indeed, in 2008 (a typical year) over 70% of the legislation passed in Ireland was of EU origin, from SI 395/2008 on mussel seed fishing to 264 on financial checks. Much of this legislation is inappropriate to Ireland, and should be repealed. ECB borrowing is not keeping the people afloat; it is simply perpetuating a particular class in power, and constitutes interference with our sovereignty.

Ireland has become notoriously expensive to live in; during its recent artistic heyday from the 1960s to 1980s, it was incredibly cheap and so young people could give their career in the arts a shot without worrying about homelessness and starvation. The official discourse around them was significantly more meaningful than now; did the Irish 26 county state have legitimacy? What was the correct relationship between church and state? Was violence justified to secure rights? Currently, young people already under fierce financial pressure, listen to pseudo-numerate financial gobbledegook fully as bizarre as talk about virgin births.

Krugman (2009, 6), in rather arch fashion, describes economic theory as similar to Wittgenstein's famous ladder; you throw it away after it has helped you to rise. That will never do; the dirty little secret of economic theory, as described in that bastion of anarchism, the WSJ, is that interest rates are calculated on the basis that all debts have been settled (Kaltsky, 2010); that unemployment is a "desire for leisure" (ibid); elsewhere, price and value cannot be aligned, and in desperation we reach out to "marginal utility" (Robertson, 1963) before that too crumbles under our grasp. The safeguards wisely inserted like FDR's Glass-Steagal, which wisely separated investment and standard banking, thus crumble in the face of economic "boom". These safeguards distinguish money made to buy as house as a central part of one's life project from speculative money. Ireland must introduce something of this sort, with regulators of higher calibre than the likes of Patrick Nary to implement them.

The incursion of the state into civil society has been egregious. Through the so-called social partnership agreements, the unions have been domesticated by the state. There is a word for a political dispensation in which labour and capital are unified under state aegis in a corporate structure: fascism. The industrial relations agreements have effectively reinstated the old English common law rule of summary dismissal at any time for any reasons. Strikes are expressly forbidden in the case of dismissal of an individual, a provision more in keeping with wartime. Enclosure of the intellectual property realm was attempted through the insane Media lab project (see Chapter 6). The perhaps intended result was the destruction of the native Irish software industry (Ō Riain 2004 describes its infinitely delicate genesis, as we shall also see below)

Michelle Smith and Cian O'Connor, the last two Irish Olympic gold medalists, were both drug cheats (in Cian O'Connor's case his horses rather than him). Music remained as one of our few areas of excellence left. Along came IMRO, the so-called Irish Music Rights Organisation, which proceeded to increase greatly the cost of putting on live music. Supposedly set up as a member organisation, it refused to protect their copyrights as they got transferred from broadcast to mechanical rights ventures, and assigned all members' copyrights to itself as it chose; sometimes in a rather personal way, as a police investigation revealed; on seanonuallain.com, the whole grisly sequence is laid bare, with the

Chairman of IMRO involved in massive theft of copyrightl. No accountability was required of it:

> "A series of controversies during the second half of the 1990s saw an eruption of suspicion, if not paranoia, about IMRO's operations … now the organisation operates with full government sanction, full support of the legal system, and with an unchallenged economic monopoly position in the Irish jurisdiction." (McCann, 2003)

In a truly egregious stroke, that whole reservoir of human experience that we call "Celtic" music was assigned to the organisation, despite public denials in Parliament by Senator Ō Murchū, who negotiated with IMRO in secret ;

> "Following a series of private meetings, Shay Hennessy, the chairman of IMRO, and Labrahs Ō Murchūs of Comhaltas Ceoltoiri Eireanns, signed a letter of agreement on the 21st December 1998 … for a nominal fee of £1000, Comhaltas contracted with IMRO for a blanket license to cover all official Comhaltas functions … in return, IMRO agreed to make financial subventions to Comhaltas … £125,000 to a Cultural Centre … run by Labhras O'Murchus' wife. The transformation of the official position of Comhaltas was spectacular." (ibid)

This is the context in which the political coup of 2004 was attempted. The writer is proud to have been part of the resistance, as the person who put Stanford e-voting expert David Dill together with the Irish Labour Party, as a member of the National Council of the Green Party whose coalition defeated the first Nice referendum, as one whose music company engaged in litigation with IMRO, and as one who won the test case guaranteeing academic tenure, and civilized treatment of other university employees. (O'Nualláin, 2004, pp. 8–13)

Let us now look at a conventional sociological analysis of Ireland. For some time, we have used the Hegelian paradigm of nation on an "as if" basis; the notion that the trope of nation exploits the sense of genius loci for political ends will suit our purposes without the Hegelian excess. What kind of society is Ireland, in the most Gradgrindian facts-based sense?

4.2 The Dummies' Guide to Irish Society: Modernisation and Incoming Capital

For three years in a row, Ireland was "ranked as the most globalised of 62 states" (Irish Times headline, 8 January 2003). It is a liberal, secular society with free access to contraception, abortion available up to term on the say-so of a minimally qualified counsellor, homosexual and heterosexual sex sharing a common age of consent of 17, divorce, free media with non-cable channels allowed to show soft porn and feature four-letter words and exotic compounds thereof (well before 10pm), porn mags on the magazine racks, and economic dynamism that up to recently was the envy of the world. All of this is in complete contrast with a mere fifteen years ago. Its republican constitution asserts the active role of the citizen in creating law, the essence of republican citizenship for writers like Bellamy (2008); the liberal wing of citizenship is well-catered for by free access to the courts to redress grievances (if one can afford the enormous legal bills involved, particularly as the state likes to use Arthur Cox, the 12th biggest law firm in Europe)

It used to be very tempting to see Ireland as a classical example of the benefits of modernisation. As modernisation progresses, secularisation increases, and family structure alters in exactly the manner it has done in Ireland (where births out of wedlock have increased literally exponentially). The model is vaguely paternalistic:

> "Modernisation theory saw world development as a process where modern societies helped traditional societies develop through the transfer of new technology, values or capital." (Tovey et al, 2003, p. 48).

So Ireland has indeed become more computer-literate, more secular, and received inflows from the EU, as we have seen, and fully $4.7 billion of US investments in 2003. Modernisation theory is obviously influenced by Comte, who discerned a path from mythological to positivistic in human societies. (Intriguingly, "Lord of the Dance" succeeded, according to the hard logical positivistic criteria of cash, by focussing on myth).

Dependency theory, by contrast, contrasts "core" countries like the EU ex-empires from peripheral countries like Ireland:

> "Dependency theory has challenged that account. It argued that the transfers were primarily in the opposite direction, from the poor countries to the rich." (ibid).

The structure of trans-national corporations (TNC's) allows them to operate differently in different countries, in particular in newly industrialising countries (NIC's) versus core countries;

> "Many sociologists therefore refer to the industrial development occurring in NIC's as dependant development. They argue that the social structure of NIC's is not converging with that of early industrialism societies. Their place in the new international division of labour means that the social structure of NIC's remains different from that of the core countries." (ibid).

To take one example, Microsoft's official European headquarters is in Dublin. Yet its prestigious European research centre is in the green and pleasant Cambridge, England. Irish people, as we will mention in chapter four, shrink-wrap Cds's and "translate" Microsoft documentation from American to British English while, in Cambridge, they invent the future. Intel was about to outsource some of its Irish software research centre in Shannon to Bangalore. The list, as we shall see, goes on.

That there has been massive growth in Irish GDP cannot be doubted. Given that the level of personal debt increased in a decade of "boom" from €16 billion to over €300 billion, and then to around €1 trillion, GDP inevitably increased. Let us recall:

> "GDP = final goods and services produced by Irish business organisations in Ireland and goods and services produced by foreign-owned business corporations in Ireland." (www.finfacts.com).

Ireland's GDP per head was indeed extraordinarily impressive:

> "The 2005 human development report, published by the UN development programme yesterday, found Irish people to be the second wealthiest in the world, with a GDP per head of $37,738 (€30,384)." (Humphreys, 2005, p. 1)

Ireland's Michelle Smyth won three gold medals in swimming at the 1996 Atlanta Olympics. A year later, she was adjudged to have interfered with a urine sample.

> "Ireland has passed out (sic) both the US and Japan in terms of development and risen to eighth place in a prestigious world table for human development" (ibid).

In the case of Cian O'Connor, it was his horse that was found to have taken drugs. As a former veterinarian's assistant, this writer can testify that horses are dangerous creatures, and recommends that all of them should take Fluphenazine before he is asked to work with them again. Anything that improves their temperament is in his opinion salutary; the fact that O'Connor's horse Waterford Crystal, suitably doped with this drug, was able to jump better, is an irrelevance. This, unfortunately, was not how the world equestrian body, the FEI, saw it.

Ireland's other major contribution to the medals in the 2004 Olympics was an assault by an Irish ex-priest on the Brazilian leading the marathon. The Brazilian lost a certain gold; the Irishman was alerting the world to its imminent demise. O'Connor's horse Waterford Crystal was jointly owned by Sir Tony O'Reilly, independent News and Media, and Waterford Wedgewood. Its urine became of urgent interest to shareholders in these corporate behemoths.

> "The report included a section entitled "Two tales of Irish poverty" which questions the accuracy of relative poverty indicators in rapidly growing economies like Ireland." (ibid).

A urine sample from Waterford Crystal was mysteriously stolen as the investigation into Ireland's sole medal of the 2004 Olympics deepened. Eventually, O'Connor and Ireland were stripped of the medal. His Irish show jumping teammate Jessica Kurten refuses to jump with him (and indeed compete for Ireland); a sport at which Ireland previously excelled has been brought into disgrace.

> "The report established that 15.2% of Irish people lived in poverty. Only Italy and the US had a higher poverty rate among 18 industrialised countries surveyed." (ibid).

The show jumping team was a 32-country example of pan-Irish excellence:

> "The report also cited relatively low levels of investment in education and health in Ireland ... In general, the report found Ireland to be one of the most unequal countries in the developed world, with the richest 10 per

> cent of the population having 9.7 times more wealth than the poorest 10 per cent." (ibid).

The story is even worse than this shameful set of surface statistics.

> "Gross National income (GNI) = final goods and services produced by Irish owned business in other countries." (www.finfacts.com).

Now let us see what Irish business is really made of. When we subtract profits made in Ireland by TNC's from GDP, and then add profits made abroad by Irish-owned TNC's, we get GNI. Many Irish accountancy and law firms work hard at creatively re-interpreting profits made by TNC's in their home countries as originating in Ireland, the new Delaware, with its lower corporate tax rate. These scams go by various names; "the Double Irish", "Dutch sandwich", and so on.

We find that in 2005 Irish GDP per head was $37,738; Irish GNI per head, even with the frenzied borrowing was $26,960. (ibid). That makes for a GDP: GNI ratio of approximately 1.4. Take it that all the claims that Ireland, along with only Finland in Europe, ever had Silicon Valley-type production levels is nonsense. It much better fits the now unfashionable dependency model.

Next time you visit your bank, take a look at its balance sheet. The money you have, perhaps proudly, deposited there is in accountancy terms a liability for the bank. That loan you don't mention to your friends comes under assets when the bank tries to talk up its share price in a desperate attempt to avoid takeover. While leading Irish banking officials like millionaire Lochlann Quinn, brother of the ex-Labour party leader, bizarrely talk about Irish ownership of its main banks as being about preservation of "intellectual capital", the reality is that Irish culture is being destroyed by actuarial fantasy.

What of the fabled technology and inward investment boom, the horribly named "Celtic Tiger"? (In his zeal to drum up business, the Bank of Ireland chief economist Dan McLaughlin brilliantly coined the term "Celtic Tiger 2" to designate the recent golden years of usury).

The academic, activist and sometime socialist activist Keiron Allen points out some home truths:

> "In contrast, Allen (2000) argues that Ireland's economic success arises from conditions in the global economy and has little to do with planned modernisation. He notes that growth rates have fallen in all major industrial economies since the mid-1970s, reflecting falling rates of profit … It has been particularly felt in the US, where business has responded in two ways: first, it has attacked the employment conditions of US workers; second, it has expanded investment abroad in search of better investment opportunities. As a consequence, investment abroad by American-based TNC's quadrupled between 1982 and 1987 (Allen, 2000, p. 22). Ireland benefited, as it was an attractive location for US investment into Europe. Particularly attractive was the spectacular low rate of corporate taxation in Ireland a young, English-speaking workforce that could be hired at rates of pay that stood at the bottom of the European average … For Allen then, the birth of the "Celtic Tiger" had little to do with Irish initiatives." (Tovey et al, 2003, p. 70)

Allen argues that Ireland is indeed a capitalist success story, but one with massive social costs. Since he wrote, however, the gains made have been dwarfed by the increases in personal debt. Moreover, exports were not enough; however, in the 1980's Ireland's attempts to target certain value-added areas did work, and this is what needs to be done again, at the expense of call centres and the like.

Lee (1985) eviscerates the Irish people for fostering emigration in order to protect their living standards. Joyce's sow that eats her own farrow, his fabled caricature of Ireland, chose to send them away. What has happened since Allen wrote, to the cheers of bankers, is an older generation again sending a younger into internal exile in order to afford a luxurious retirement. In the manner of Carlos Castaneda's (plagiarized, as ever) "Journey to Ixtlan", you can stay in Ixtlan, your home place, but it will not be home any more. The socially permissive legislation, never voted on by the populace (who, according to any decent democratic criterion, in fact voted against divorce in the mid-1990s) imparts an air of negative moral eschatology. The radio waves thicken with obscenity. In the words of Ariel Levy (2005), you see Britney Spears withering semi-naked on public TV so much that you feel you have "dated" her (Ariel's delicate term).

Most of all, everything is unforgivably expensive, and simple, cheap pleasures like a chat over a pint of beer have become hugely self-conscious forays into credit card debt. Then you go to your humble home, which you bought for over a hundred times what your parents paid for theirs (this is often literally true for anyone born before 1970 and buying after 1998, and McWilliams, 2006, cites his parents' house going up a thousand-fold in price in 50 years). What remains of Ireland?

4.3 Civil Society

Their state has spectacularly failed the Irish people; in its childish urge to be associated with good news, the government has neglected its fiduciary, legal, not to mention its moral duties. As it behaved in this way, the state expanded into what were traditionally areas of civil society, exemplified by its domestication of the unions in the so-called partnership agreements. For selling out their members, union bosses get perks, post-retirement, like seats on the board of the recently privatised telecommunications company, Eircom and the Central bank (both of which actually happened). Eircom was eventually in 2006 to petition the government for funds to roll out broadband, as it had failed to do so.

Alexis de Tocqueville famously commented on the American drive to association (Aron, 1965). As a teacher at UC Berkeley after 30 years in the Irish educational system, I am as astonished as Tocqueville at the willingness of students to organise into groups, and take on the educational thrust of the class as a joint crusade. Civil society is a paradoxical term. In many ways, community, with which it is often confused, is an outgrowth of family. Civil society refers to voluntary associations like the United Way that sprung from non-familial joint projects.

While Tovey et al (2003) fail to make this distinction, and conflate community with civil society, their account is otherwise, as ever, helpful and informative. They distinguish integrationist societies like Muintir na Tíre (the people of the land), a priest-led society that was state-friendly, and oppositional groupings like the equally priest-led Glencolumbcille *de facto* commune (op.cit, p. 116). The major achievement of what one can only term the Bertiestate has been the assimilation of many civil society movements to the state. It was Ahern, as Minister for Labour in 1987, who drew up the first partnership agreement at the instigation of Charles Haughey. It is unlikely that the restriction of individual freedoms in these agreements, which has led to an epidemic of workplace bullying and indeed suicide, would survive a challenge at the EU court of human rights. The control of Irish musicians through IMRO has been aided and abetted by the state's refusal to prosecute egregious breaches of copyright law by IMRO management.

As mentioned later, Ahern's daughter married a member of one of the boy and girl bands (I forget which) who sprung up like mushrooms on a dunghill in the late 1990s. Coincidentally perhaps, the group in question, Westlife, had an unprecedented run of No.1 hits (in Britain and Ireland, even flamboyant bookmakers like Paddy Power refuses to take bets on the pop charts, which are trivially manipulable). Then they got into property development, and their leader was declared bankrupt in Britain.

Struck by artistic genius, Ahern's other daughter became a publishing phenomenon with the Murdoch-owned Harper Collins, just as Murdoch was increasing his grip on IMRO. However, none of these is Ahern's major achievements of appropriation to the Irish state of civil society structures. That honour falls to his gelding of the "provisional" IRA.

Ahern's father con was himself an irredentist IRA member. In the late 1930's, the IRA convened a meeting of the remaining anti-treaty parliamentarians of 1922 just as de Valera's constitution was being put to the Irish people. These parliamentarians, *ultra vires* as one could wish, selected the IRA council as the real government of Ireland, just after the 1937 constitution had laid claim to the whole island. Until 2005, as exemplified by its "Nightmare before Xmas" type offer to Robert McCartney's sisters to kill the men who had killed their brother, it purported to hold the power of life and death on everyone on the island of Ireland.

Or will so purport until, as inevitably will happen, they go into coalition with Fianna Fáil. "Irredentist" does not even begin to describe the IRA's claim on the whole island of Ireland. Their refusal to enter parliament in the republic probably cost them the balance of power there in 1981; the later stated acceptance to do so led to a major split. (Moloney, 2002, p. 197).

Once the genie of national unity was out of the bottle, it was going to be near impossible to control it. The initial desire to reform the state became quickened by the desire to unify with the south, once ill-trained British soldiers arrived in Northern Ireland in 1969 (op.cit, p. 84). Gerry Adams was faced with a dilemma. The British did not mind losing a few squaddies to mad Paddies just a short ferry ride away; this capacity to train soldiers in active service helped them to win the Falklands war. Undoubtedly correct in so doing, Adams decided to stop the bloodshed.

Theological slights of hand had to be performed. In the meantime, effective IRA operations were mysteriously betrayed to the British (op. cit, p. 318). The demand for full British withdrawal from Ireland was converted into a statement of political withdrawal, of a concession that the British no longer had any strategic plans in Ireland (394). Self-determination for the Irish people, another holy of holies for the republicans, was glossed by recategorising the equally unmovably British unionists as Irish. Even old military men like Joe Cahill (295) and Brian Keenan eventually came on board.

Ahern has since managed to convince the IRA to disarm. The way is now clear for a grand republican coalition of Fianna Fáil and Sinn Féin. The extent to which even such a fearsome combination would actually rule the country is debatable (although my money would be on them).

As would the money of the ex-hunger striker Anthony McIntyre (2008). He is clear that the IRA lost the war, which was about driving the British from Ireland, and that the British won it. He is now somewhat bewildered as to whom he was fighting for, as distinct from against, becoming somewhat obsessed with Sinn Fein's president for life;

> "When we took part in the Adams war....we deluded ourselves that we were fighting for Ireland when all we were doing was fighting for Adams. He became the author of our meaning." (222)

To support his view that the Good Friday agreement (GFA) is nonsense, he quotes an Irish diplomat speaking at Oxford;

> "The GFA is a delicately balanced compromise that can be destroyed by truth ....honesty and straightforward talking must be avoided at all costs" (307)

McIntyre shows further acerbic brilliance while commenting on the implementation of the GFA; the end-point is one in which Sinn Féin has accepted partition, acceptance of the unionist veto of a whole-island country, and the making illegal of the IRA. As he points out, with these views he would have been in the loyalist wing, not the republican wing, of Long Kesh prison. Adams himself keeps denying his own membership if the IRA, while Moloney has adduced evidence that the Ballymurphy contingent he led pioneered the car bomb, and the Armalite (253).

Yet the most trenchant aspect of McIntyre's criticism is the drawing –out by Sinn Fein of the peace process; for example, sacrificing David Trimble by sending him out with no compromises from them at the 2003 elections, when it was clear that Trimble's successors would give them a worse deal;

> "The trick of the peace process is to keep people endlessly participating in a process that somehow never seems to bring about peace."

Crises are manufactured in order to keep Sinn Fein on the news in the republic and - a point that McIntyre misses - in order to ensure that Ahern was able to deflect criticism for his handling of other affairs of state, pleading his preoccupation with peace;

> "Such crises are what maintain the peace in a state of process rather than allowing it to come to fruition as a solution…central…is the continuing existence of the IRA…with the IRA off the scene, the peace process comes to the end of its shelf life and beds down as a solution"

He again becomes wonderfully absurdist;

> "Yes, peace process, you are the most exemplary of all pace processes" (221)

Clearly, it will help us all as Irishmen and women to delegate this nonsense to Ulster as a province in a federation, lest it continue to absorb excess amounts of our scarce national resources.

Similarly far from the gentle face of civil society, Tovey et al (87 ff) pointed to a power elite hypothesis of Irish rule, an interlocking set of financial interest revealed by government-funded tribunals from the mid 1990s onwards. (The tribunals were essentially an admission that then as now, the Irish criminal justice system had failed). This centralization was minor indeed compared to the revelations due to the banking crisis.

In fact, it is likely that the centralization of the Irish apparatus of state, and the failure to prosecute white-collar crime, facilitates the perpetual emergence of power elites. Committing crimes that involves the theft of tens of billions from the taxpayer can be finessed by sleight of hand, rather than prosecuted,; continued by judicious (if only slightly legal) use of Ireland's gargantuan law firms to guard against any "libellous" open discussion, and subsequently turned into a political debate between the two tweedles about whether NAMA is correct. The fact that the chairman of Anglo Irish in resolution, Alan Dukes, is an ex-leader of Fine Gael, and that another such, the late Bilderberger groupie Garret Fitzgerald, supported NAMA tells one all that one needs to know; or would, were it not for the fact that the right wing of Fine Gael attempted a leadership coup in 2010 immediately before a vote of no confidence in the Prime minister, arising from trenchant criticism of his role in the financial crisis by the IMF and independent Central bank. .

Clifford et al (2009) trace the origins of the "Drumcondra mafia", its capo being Ahern, as they morphed from informal gang to gain control of the apparatus of state. In particular, senior civil servants in all departments issued Ahern with summaries on Thursday nights which were processed in Drumcondra on Friday. More recently, the evanescent liquidity in the international money markets that characterised the late Greenspan years allowed the entrance of a "property" cabal for which two generations of Irish will pay.

The vanishingly small membership of the cabal, and its elusions of grandeur, are treated well in Macdonald et al (2010). Commenting of Bono's bosom buddy, Sean Mulryan, who actually gets name-checked along with other developers (Mulryan apparently has successfully invited Bono to his ancestral cottage) on the most recent U2 album (I'm no expert, but is this rock'n'roll?), the following is pointed out;

> "The scale of what Mulryan is building or planning in London Docklands is quite staggering" (233)

It better be good, as our grandchildren will be paying for it. As for Mulryan's fellow U2 dedicatee, and fellow investor in his own eternal salvation by getting his name inscribed at our expense in the Vatican, Derek Quinlan:

> "The most sensational coup of the Celtic tiger era was the acquisition for E750 million of the Savoy hotel group by a syndicate of wealthy Irish investors led by former tax inspector Derek Quinlan" (235)

Sicut est in terra atque;

> "The Clarence hotel, which McKillen and Quinlan are partnering U2's Bono and The Edge" (237)

Needless to say, McKillen is yet another dedicatee, and investor in his own eternal rest with our money at the Vatican. His attempt to buy the hotel outright from Quinlan led to one of the great recent courtroom farces in British courts, where he was publicly accused of having "no money"!

When considering, with Tovey, the Power elite hypothesis of Irish society – which seems on the face of things utterly proven by the unashamed attempt to get us to pay for the goings on of this bunch (including Sikorsky helicopters for him'n'her, 50-100 racehorses, and Debbie Harry performing for one's 50th – and that's just Mulryan) - it is tempting to echo Mussolini:

> "Everything in the state, nothing outside the state, and nothing against the state" (Goldberg, 52).

For Goldberg (23) "Fascism is a religion of the state". Ireland's apparent immunity to this political movement must be reviewed, given De Valera's *desiderata*:

> "The reality was that de Valera believed in the state control of all aspects of Irish life" (Ferriter, 2004, 365)

Indeed, Ferriter (op cit) points out that de Valera explicitly stated that the vast smorgasbord of the nation's life in all its aspects should be subject to a single will. This coheres with his micro-management of the Irish Press group; apparently, his major concern on viewing news enterprises in the USA was how they were controlled (O'Brien, 2001) versus how the news was collated, and so on. His successor Lemass had massive power in finance (374); this is the candy shop that Ahern raided.

The Irish state, this writer argues, is at this point a new, virulently cancerous overgrowth on 10 millennia of Irish civil society. So far, it is relatively superficial, and can be extirpated to allowed civil society structures to flourish again (Ferriter, 374-378). Ferriter is clear about the alternative (359) as he comments on "...what was becoming a crusade for complete state centralization on the part of the Irish government"

Brisard et al (2002) take time out from analysis of the Bush-bin Laden connections on which their book focuses to visit the bizarre bestowal of Irish passports on sheikh Mahfouz and his retinue by Haughey (138). This, in retrospect, facilitated the emergence of Ireland in the late 1990's as a maternity ward for much of West Africa. In short, the way power works in Ireland leaves everything up for grabs, and unaccountably so; citizenship, the country's treasure, and political power divorced from the electorate.

Likewise, the administration allows for absurdities like a situation wherein the natives of Meath were not allowed build anywhere near Tara, but a motorway has been rammed through just beside it. A federal system based on the ancient provinces is nowhere near as absurd as what currently obtains. Ulster can be considered with respect to the cross-border bodies that currently exist, and the British should hold on to it for as long as they are prepared to pay for it. It is our showpiece; see how these Christians love each other!

An alternative is good old-fashioned Mussolini-style corporatism, with inevitable compromise of individual rights. It is hard to imagine the banks gently giving up their current role in the pecking order of Irish society; as they bleed the people dry, only forces equivalent to a revolution will dislodge them. Ahern's post e-voting vision was possibly very similar to 1930s Italy in its political structure, rather than dynamics. This uneducated prime minister, who has frequently falsely claimed attendance at LSE and UC Dublin, would have made a delightful Duce.

The church may return in some form or other; while it is morally bankrupt, its extensive land holdings, much of which was acquired during the great Famine, makes it financially extremely solvent. Women will not put up with their former role:

> "The mores of the church and practices of the priest provided a powerful model for child rearing, as mothers initiated the social and moral perspective of the religious." (Tovey et al, 2003, p.26)

However, there is certainly enough money in the Irish Church's kitty (including money sent there by the Canadian Church to avoid having to pay off the sexually abused in Canada) to engineer a charismatic religious revival on foot of a papal visit, perhaps presaged by the 2012 50th Eucharistic congress in dublin. In the meantime, amid the new religious movements developed in Part I of Tovey et al, 2003, the Cistercian monk Brother Turner is fashioning an admirable mystical Christianity. (O'Nualláin, 2004, 217–218)

Classical civil society organisations like the Gaelic Athletic Organisation (GAA) will continue to thrive. The extent to which the GAA has connected with modernity is deeply impressive; no longer are its players forbidden to play foreign sports, and its use of rock music in video clips reminds one rather of the ice hockey "Rock em sock em" heyday. The two nations of this book's introductions have, finally self-aware, come together.

Comhaltas Ceóltoiri Éiream (CCE), the flagbearer for Irish traditional music and dance, is fatally compromised, as is the now state-assimilated IMRO. The report of the Arts Council of Ireland (2004, p. 21) frets:

> "The committee notes with some concern the agreement that arose between IMRO and CE, in which Comhaltas agreed to pay IMRO an annual fee for a blanket licence, and in turn received financial subventions over five years."

Only with the reversal of this enclosure of the commons will Irish musicians begin to make an impact internationally again. Only with a withdrawal of the Bertiestate from precisely the informal organisations that once made Ireland a dynamic and fascinating place (excluding, of course, the IRA) will the country as a whole begin to breathe again.

CHAPTER FIVE

SO FAR FROM GOD, SO BETWEEN BOSTON AND BERLIN: IRELAND IN THE WORLD

> "It is clear from the strategies outlined and the models that have been projected for Ireland's economy....that unemployment will continue to rise, unfortunately, before things get better"
> —Prime Minister Brian Cowen speaking in Parliament, July 1, 2009

5.1 Ireland's Wirtschaftswunder

Ashby Avenue, in Berkeley, winds its way east from the Pacific through some of America's prime real estate before turning into Highway 13, which cuts through the Hayward fault valley. The traveller feasts her eyes east of Telegraph Avenue on houses inspired by the work of local architectural heroes Julia Morgan and Curtis Maybeck. Suddenly, the boulevard becomes a highway, but with a difference. The dividing line is, in fact, a cement wall, with crude designs. There used to be many such in the United States with much more elaborate designs than Highway 13 which made driving an aesthetic experience; the Sunday afternoon drive was planned as a pleasure at many levels.

After its military defeat in 1945, Germany became the subject of many economic experiments. The result was a *wirtschaftswunder*, an economic miracle. The millions of Germans who starved to death between 1945 and 1949 might have had other terms for the economic policies of this period. The removal of highway dividing art in the design of *autobahnen* was a minor detail in comparison. Other national test tubes for American economic experimentation since then have included 1970s Chile, where the Chicago School of Economics, led by Milton Friedman, was given a country to play with.

Ireland is hardly more free economically than Pinochet's Chile, where the economic experiment led to mass emigration. There is a scene in John Le

Carré's (2001) *The Constant Gardener*, in which the central love affair in the book begins unpromisingly:

> " 'So when is a state not a state, in your opinion, Mr. Quayle?' Tessa inquired sweetly."(p.143)

The middle-aged dilettante, Justin Quayle, played by (the partly Irish) Ralph Fiennes in the movie replies:

> "A state ceases to be a state when it ceases to deliver on its essential responsibilities." (op. Cit. 145)

Pressed on the point, he enumerates these responsibilities:

> "Electoral suffrage … protection of life and property … justice, health and education for all, at least to a certain level … the maintenance of a sound administrative infrastructure … roads, transport, drains, et cetera" (ibid.)

(Remarkably, John Le Carré has used the trope of birth out of wedlock to an Irish mother at least 3 times in his books to compromise our view of the protagonist – The Tailor of Panama, Our Game, and "Absolute Friends", the last an appropriately paranoid examination of the W. Bush world)

The facile and ridiculous narrative (exemplified by Garvin, 2004) that sees Ireland as emerging from a priest-ridden miasma into the clear light of twenty-first century Anglo-Saxon nationhood must be seen in this light. Up to recently, health and education were mainly taken care of by the great Irish religious nursing and teaching orders. We shall see later that electoral suffrage survived in Ireland only after an intense struggle. More to the point, its exposure to global capitalism ensures that Ireland is not in a position to guarantee a decent life for its citizens.

In Anglo-Saxon countries, mortgage rates fluctuate somewhat wildly. The federal funds rate charged on overnight loans between banks (Ip, 2005, p.1) can be adjusted by a central bank; in the case of the US, by the private Federal Reserve, successively headed by Paul Volcker, the Ayn Rand follower Alan Greenspan, and the academic Bernanke. The career bureaucrat, Wall Street booster, and tax dodger Tim Geithner now heads the Treasury. With respect to these particular appointments and the dreary conservatism of Obama's economic policies, Baker (2009, 37) comments sadly:

"Barack Obama is moving prudently, carefully, reasonably toward disaster"

Baker would prefer an FDR like situation where it is accepted that Labour, business and government are different stakeholders each with their own agenda to the Obama/Hoover fantasy that "we" as a whole can work things out. That strikes this writer as also correct for Ireland.

In order to control inflationary pressure, the fed raised its short-time interest rate eleven times between June 2004 and September 2005. Up to June 2004, this rate had been at wartime low levels.

Let's see what then happens:

> "Longer-term lending rates will be little affected, however, US bond markets, where long-term rates are set, had anticipated." (Ip, op. Cit. 6)

The bond markets in the US are in fact largely controlled by the Chinese and Japanese economies. China's exporters need to keep the dollar pegged to a relatively high level against the yuan so that US consumers can afford their products. Their purchase of US treasury bonds effectively keeps mortgage rates low, and fuelled a real estate frenzy in the US.

The 2008 collapse was inevitable.We shall dwell for a moment on some little-known twists that have turned a recession into incipient depression. The first is the strange cast of criminals who get to the top in high finance, from Gordon Gekko/Ivan Boesky (who went to Wall Street after bankrupting the family strip joint business) to Alan Stanford (ditto for the family health studios). Ireland surely needs to insulate itself from Wall St. (The fact that Ireland has, if accidentally, seized enough of Allied Irish bank to ensure that the state can print and distribute money may ironically work in its favour, as may the huge amount of modern housing which can be sold off to its diaspora). The second is the role of the "Quants"; scientists trained in quantitative methods who took jobs in finance. For example, the Black-Scholes formula was touted as a means of portfolio insurance by pricing options:

> "The model is based on the assumption that the trader can suck all the risk out of the market by taking a short position and increasing that position as the market falls" (Lewis, 2008a, P. 132)

It is worth noting that the Black-Scholes formula uses a model of heat diffusion developed by Fourier in the 19th century; in retrospect, it was too much to ask for it to work in finance (putting it gently). In fact, Lewis (ibid.) points out that the formula failed spectacularly in the 1987 crash. Yet the model involved was responsibility itself compared to the excesses growing up around subprime (Lewis, 2008b, P. 120):

> "In 2005, there had been $130 billion in subprime mortgage lending, with $55 billion of that repackaged as mortgage bonds. But in 2005, there was $625 billion in subprime mortgage loans, $507 billion of which found its way into mortgage bonds"

These figures are frightening enough, but that is not where the damage was done. The problem arose with securitization, the packaging of these subprime bonds with other bonds in the context of a truly baroque mathematical theory that raised the credit worthiness of the subprime bonds:

> "This was the engine of doom........Wall Street had used these BBB tranches – the worst of the worst – to build yet another tower of bonds: a 'particularly egregious' C.D.O."(123)

The rating agencies, paid by the very investment entities that they were rating, would declare these to be AAA (154).

Investors like Steve Eisman bet against these bonds only to find that "When Eisman bought a credit-default swap, he enabled Deutsche Bank to create another bond identical in every respect but one to the original...In fact, there was no mortgage at all" (156)

In fact, an argument can be made that there is something much darker going on. Very socially cut off Asperger's types (the "quants") are given the world's economy to play with using mathematical models that really exist only for them as no-one else understands them. For a while they make a lot of money for their uncomprehending but grateful employers, and then a crash happens as reality bites and the production in the world economy is matched against the notional figures in the models. Never mind; just create an Obama figure from whole cloth, fund him through Goldman Sachs, and allow him, once in place, to perpetuate the theft by intricate dance between the Fed and Treasury that diverts all spare capacity in the economy back to the financial firms that caused the trouble in the first place. No, there won't be a revolution; the entire W security apparatus is still in place. Ireland can do better than this, particularly as it was Geithner who insisted that we pay off all bondholders after the IMF showed a willingness to cut us some slack.

Altogether close to $1 quadrillion of unreal money has been created by sleight of hand like this. It will take perhaps a decade to deflate it. Grant (2008) argues that we have been here before (in 1837, 1857, 1873, 1893, 1907 and so on), and implicit in his argument is that some kind of return to a gold or gold/silver standard will be necessary. This book is dealing with the consequences in one small country of a sudden flood of incoming capital which, for a full decade, utterly changed how the country worked.

A third factor exacerbating collapse of the world's economy is the revolving door between Wall St. and government. Sorkin (2009, 177) documents the peculiar sequence of events that resulted in the 2008 collapse of Lehmann brothers and the colossally expensive rescue of AIG. Hank Paulson "regretted signing the original ethics letter agreeing not to get involved in any matter related to Goldman", his previous employer. Magic was performed, and "Unknown to the public, Paulson was now officially free to help Goldman Sachs" (ibid).

Greider (2009, 18) delivers a trenchant analysis:

> "Some Wall St players suspect that certain bailouts engineered by the Treasury and the Federal Reserve (including Timothy Geithner..) were motivated by a logic never revealed to the public....If AIG went down, it would threaten Goldman and other holders of AIG's collapsing derivatives contracts....Something similar is suspected about the Bear Stearns bailout. The intention may have been to protect JP Morgan Chase, the commercial bank with the largest holdings of vulnerable derivatives. Morgan Chase demanded and got full federal financing for any losses..."

In that pithy phrase, privatized profit and socialized risk has become the norm. In fact, the mechanisms making the money "markets" have acquired a social safety net. It is perhaps only a slight exaggeration to state that only China's continued forced investment in American bonds have allowed this corrupt and inefficient farce to continue. Famously, in an earlier incarnation, one in which it is not clear which side he favours, Lewis (1989) depicted the obscenity and abuse characteristic of bond trading houses both in New York and London. Several of the heroes of that earlier book were central to the late 1990's crash - and in the case of Meriwether, lived on to crash and burn another day in 2008. Greenspan's monomaniac refusal to countenance regulation for over the counter derivatives, even in the wake of Meriwether's LTCM crash, and the horrendous consequences for the world's real economy, are now the stuff of legend.

At this point, we are perhaps in a position to ask what exactly money is. The current "market" answer is that it is a totally fungible means of exchange – fungible in that it is assumed that the coin one uses to buy one's bread is the same species as junk bonds, as exotic derivatives, as CDO's. Should money be so fungible that mortgage contracts, the biggest deal most people make, be bundled together in their millions with pork futures, bets against share prices, bets against these bets, and sold a few thousand times a week?

The eventually fugitive John Law used a Thomist argument about money (Gleeson, 1999); price is that by which an article is bought, not that for which it is bought (confer Aquinas; Man is rational BY his soul). Money reflects the action of a metric; it should not be an autonomous agent in a society. As things stand, the totality of life which a nation-state should reflect requires that life be de-economized, that people should stop feeling that their every activity should be quantified in money; and, to take matters further, the economic system should be de-financialized, removed from math abstractions to the point that even a gold/silver mixture underlies it in the extreme.

Remarkably, the admission of colossal failure of regulation that is NAMA allows a better way. Articles like those by Shah (2010) and the same week in the Economist (2010) have suggested to some that an Anglo conspiracy to destroy Ireland is at work. There are some of us who say – "So much the better. We can now run the country away from the scrutiny of people who do not understand the genius of its people". We can avoid the debauching of national identity pointed out astutely by Lewis (2010);

> "The tsunami of cheap credit that rolled across the planet between 2002 and 2007 wasn't just money, it was temptation. It offered entire societies the opportunities to reveal aspects of their characters….Germans wanted to be even more German. The Irish wanted to stop being Irish"

We now may want to be Irish again; committed to culture and conviviality, anti-authoritarian, and good at a wide range of human activities Ironically, it may soon be possible for the Irish government to loan directly to its citizens for house purchases, with only a rubber-stamping mechanism by a zombie bank (itself on the brink of nationalization or nationalized like allied Irish) intervening between the two. This is unlike the USA, where the bizarre relationship between the Fed and the Treasury department has the latter essentially acting as a printer for the former.

This has of course led to calls for closure of the Fed; more recently, Obama's allowing investment banks borrow Treasury money at 0% and then invest that in treasury bonds yielding far more is sinister in the extreme; particularly given his close ties with Goldman Sachs. Bailouts of any description destroy the major moral impetus and structural benefit of capitalism, and the market is indeed a vital mechanism. Regulation like the Glass-Steagal act that Clinton renounced is an urgent moral imperative.

Elsewhere, Lewis (2009) examined perhaps the only European country that has suffered a bigger blow than Ireland: another small country, Iceland. (The joke used to be that the only difference between them was a letter and a few months; it is now clear that the ECB is determined to ensure that Ireland's collapse is more orderly.) An aggressive nationalism infected Iceland's apparent financial genius:

> "He examined Kaupthing's annual reports....this giant international bank had only one board member who was not Icelandic" (147)

> "Icelanders... had their own explanation for why, when they leaped into global finance, they broke world records: the natural superiority of Icelanders" (174)

The pressure on the European Central Bank to raise interest rates is lessened by low bond rates in the US. Banking systems in countries whose population are savers, like France and Japan, now need to make profits by loaning to other markets. Consequently, Ireland became flooded with borrowed money, and house prices quadrupled in many places. Like Iceland, we were continually lectured about precisely what aspects of our system made us world-beaters.

In 2010 the only process saving the Irish government from having to nationalise all its banks prior to Iceland-style bankruptcy was a sleight of hand whereby the ECB loaned to the Irish banks to buy Irish state treasuries, and then proceeded to buy them directly, while denying it was doing so The quid pro quo is that Ireland cannot inflate its way out, but must allow the economy contract while saving the banks and repay their foreign creditors. Moreover, in 2009 the National Assets Management Agency (NAMA) was founded; the treasuries board head Michael Somers, under whose aegis it was meant to run, explained in front of a parliamentary committee in Spring, 2009, that he had no idea how it was to run, or how he was going to hire the thousands of employees required to manage the E90 billion or so in property "assets" (derelict golf courses and hotels, condos in Florida, and so on) that the state was about to buy. Somers' statement is the surest indication that NAMA was planned by a cabal several years ago.

Since then, several things have become clear. First of all, Anglo-Irish bank collapsed, and had to be nationalized. It was found that 15 debtors had debts exceeding E500 million. The Ahern government had been notoriously close to property developers, and there is every indication that all 15 are "developers". Secondly, it was clear that the ratio of depositors to debtors of the bank was in three figures; it was a very select group who were allowed borrow money, versus the 300,000 who deposited money. Since nationalization, the bank has continued its policy of not loaning outside a charmed circle. Thirdly, it was clear that no interest payments on the debt were really being made, and that in fact the bank was often loaning money to "developers" who only pretended to want to pay it back; in another notorious incident, the bank loaned money to a "Golden circle" to buy its own shares, with the shares themselves used as collateral. This investment was lost, with the taxpayer eventually paying.

There is a parsimonious explanation, which looks dreadfully plausible. No attempt was made to conduct anything resembling real business. Arbitrary amounts of "money" were, if briefly, available on the international markets; therefore, what remained was simply a formal game of deciding just how high to push Irish property prices. Anglo-Irish bank led the way; but from 2005 on, the other two main banks followed it into the trough.

In 2007, Ahern managed to inveigle the Greens into government, and copper-fastened it by also inviting a motley crew of socialists, crooks, and neoliberals in case the Greens bolted before their time. The 2009 local elections was well past that critical time; the future of the Greens was now interlocked with Fianna Fail. Time came when the scam whereby these property developers did not pay interest on their enormous loans, let alone on the principal, came to light. No matter; at that point, the "greens" ere fatally compromised.

NAMA ensured not just the death of the "greens", with the Donegal section withdrawing from what they insisted was an "alliance", not a national party, but that there will not be a dull moment in Irish politics for a few years as the public becomes anxious to know just whose billionaire bank account they are subsidising in this neo-feudal system. It increasingly looks as though general elections could be fought and won, and effectively were, on the rounding error of the massive deals. It does seem to be the case that the banks came under enormous political pressure to go easy on certain property developers.

The punch line; Michael Somers need not have worried. The banks will be handling this new addition to the national debt. In fact, everything is consistent with the theory that this was planned all along as plan B, and all that they had to do was hook the "greens" for enough time that they in turn feared a new general election. The property developers keep the bulk of their property, insofar as they ever owned it; in fact, insofar as they were ever property developers in the first place. What is really happening is solidifying a massive transfer of power and wealth in Ireland from the taxpayer to a clique around FF. Ahern also managed to take out his erstwhile critics in the "greens" en passant; it may be his single stroke of political genius.

Personal debt during a decade of supposedly unprecedented economic boom rose from €16 billion to over €300 billion to over a trillion. Per unit of gross national income per person, the Irish racked up the whole US personal debt every eight months or so, due partly to the so-called "Financial services" industry, until it grew to over $1 trillion. Not to worry, say the bankers, who are given bully pulpits in Irish Times columns without so much as an advertisement banner, let alone a health warning. So, as a 2005 article went, there are 1.5 million dwelling units in Ireland, each worth on average €300,000. (We see amplified such figures below).That makes €450 billion, with perhaps another 300 billion extra in the pipeline due to price increases, so keep borrowing and building. This is the narrative that ensured that the IMF's colonial visit in 2010 went unprotected.

As indeed the Irish did, with a fervor that can truly be described as religious. (The state has openly connived with the realtors; a 2004 Department of the Environment report claiming house prices were decreasing was rubbished by the estate agents, Sherry Fitzgerald, who successfully persuaded the government to calculate house prices their way therefrom.) In 2004, 77,000 houses were built in Ireland for a net immigration of 40,000. Since the average Irish household is almost exactly

3, that leaves a shortfall of about 200,000 people to occupy these houses. It gets worse; the 1.5 million figure above, cited by the Bank of Ireland's chief economist, Dan McLaughlin, meant that there are currently over 170,000 empty houses/apartments in Ireland in 2005, even before the real madness started. Conservatively put, we had a population of 4 million and housing for 5-7 million, with the housing supply rising at about five times the rate it should even were supply and demand in equilibrium.

The response from the financial markets has been to see Ireland as El Dorado for mortgages. The state has openly colluded in serving up its citizens to international capitalism. No appropriate bankruptcy protection is available; the US, faced with a minor personal debt burden by comparison, expected 1.8 million personal bankruptcies in 2005. The UK radically raised interest rates, and personal bankruptcy levels, in the face of what was – again relative to the size of the countries – a very minor bump, not a bubble. .

To adapt Quayle, then, a nation-state should be able to insulate its citizens from international usurers, at least to the extent that its control over its own land allows. The Irish state has 1% of the European population and has been at a completely different part of the economic cycle to the dominant French and German economies ever since it joined the Euro Club. Nor does it any longer have control of many common law issues, let alone state subsidy of business, competition, and corporate takeovers.

In the summer of 2005, a financial services advisor called Eddie Hobbs hosted a TV program on Ireland's national station called "Rip-off Republic." Apart from the record viewing levels, the extent to which this rather boring series managed to push down the government's approval ratings is astonishing. Yet, given its proxy and actual memberships in the Anglo-Saxon financial club, the EU, the OECD, the WTO and so on, there is nothing Ireland can do. To regain sovereignty — as it must — Ireland will have to modify the terms of its membership in or leave some of these organizations. In the meantime, they praise Ireland for spectacular and totally misleading GDP figures; the state lives off its profligate citizens. Let us see what friends Ireland might lose by having the courage to care for its people.

In this period, Ireland continued to be praised by international capitalism (Coleman 2005a) just as the Roman Catholic Church praised it for "keeping the faith". The Roman Catholic Church established itself in the

Anglo-Saxon world through the newly Anglophone nineteenth century Irish, exactly as the Oxford convert John Henry Newman prophesied. The feats of individual heroism by Irish religious in educating and caring for generations of others' children within and despite the imperial strictures of their church has been forgotten about in the rush to publicise the extreme minority of sexual deviants in their ranks.

The new economic faith will remain as impenetrable a mystery as the Trinity to the Irish (Coleman 2005b). And not just to the Irish; the persistence of low interest rates world-wide (not just the US) during this period remains a mystery to the best economic commentators, who are forced to resort to an argument along the lines of much capital, little investment (cover story, Wall Street Journal, 13 Oct 2005). One obvious possibility - perhaps too obvious? - is that vast amounts of unreal money were being manufactured by the new financial instruments in Wall Street and its satellites by Quants.

The signs as this book is being completed are those of economic meltdown in Ireland, with almost inevitable default being nuanced by EU incursion into the country. The neoliberal agenda cannot be implemented without state impetus behind it (Cahill, 2009) We will visit this later, after a more in-depth look at Ireland's peculiar relationship with the USA.

The persistence in Ireland of the neoliberal consensus – open markets, light-touch government regulation, low taxes – can perhaps be explained in the same terms as its hanging on to an old date for Easter, or Jansenist clericalism in the 20th century. Economists can indeed calculate many useful things about productivity. The problems emerge when they overstep their discipline, and argue for a view like neoliberalism that has profound socio-political interactions.

The fact is that neoliberalism is couched at way too high a level of abstraction – in the same way as Marxism is so couched – to be useful as a guide for getting out of a specific troubled situation. Many successful "open" economies like the US, Britain, South Korea and Switzerland used protectionist policies before, now ready for prime time, they opened up their economies. This is exactly what Ireland should no revert to, with mild protectionism being used to foster areas of promise. In so doing, the state should assert its main motivation as cultural, not economic; that it nurtures its people.

Simultaneously, a definancialization of the economy should be implemented; perhaps indeed to the point at which citizens feel comfortable about entering into political debate without knowing what CDO's are (let alone CFD's). In this writer's lifetime, we turned the economy around incidentally, while being essentially concerned about buttressing the culture in every way, including the political. We can do this again, and enter free trade areas when we are ready to do so.

5.2 Ireland and the US

It is arguable that Ireland owes its existence as a somewhat independent state to the Irish community in the US. It is indeed arguable that the Irish owe their survival as an identifiable ethnic group to the same people. The links arguably go back to pre-mediaeval times, but more concretely, Wilson (1998, p. 95) states:

> "To be American, in this view, was to embrace the principles of democracy, the program of civil and religious liberty for which the United Irishmen had fought in their own country during the 1790s. In the process, the educational system, broadly conceived, would produce nothing less than a new citizenry for this New World. No group of people threw themselves more wholeheartedly into this endeavour than the United Irishmen."

The natural law system that Tómás O Cléirigh, impressed by the philosopher Suarez, had attempted to develop, fell to English common law, precedent alone without any written constitution or articulate notion of a natural order, in the Tudor shake-out (Carroll, 2001). The US Irish now were citizens of a country with a constitution. After the relatively privileged United Irish were well settled in, the huddled masses of Irish came to the US in droves from the mid-nineteenth century. Their success in transforming a priest-ridden peasant culture into the most successful ethnicity in the US has rightly inspired much writing.

What kind of country did these Irish find? Let us start with the loftiest possible description, that which sees the US as an incarnation of a new movement in the human psyche, that which exploits the trope of nation to educate new movements of the spirit. Needleman (2002), in this vein, goes beyond the 1775 Declaration of Independence, with its borrowings from the English Civil War and Rousseau. The now-creaking eighteenth century constitutional congeries of checks and balances that is republican, rather than democratic, and has recently not hesitated to compromise universal electoral suffrage (Miller, 2005) is not particularly to be lauded, either. The egregious disenfranchisement of African-Americans and other poor minorities, likely democratic voters, in 2000 and 2004 does not engage Needleman. America, he argues, seeks much bigger game:

> "Without a doubt, every hero of the American pantheon is a representative of the idea of freedom ... the deepest spiritual source of the early colonists' rejection of political and religious tyranny was that such tyranny prevented them from searching for inner freedom." (Needleman, 2002, p100)

While granting that there were economic, political and military factors involved in the movements of peoples from England and Europe to America and the westward expansion of the United States (op cit., p. 101), Needleman will not be budged on this point. Manifest destiny, the westward and southward impetus of the US, is currently destroying Iraq and Afghanistan as it turns East. Yet is true that

> " ... very many ... brought with them plans for a life of interiority, even to the point of various forms of monastic communitarianism"(ibid, p. 14)

Needleman acknowledges the genocide of the Native Americans, but insists that the US Constitution had Iroquois influences. Yet the Constitution itself has deeper meaning for him:

> "If Lincoln is our icon of individual consciousness, as we shall see, Jefferson represents the interconnectedness of metaphysics, spiritual psychology, and practical political organization." (op cit. p. 150)

(We shall note that McGuire (2003) deeply dissents about the Constitution.)

> "With respect to life, liberty, and the pursuit of happiness, the happiness Jefferson spoke of is a matter of the spirit of man." (op cit. p. 149).

The US, it can plausibly be argued, is currently irrevocably torn between its imperial ambitions and the protections for the individual embodied in the First Amendment, the first element of the Bill of Rights:

> "Congress shall make no law respecting the establishment of religion, or prohibiting the free exercise thereof; or abridging the freedom of speech, or the press; or the right of the people peaceably to assemble, and to petition the government for a redress of grievances."

The late Chief Justice Rehnquist interpreted this minimally as neither more nor less than a prohibition on the creation of a state church. It is undoubtedly a huge step for a state voluntarily to assent to limitations on its powers; however, Rehnquist's minimalism, exemplified by the restrictions that the post-9/11 US put on free speech and assembly through the Patriot Act, made the First Amendment a dead letter. A tireless advocate of states' rights against the federal government, Rehnquist reverted to Republican type in stopping the 2000 presidential election recount.

So a hypothesis emerges; the US has an absurd, lumbering, antiquated constitution and farcical college electoral system with a Bill of Rights that gets torn up when reasons of state dictate it, as in 2001 and 1919. When this happens, the political left indeed retire into interiority and write carping notes to each other in the tiny non-corporate free press. Unlike Ireland, few political protestors ever show enough sincerity to get arrested, let alone go to jail. Only in Ireland have protestors like Ciaran O'Reilly and Mary Kelly damaged US warplanes, at great risk to themselves. The First Amendment is used more often to permit puerile and violently misogynistic pornography, as recounted in Milos Forman's *The People versus Larry Flynt,* than to facilitate dissent. Above all, money talks and in many ways *is* life, liberty, and the pursuit of happiness. (McGuire, 2003)
It is the view of this book that the US oscillates between this extreme and my friend and colleague Jacob Needleman's Parnassus. The *reductio ad absurdum* is of course the McCarthy years; no responsible newspaper could ignore McCarthy before his censure by the senate. (Bayley, 1981, p.151) During the censure proceedings, Noam Chomsky supported McCarthy. Go figure.

Gibbon's (1963, p.74) is the classic account of what Chalmers Johnson (2006) has called "the sorrows of empire."

> "During four-score years ... Rome groaned beneath an unremitting tyranny. In the conduct of those monarchs we may trace the utmost lives of vice."

The mad Iraq imperial adventure, based, as the publication of the Downing Street Memo further amplified, on the egregious untruth before and lack of concern for the aftermath of adventure, is the veritable elephant in the room in geopolitics. Given that South-east Asia's GDP is now the equal of that of the US, it does rather seem that the Anglo-Saxon dominance of world affairs has run its course.

Ritter (2005), whose infinitely courageous attempts (following his UN work with Unscom) to pre-empt the pre-emptive war were what convinced many of us vigorously to protest it, is clear that the die was cast well before the infamous Downing Street Memo . The CIA had "made a decision that, rather than fight Unscom and thereby...compromise their secret coup plans" (133), Ritter was to be allowed use a grab-bag of skills and other nations' intelligence services (like Israel, 144, and Britain) so long as room for doubt remained about Iraq's WMD capacity. When Ritter seemed to on the verge of extinguishing this doubt – which perhaps even Saddam did not want to happen, as it would make him vulnerable to attack from Iran – he was removed. Indeed, Ritter's operation was compromised from within by the CIA (217):

> "The CIA had been sabotaging the Unscom SCE (intercepts within Iraq - this writer's note) effort from day one....the USA was using the SCE as a cover for one of its own operations"

These operations included a botched CIA-planned coup against Saddam in 1996, abandoned after Iraq gained control of a CIA spy satellite. A further military adventure was planned for 1998 (277);

> "Everyone in the US chain of command was confident that there would at last be a window for military action against Iraq. Our inspection diplomacy...put an end to those plans"

In fact, "inspections had worked, after all "(289)

Ritter ended up reporting at the UN to the Australian Richard Butler, who promptly began working for the USA. As in Lindsay (1979), where a Prime minister is forced to resign due to potential exposure of CIA interference in Aussie domestic politics. it is clear that Australia does not have an independent voice in world affairs;

> "Richard Butler had given up trying to produce an authoritative assessment of Iraq's unaccounted for weapons....an investigation into concealment was the only way to break this deadlock "(Ritter, 2005, 287)

Even the Blix investigation, with its far superior technology, was not allowed give Saddam a clean bill of health on this issue. Ritter (290) concludes with a tragic assessment;

> "The US government...were willing to promote what even their own intelligence services classed as highly dubious documents"

The final (for the moment, metaphorical) bombshell (291):

> "As far as the CIA is concerned, the issue of fixing intelligence around policy predates July 2002, reaching as far back as 1992"

This is the issue on which Ahern wanted the Irish to join the Anglo-Saxon club. The repeated use of Shannon and Dublin airports for torture/rendition flights from 2001 is documented in Grey (2007, 294-318). This must have had Ahern's personal approval.

The American Revolution is best understood as an internal Anglo-Saxon family spat with the French joking in as a grudge rematch against the English of their earlier defeat on a continent no longer particularly important to them. Underlying it was a more serious argument about how quickly to exterminate Native Americans. (Mann, 2005, argues that pre-Columbus, America was as metropolitan, populous and technologically advanced as Europe.) The Irish, soldiers in everyone's army but their own, may have enthusiastically joined in the slaughter. Intriguingly, and often without any or with just a few bases of DNA, up to 30 million Americans now claim native heritage. Ireland may show them how to reacculture the continent; a start would be to follow Ecuador in publishing government documents in local native languages.

In June, 2004, "President" George W. Bush visited Ireland. The Irish prime minister, Bartholmew "Bertie" Ahern, (called Taoiseach in the language he himself does not speak) was at the time swinging the world by the tail. Ahern had made his career as bagman and apologist to ex-Taoiseach, Charles J. Haughey, who was later excoriated by a government tribunal. Now, however, Ahern was President of Europe, according to the system that rotates this position among member states every 6 months. His historical moment had come; first of all, find a centre-right President for the European Commission. *The Economist*, which has followed the Roman Church in praising the Irish whenever they comply with its incredible belief system, encouraged him to select himself, as a classical centre-right politician (within two months and after the disastrous local election result we note below, Ahern declared himself a socialist). Ahern demurred; he had bigger fish to fry. The man who did not hesitate to nullify the historical Irish claim on the whole of the island wanted to play with the Anglo-Saxon big boys, rather than some foreigners who didn't even speak English!

The poisoned chalice of the presidency was handed to Portugal's neoliberal Barroso, and the rest is indeed history. The momentum of the European project has been stayed. That much Ahern, perhaps, predicted. As a veteran moral prostitute, an initially wholehearted supporter of the mad Iraq adventure (we're happy to have helped get rid of a dictator, he declared not mentioning who created that dictator) and a narcissist whose annual makeup bill equalled the average Irish industrial wage, Ahern had a high card that he wanted to play.

The Abu Ghraib scandal had just come to light, and Bertie saw his opportunity. "These things happen", he declared. The reputation of Ireland has rarely been in greater peril than at that moment. Ahern got trounced in the local and European elections immediately afterward, having failed to emulate his new friend in introducing electronic voting. (The prospective Irish system, as we shall see, was particularly egregious.) Though Ahern's response was to rush desperately over to the centre-left, forswearing his previous support of the Iraq war, the electoral damage was done. What looks frankly like an attempted political coup during the years 2003–2004, with massive privatizations and a US-type cessation of democracy, had been aborted. Let us look closely at the new friend that Bertie wanted to woo.

Torture was introduced as state policy in the US as a result of legal opinions written by John Yoo, an academic lawyer. Ironically for Ahern, Yoo exploited a previous ruling at the European Court in 1977 when Britain, sued by Ireland, reserved the word "torture" in a truly gothic way; "Torture is not torture if the torturer was … seeking information." Only gratuitous or purely sadistic torture qualified as torture. Moreover, to meet the definition, the pain caused had to be the equivalent of losing an organ or bodily function, or dying. (Holtzman, 2005, p.22). Cutting off a finger is not torture. Yoo still stands by this and argues that Al Qaeda has the same potential to harm as a state.

Yoo in person is deeply unimpressive, and has chickened out of debates even in his home university, UC Berkeley, where the campaign to fire him was stayed on the grounds of "academic freedom". (A personal note; attempting to avoid exposure now that his supporters are out of power, Yoo plays squash under a pseudonym, as I have witnessed in Sf's Bay Club) In particular, he cited security concerns for refusing to debate veteran Irish-American lawyer James Brosnahan, a man who keeps the ancient Irish passion for justice alive. Forced to speak unopposed, Brosnahan related how he repeatedly received death-threats while defending the so-called American Taliban, John Walker Lindh. He continued to defend Lindh.

The viciousness of the Bush administration was equalled only by its incompetence and treason:

> "A survey of 168 cities showed that 90 per cent of them had not received any additional federal assistance since the 9/11 attacks. Emergency services, organizations were understaffed … " (Clarke, 2004, p.259)

The former inhabitants of New Orleans can attest all this. Just as it looks as though the Irish e-voting system was actually a cover for a neoconservative political coup in a European country, so does it seem that those neocons had no political agenda beyond controlling Middle East oil.

Palast (2006) argues that they were ultimately trying to destroy OPEC, and in fact lost the battle with the big oil companies on this score. In particular, Palast comments that the neocon plan to undermine OPEC was defeated by the more modest plan to make massive profits for the oil companies by restricting supply of oil. Posting a bare minimum of soldiers, contrary to military advice, avoids the problems of drafting middle-class college students. Who cares if trailer-trash from the boonies and green card-seeking wetbacks get killed securing oil pipelines? Over 20% of the military in Iraq, particularly the security detail that guard administration officials, actually came from private contractors, who are rather better able to take care of their employees. Steve Coll, whose work on Afghanistan we have already witnessed, contends that Exxon is in many ways a state with its own interests.

It is difficult to imagine any appropriate fate for Bush, Cheney, Rice, and Rumsfeld other than criminal charges for illegally starting a war, and a future international war crimes tribunal. Intriguingly, none of this administration has seen military combat; Bush, and less famously but more intensely, Dick Cheney, went further than most Berkeley draft-dodgers in ensuring their CVs remained free of actual real war in which they were in harm's way. This recalcitrance has now been passed on to their children, as indeed the children of all but one of the elected representatives on Capitol hill, who voted near-unanimously for the war.

Their Svengali, Karl Rove, the eminence gris of the Bush family, had the audacity to follow his maxim, "attack their strengths" in the 2004 election by using John Kerry's combat record against him. Rove periodically gets fired by the Bush family when he goes too far, as in 1992. In 2007, he potentially faced a treason investigation for outing the name of a covert CIA agent in order to take revenge on ex-ambassador Joe Wilson's refusal to go along with the "weapons of mass destruction" charade (the CIA agent, Valerie Plane, is Wilson's wife.) It is hard to believe that these people are patriots as distinct from apparatchiks of a wealthy power base in American society.

At the nadir of modern American politics, the first G. W. Bush administration, the Irish Deputy Prime Minister, Mary Harney, announced that Ireland felt spiritually closer to Boston than Berlin. It is unlikely that Harney meant that the Irish experienced less affinity to the Rhenish mystics like Meister Eckhart than to Yankees like Emerson with their emphasis on the oversoul. (For Needleman (ibid), as for other American writers like Ken Wilber, Emerson and his contemporaries achieved a spiritual break from Old Europe.)

Nor did Harney refer to the large Irish-speaking population in Boston, a population whose apotheosis in Sean O'Mainín's infinitely courageous bid for the light-heavyweight world boxing crown is documented in the brilliant TV documentary "Aisling Ghear." O'Mainín was eventually beaten in a title fight by Mike McCallum, pound for pound one of the greatest boxers of all time, and seems to have suffered dreadfully. Intriguingly, O'Mainin saw himself as fighting not for glory or money or anything so prosaic; as a native Irish speaker, he saw himself as fighting for a Gaelic Ireland in the 1980s and 1990s.

Berlin, as the results of even the German 2005 and 2009 general elections show, is largely social democratic with Merkel and Stauble having gone too far to the tight. What the ponderous and extreme right-wing Harney wished to prescribe was an Ireland with the same relationship of state, market, and people as the US. After September, 2005, and the botched operations both pre and post hurricanes Katrina and Rita, it is clear that, when it comes to issues of social welfare, the US state has broken down. Let us look again at this odd combination of Christian fundamentalism and libertarianism that Harney would have the Irish imitate.

The Christ of the gospels chides the damned at the last judgment for not visiting prisoners; conversely, the blessed are those who helped prisoners.

The Christian right in the US are most unbiblical. As the CIA director, Porter Goss, told the Senate Intelligence Committee on February 16:

> "Torture doesn't work. There are better ways to deal with captives."

So torture has an entirely different purpose:

> "This is torture's true purpose: to terrorize — not only the people in Guantanamo's cages and Syria's isolation cells, but also, and more important, the broader community that hears about these abuses." (Klein, 2005)

Nguyen (2005) adduces evidence that fully 20,000 people of Pakistani ancestry have left the Midwood neighbourhood of Brooklyn since 9/11. The atmosphere post Patriot Act is truly Kafkaesque; detention of indefinite duration without charge is allowed, and the human rights situation is pre-Magna Carta. Dawn raids are performed by the FBI, and interrogations involve questions like whether the interrogee knows anybody who has been at flight school (ibid). The terror affects non-white people wholly disproportionately. In the meantime, Cheney was smarting from Watergate to the point of supporting a version of executive power that has seen Bush subvert the legislative process. For example, "Signing statements", in which the president does not veto legislation but signals the wish to make it a dead letter, were extremely rare until 2000; Bush's tally was a large multiple of all other US presidents. The current Democratic president rescinded few of these new powers and shows a Playstation addiction to drone attacks.

As in Kafka's *The Trial,* that disturbing masterpiece about the imposition of automaticity on individuals under a bureaucratic regime, the accusers are themselves not of the finest moral calibre. It is doubtful that patriotism really is the last refuge of the scoundrel; even if rejected after he offers to do the dirty for his country, his church will accept him. In the US, with its post-addiction chief executive, that will allow him to return to the warm bosom of his country's approval.

William Hager is a case in point. He was a Bush appointee to the "Advisory Committee for Reproductive Health Drugs in the Food and Drug Administration (FDA)." (McCarvey, 2005, p.11) As such, he was scheduled to take part in decisions about the so-called "morning-after pill." He is in no doubt about his divine vocation:

> " 'I want to share with you some information about how God has called me to stand in the gap ... Not only for others, but regarding ethical and moral issues in our country.'" (ibid)

It is probably superfluous to mention that:

> "his ardent evangelical piety anchors his staunch opposition to emergency contraception, abortion and premarital sex." (ibid.)

His wife, Linda Davis, testifies that, once married, anything goes with David:

> "Davis alleges that between 1995 and their divorce in 2002, Hager repeatedly sodomized her without her consent ... it was the painful, invasive, totally non-consensual nature of the anal sex that was so horrible." (McCarvey, 2005, p.13)

David's ban on premarital sex does not extend to himself:

> "Sometime between the births of Neal (in 1977) and Jonathan (in 1979), Hager embarked on an affair with a bible-study classmate who was a friend of Davis's." (op cit, p. 16)

However, it being America, Boston not Berlin, the business of the country was business:

> "By the 1980s, according to Davis, Hager was pressuring her to let him videotape and photograph them having sex. She consented, and eventually she even let Hager pay her for sex she wouldn't otherwise have engaged in - for example, $2,000 for oral sex." (ibid.)

Interestingly, David is an obstetrician and gynaecologist. One can safely assume that the crony capitalist gang that comprised the Bush regime abounded with such creatures from time to time, as in the case of Michael Brown, himself a federal emergency disaster, their incompetence becomes visible and thus embarrassing enough to merit resignation. Romney's team will be very similar.

Yet, this posturing on sexual (as distinct from moral) issues is probably utterly calculated. George W. Bush did not hesitate to state in their third debate, contrary to Kerry's insistence that any Supreme Court judge he (Kerry) appointed should uphold Roe v. Wade, that he (Bush) had no such litmus test. Heuvel, (2005, p.3) is very clear on this point:

> "The Bush clan takes on no issue without political calculation, and here the math was precise. The religious right remembers well that grandfather Prescott Bush was Planned Parenthood's best friend in the Senate and that father George H. W. Bush was staunchly pro-choice up to the moment of his selection as Ronald Reagan's running mate." (Heuvel, 2005, p. 3)

Yet the 2000 presidential election was decided ultimately by massive vote fraud in Florida. Echoing the repressive Jim Crow Laws of a century before, and documented in minute detail since then (Miller, 2005) tens of thousands of people of colour were systematically disenfranchised, often by invented fictitious criminal records for them. The director of elections for the 2004 theft of the Ohio vote was "Secretary of State Kenneth Blackwell, the co-chair of the Bush-Cheney campaign in Ohio." (Miller, 2005, p. 61) Blackwell's correlate in the 2000 election, Katherine Harris, is a fundamentalist Christian who saw herself as being directed by God:

> "Neither Bush brother ever misses a chance to prove his Christian-right allegiance." (ibid.)

In Irish political history, only Oliver J. Flanagan of Fine Gael gained much electoral leverage by proclaiming his adherence to Canon, rather than state law. Secularism was always implicit in important Irish issues. The last Republican primary campaign saw Santorum take extreme Catholic positions not seen in Irish politics for a generation.

Vote-rigging is implemented in the US primarily through disenfranchisement. The organization that performed this task, Choicepoint, is controlled by a convicted drug smuggler. Secondly, the unaccountable e-voting systems were created for Ohio primarily by Diebold, whose CEO, Walter O'Dell, promised before the election to deliver Ohio for George W. Bush. Many counties in California have since banned e-voting. As a personal note this writer can testify that the very same Diebold manufactures ATMs that, unlike their Irish counterparts, never fail to return a receipt. So the technology for accountable e-voting is there, but unused.

The Bush dynasty functioned on electoral fraud and religious hypocrisy. To adapt St. Augustine: "Lord, let us overturn Roe versus Wade, but not yet." Roe versus Wade is far too useful, as a bargaining chip, and Romney will [play the same game; it garners support from the religious right who can eventually be dispensed with and the hysterical response from the left, who often insist on the right to state-funded abortion at all stages of pregnancy (which Ireland allows), heightens the emotional temperature.

There can be little doubt that some of George W. Bush, like Romney, was a sincere Christian; Christ may have helped him recover from cocaine addiction. However, the sinister nature of his regime is exemplified by an (admittedly unnamed) Bush official in an interview with reporter Ron Suskind:

> "We're an empire now, and when we act, we create our own reality. And while you're studying that reality — judiciously, as you will — we'll act again, creating other new realities, which you can study too, and that's how things will sort out. We're history's actors and you, all of you, will be left to study what we do." (Alterman, 2005, p.11)

The analogy is too good to pass up:

> "War is peace. Freedom is slavery. Ignorance is strength. … the sun had shifted round, and the myriad windows of the Ministry of Truth … looked grim as the loopholes of a fortress … Only the Thought Police would read what he had written, before they wiped it out of existence and out of memory." (Orwell, 1949)

Winston Smith of course eventually succumbs:

> "He accepted everything. The past was alterable. The past never had been altered." (ibid).

Milan Kundera has famously documented the struggle of memory in totalitarian societies. In recent years, the Irish bureaucracy began to learn a few tricks of this particular trade. (It is likely that the Irish bureaucrats styled themselves on the arrogant and unaccountable Bush administration). The unjust imprisonment of the Rossport Five, as described in the preface, was spun by Minister Noel Dempsey as an exemplification of the principles of the 1916 rebellion. Since the men were technically in jail for contempt of court, Dempsey proudly declared that their very presence in jail showed that Ireland had its own judicial system. The fact that the jailing was done at the behest of the multinational Shell who gained ownership of the gas in question through an egregious deal with Dempsey's fellow party member and convicted criminal Ray Burke, perhaps indicates that the 1916 leaders Pearse and Connolly might not have been as enthusiastic as Dempsey about the jailing of five Irishmen.

More to the point, the High Court that refuses to release the men is a joke even in the English Bar for its impenetrable language and nostalgia for the ways of Empire. The Rossport case, taking place in a completely financially bankrupt country that prides itself on its wealth in precisely the same manner as it prided itself on its equally unreal capacity to get its populace into a non-existent Catholic heaven, shows that a social process not far from revolution is urgently needed in Ireland:

> "Make no mistake: the Bush administration and its ideological allies are employing every means available to undermine journalists' ability to exercise their First Amendment function to hold power accountable ... Bush himself, on more than one occasion, has told reporters he does not read their work and prefers to live inside the information bubble blown by his loyal minions". (Alterman, ibid.)

The Ireland of the 1970s was full of minority journals like *Hibernia*, often motivated by entirely different takes on what the political and administrative consequences of the 1916 revolution were than that being peddled by the official state. (In this vein, Plowman (2003) writes about an intriguing US linkup between anti-colonial Irish and Indian nationalists in the American spin-off, *New Hibernia Review*.) The type of news management perfected by the G. W. Bush administration is unnecessary in Ireland, where the concentration of media ownership is greater even than in the United States.

> "The overwhelmingly important indigenous media player in the private sector is the *Independent News and Media* group. It has a dominant position in the Irish newspaper industry, accounting for two-thirds of all daily Irish newspaper sales and a large proportion of Sunday newspaper sales. The company is also a global media player with interests on three continents and a global workforce of 12,000." (Tovey, et al, 2003, p. 431)

In the most blatant media political intervention in Irish history, the *Irish Independent*, in 1997, urged the electorate to oust the social democratic government, which had managed to maintain high rates of conventional economic growth while maintaining a social safety net, for a mixture of economic noecons, neoliberals, and liberal democrats. The state radio and TV station, Radio Telefis Eireann (RTE) has fortunately remained largely independent despite the attempted depredations of this government, *in situ* from 1997 to 2011.

Talk radio is beginning to proliferate in Ireland, though we have some ways to go before the political excesses of Rush Limbaugh, Savage Nation, and the John Ziegler Show, described by its host himself:

> "The underlying premise of the John Ziegler Show is that, thanks to its socialistic leanings, incompetent media, eroding moral foundations. ... the US as we know it is doomed." (Wallace, 2005, p. 52)

The drug-addict Rush Limbaugh described the torture in Abu Ghraib as essentially a frat party; however, there is a more general observation to be made:

> "Maybe it's better to say that he is part of a peculiar, modern and very popular type of news industry, one that manages to enjoy the authority and influence of journalism without the stodgy constraints of fairness, objectivity, and responsibility that make trying to tell the truth such a drag." (Wallace, op cit, p. 53)

The record budgetary deficit levels of the Bush administration need no rehearsal here. Currently the US economy is shored up by labourers in China who produce a sufficient surplus for that country to buy US treasuries. Yet the warning signs were there for years:

> "Alan Greenspan is walking a tightrope. Investment guru Warren Buffet cites hedge funds and housing prices as economic flash points ... Historically, easy money, if left unchecked, has ignited an upward spiral of wages and prices." (Abate, 2005, p. 1)

> "The financial profession warns us of risk, but it has adopted an overly precise pseudoscientific approach. Investors are told to 'balance' portfolios (rather than to select stocks) to 'allocate' (rather than to 'invest') their assets." (Lowenstein, 2005, p.20)

The response of the Irish government to this new financial Disneyland has been to try and associate itself with any good news that came along and to evade responsibility for the financial calamity it imposed on its people. Ireland was effectively turned into a debtor's prison, while newspaper headlines scream to the populace in sheerest Orwellian echo that they are, in fact, in the second richest country on earth. (Humphreys, 2005). Again, thi softened up the citizenry for the inevitable coup. (The last print media solace, the *Irish Times* was turned over to a far-right editor and chairman of its mysterious trust after a near-bankruptcy in 2001.)

Tiny Ireland, buffeted on the tsunami of international commerce had a choice. It has decided to free its banks from the consequences of their own greed and incompetence by adding enormously to the national public debt. Alternatively, it could have acted more in line with the principles of the revolution on which the state bases its legitimacy. It can introduce precisely the "fresh start" Chapter 7 bankruptcy legislation that the Bush administration, under pressure from its credit card company friends, scrapped in October, 2005.

It could have guaranteed roofs over the heads of any evictees by using its frequent current account surplus to build social housing on land it was free to rezone. If that were to cause its banks to collapse due to bad debt, then so be it; they collapsed anyway. (The Irish people have seen the CEO of the second-biggest bank being forced to resign for surfing escort agency porn sites during work hours prior to a trip to the US, and his peers being forced to resign. They did not shed a tear at several banks' collapse, but cried bitter tears at the bail-out.) Finally, the state now owns a vast portfolio of property through NAMA that it could use to house the homeless.

There was perhaps no alternative in this post-collapse scenario other than a nationalisation of the major banks; what happened in Ireland, rather, was a bankaliztion of the state. The state should be in control of wealth generated in its jurisdiction in these types of fiscal emergencies; what else does independence mean? If Ireland then has to leave the Euro, or engage in a parallel currency scenario, then so be it. Subsequently, in the reality that hits, it can reflect on the dreamworld it entered from 1997–2007, fully as absurd, harmful, and viciously imposed as anything that the Roman Catholic Church forced on Ireland at the zenith of its power there.

From 2009, a subterfuge was played out involving the ECB, the Irish state, and the Irish banks. The ECB quietly loaned money to the banks. They then bought the bonds issued by the Irish treasury. This ended very badly. .

A final, more imaginative alternative is to anticipate the potential collapse by the systematic introduction of a parallel currency before the collapse due to the "chapter 7" scenario. Following historical precedent, we'll call the new currency the púnt. Personal debt owed within Ireland to Irish financial institutions would be redenominated in púnts from Euro in this scenario. The new self-elected Irish elite would immediately lose all its new friends in the WTO, IMF, EU Central Bank, and so on; the people of Ireland would not notice the difference. The major financial institutions, and in particular the Bank of Ireland and Allied Irish Banks, would be nationalized in this scenario, and taken off the current ECB life support system.

Until the unlikely scenario emerged wherein Ireland was ready to be re-exposed to the hurricanes of international commerce, a protected part of the economy dealing with housing and other essentials would be dealt with in púnts. This is similar to what is happening with the increasingly clear distinction between investment vehicles and what are effectively "building societies." The attraction of Ireland for corporations would remain undimmed; they come for the low corporation tax, not any love of the people. As in Cuba, the housing púnt would be non-convertible, and reserved for Irish citizens. Of course, this seems absurd on first reading; but it is no more so than the current *status quo*.

The current Irish capitalist credo was fully as eschatological as millenniar Christianity. In an already saturated housing market, with rents plummeting in an unprecedented fashion (see www.daft.ie and pick exactly where you would like to live cheaply in Ireland), the Irish mortgage market was announced in the *Irish Times* of 17 September 2005 as due to grow. The motor for all this, of course, is the state's coercion of its citizens, and manipulation of land costs; yet we have just seen it end in tears, with the State's lack of real power now clear.

However, the attempt to marry native greed with Bush-style destruction of the welfare state could have been much worse. There is substantial evidence that Ireland initially planned to be part of the "coalition of the willing" which invaded Iraq; indeed, Bartholomew "Bertie" Ahern stated, as we have seen, that he viewed even the minimalist offering of Shannon Airport as a stopover both for US troops and future "rendition" torture victims as, Spike Milligan-like, his part in Saddam's downfall. (We have seen that conspiracy theorists will be extremely encouraged by the revelation in the Irish Times of 13 October, 2005, that the contract for the 372 million Euro Shannon tunnel went to a Halliburton subsidiary.)

As Ahern spoke, the government had suffered a recent referendum loss on a further strengthening and centralisation of the EU by dint of the left's appealing to traditional Irish state neutrality in pointing out that Ahern's government had broken an election promise by pushing Ireland without a referendum into the NATO twin, Partnership for Peace (ppf). His nose bloodied, Ahern received a bribe of several hundreds of millions euro from the EU and a meaningless written acknowledgement of Irish neutrality in the revised Nice Document, which was put to the Irish populace post-9/11. The anti-Nice vote actually went up; however, the Nice contingent, comprising all the major political parties and the union movement, mobilised sufficient support to win. (The unelected eurocrats have always supported a new principle of democracy as it centralised its power; vote and vote again until you give us the result you want. As of 2012, the Irish have stopped voting in any but risible numbers in these referenda)

The incompetence and inter-departmental competition between the FBI, CIA, and other government agencies, and the mysterious collapse of WTC tower seven have been documented elsewhere (eg, on WTC7.net). Al-Qaeda was in bits at the time of 9/11:

> "Perhaps one of the most important insights to emerge from the computer is that 9/11 sprang not so much from al-Qaeda's strengths as from its weaknesses. The computer did not reveal any links to Iraq or any other deep-pocketed government." (Cullison, A., 2004, pp. 56–57)

Let us note that this is a computer left by al-Qaeda in Afghanistan:

> "What emerged was an astonishing inside look at the day-to-day world of al-Qaeda, as managed by its top strategic planners - among them bin Laden, al-Zawahiri, Atef, Ramzi bin al-Shibh, and Khalid Sheikh Muhammad, all of whom were intimately involved in the planning of 9/11, and some of whom (bin Laden and al-Zawahiri) are still at large." (Cullison, op cit., p. 56)

Conspiracy theories are not our business, yet, undoubtedly, crucial evidence was ignored on the run-up to 9/11. George H. W. Bush was undoubtedly meeting through the Carlyle group (who are the co-owners with the British military of the security routines for the Irish e-voting system) with Osama bin-Laden's brother as 9/11 happened. The Taliban are effectively a CIA creation, being personally visited by CIA director Bill Casey as he delivered the anti-helicopter armament that helped defeat the soviets in Afghanistan. None of that was Ireland's business as issues to be rectified; it is American liberals who need to start engaging themselves in such thorny issues for the sake of the whole world. However, George W. Bush's response was to quicken his plans for invading Iraq (Clarke, 2004).

Juhasz (2007) spells out the catastrophic sequence of events that ended with perhaps the worst presidency in US history, and according to Miller (2005), the most fraudulently obtained one. In 1992, a defence planning guidance group was formed which in 1998 metastasized into the project for a new American century. Also in 1992, Cheney as secretary of defence oversaw the first handing over of a military logistics contract to the private company KBR, before in 1996 becoming CEO of Halliburton with no previous business experience. In 2002, these persons, now in power, formulated a national security strategy that emphasised prevention, not pre-emption. Anyone could be attacked, anytime. The takeover of Iraq culminated in legislation resembling nothing so much as the post-Cromwellian “Act of Good affection” passed in 1652 (O'Callaghan, 2000, 44-46).

While the latter legislation involved ethnic cleansing, in many ways Consul Bremer's orders are no less radical (Juhasz, 2007, 200-222). Massive privatisations of all state-owned enterprises, with Bechtel importing cheaper labour instead of employing the locals (223). Neither water nor sewage was done properly (236). The media was to be restricted, and masses of civil servants and army personnel were to be fired. (Juhasz, ibid. 68-83, also comments on the nature of the type of structural adjustment program that the IMF may now impose on Ireland, with cutting of government spending, no tariffs like Iraq, etc. Unlike Argentina, which has largely recovered, Ireland no longer has a native manufacturing base for the workers to expropriate).

Palast (2006) amplifies these points, with his added special genius for acquiring documents that we weren't supposed to see. One such document suggests;

> “Countries with less attractive geology and governance such as Azerbaijan have been able to overcome their risk profile and attract billions of dollars of investment “ (100) essentially by offering the rest of the country for sale at a discount, as Ireland may well do soon.. The system is very simple; a middleman is appointed to bribe the ministers involved (like perhaps Ray Burke in Ireland), and funds are released to them once the contract is signed. In that vein, a full $4.2 billion was made in Kazakhstan by Hurricane Hydrocarbons for a $51 million investment, and the people got none of it;
>
> “$51 million on payment to the broker ended up ...in the Swiss bank accounts of the president and oil ministers” (101)

While the Anglo-Saxon genetic impact on Britain was perhaps overstated, certain diehards on the council of foreign relations insist that there is an Anglo-American Way (Mead, 2007). It adjudicates intelligently between order and liberty. It is a Hegelian universal force, and coming soon to a neighbourhood near you, as we simply know that it's better and you must have it. Its economics were established in the 18th century; there is an unseen hand that ensures that a market full of rational actors behaving selfishly will stabilise. The South sea Bubble failed to dent this confidence, like the 3 busts and booms since 1998; for Anglo-Saxon common law is similarly precedent alone, and the notion of civil law is anathema. This word is not chosen lightly; for was it not the unseen hand that motivated Abraham to act on faith? Remarkably, Mead can say all this in public without laughing.

Miller (2005) insists that the right-wing in the USA sincerely believes in its mission:

> "We believe that the word of god must be applied to all of life" (131).

For Val Finnell, "The Christian worldview is the answer" (ibid.). The EPA is called "The Gestapo of government" (70). In that vein, it might well be noted that Macdonald et al (2006, 13) document 85 first warnings issued by the EU to Ireland in Ahern's first term, twice that of France. Tara is described by Ahern's department as "a row about who was there five thousand years ago" (ibid., 33).The Shell saga is well described (266-269); in general, the government's environmental policy has been flagrantly to disobey the law, even when EU law is added to the Irish statute books.

The disgrace which is US policy on torture did not faze our Bertie. Grey (2007) painstakingly lists the numerous CIA rendition planes that have used Shannon or Dublin on their way to commit the unspeakable. In the meantime, supposedly right-wing Denmark simply does not allow CIA planes in its airspace. (Granted, the diplomatic standoff between Demark and the USA concerning Greenland may have a role here).

Once bitten, Ahern was not prepared to risk a further referendum. The Irish outpouring of grief to 9/11 victims was sincere; the number of Irish surnames among the slain testify to the extent to which the Irish have lifted themselves up from their peasant origins to roles in the commercial elite slain in the twin towers. Ireland was to enter the world of the Anglo-Saxon elite by stealth; Ahern's chairmanship of the fractious Europeans during his presidency was to be a harbinger. A neoconservative Ireland could be socially engineered in a thrice by an appropriate inversion of the Christian myth in the educational system. If Jesus died to save us in the old version, Bertie could keep leading so that we continue to have loads of money in the new.

Electronic voting was to be introduced on Mayday weekend, 2004, simultaneous with an EU summit in Dublin. It is deeply indicative of the strength of Irish democracy that the panel picked to usher in e-voting then utterly refused to endorse it, and that a follow-up report in 2006 about amended software was almost as negative. It was revealed that, with just over a month to go to its first deployment, no program code was ready. The database to be used was Microsoft Access, which is rather like trying to fly across the Atlantic in a child's kite. The response of the *Irish Times*, now the paper of record in Ireland, was to relegate the e-voting story, and to put two rather flattering photos of the prospective president-for-life Bartholomew Ahern on its cover. Ahern's response was to try and force the early retirement of Judge Smith, who chaired the e-voting panel. The electorate's response was to give Ahern's party the greatest electoral drubbing they had received since their days as hard-done-by victims of state malfeasance and torture in the 1920s. Shortly before the 2009 local and european elections and their even greater drubbing of these miscreants, e-voting finally was abandoned.

Miller (2005) documents, in sometimes excruciating detail, the malfeasance of the 2004 US elections. When criminal Christians were caught, they were encouraged to "just visualise Jesus standing behind you" (70). Like Palast, Miller documents physical intimidation of voters, filming of voters by private detectives, deliberately wrong polling information, and absentee ballots requested by suspicious people. (228-233). Remarkably, Choicepoint, founded by a drugrunner, whom Palast had fingered for the removal of African-Americans from the voting rolls in Florida in 2000, was given access by the department of homeland security to its archive of foreign nationals. In Craven county, New York, "Bush/Cheney got 11283 more votes than the entire number of votes cast for president" with much evidence of vote-flipping, where voters saw their vote changed on screen.

It is important to note that many consider the Voting Rights act of 1965, which has been reaffirmed and strengthened many times since, perhaps the single most successful piece of legislation in the history of the USA. So when Palast (2006) documents "Hispanics put then in front of an old shoptronics machine and...one in 13..did not register a vote for president" (224), we know that something terrible has gone wrong. When Bob Fitrakis asked for a recount, he was told "the backup tapes have been destroyed so as not to conflict with the original tally and create confusion" (229). The "privatization of the voting system...outsourcing the blood and bones of vote counting" continues apace.

Ahern's party was routed in his own heartland of Dublin City Centre in 2004 and 2009. Of the 13 constituencies contested, fully seven were topped in 2004 by Sinn Fein, the political wing of the Provisional IRA.

Labour, which is dominated by ex-"official" IRA (think People's Judaean front and Judaean people's front) topped four. The result is that, at a local borough level, Dublin was now effectively run by IRA veteran fellow travellers. The 2009 locals amplified this result, with Ahern failing even to get his own brother elected either to the national parliament of the local council.

I have no wish to romanticise the "Irish democratic spirit" or overestimate the *nous* of the Irish electorate. However, the final declaration of the "jury of conscience" in Istanbul, June 27, 2005, is devastating;

> "The invasion and occupation of Iraq was and is illegal. The reasons given by the US and UK governments for the invasion and occupation of Iraq in March 2003 have proven to be false. Much evidence supports the conclusion that a major motive for the war was to control and dominate the Middle East and its vast reserves of oil as part of the US drive for global hegemony." (in Roy, 2005, p. 24)

By the time this is being read, several thousands of the flower of American youth will have died in the name of an insane plan cooked up by chickenhawks calling themselves the Project for a New American Century. In the meantime, the US inflicted well over 100,000 Iraqi casualties:

> "Little popular support was necessary for such attacks, though popular support was growing … The Americans knew it, too. Even within the Green Zone, they derided their home as 'The Bubble.' But they could not stop themselves from their retreat." (Langowische, 2004, p. 62)

Their attitude to legal affairs in the cradle of civilisation resembled the old British adage that foreigners will understand if only you speak loudly enough in English to them:

> "Working … under Bremer himself, the lawyers essentially drew up a new nation." (op cit, p. 88)

The tension between Anglo-Saxon common law and the more sophisticated Iraqi civil law echoes that between the Anglo-Irish and Brehon legal systems.

Ahern's attempted political coup, with its sweeping privatisations, destruction of democracy, and engagement in military alliances, had been defeated. His response was to fire his Minister of Finance, whose aggressive neo-liberal leanings and monoglot linguistic orientation has not helped him in his new post in Brussels. Ahern's attempted return to the centre-left was stymied by his libertarian coalition partners, the progressive democrats. Though he did finally get their leader to enunciate a comforting belief that earnings over €200K should be subject to 20% tax, the coalition was doomed. For the moment, at least, Ireland was safe from a toxic combination of Catholic nationalism, Clemenceau-type verbal republicanism, and international capitalism. The 2007 coalition was a much more uneasy creation; various socialists and disgraced independents together with the doomed "Green" party.

For all its posturing, the American administration that Ahern was so keen to favour over Berlin was as incompetent as it was immoral. George W. Bush's initiative in attacking the wrong enemy in Iraq will go down in military history as a blunder of gigantic proportions. The lies told about weapons of mass destruction are on the public record. However, even the Middle East as a whole is unlikely to remain quite as much in focus as it is currently:

> "No matter how successfully our military adapts to the rise of China, it is clear that our current dominance in the Pacific will not last ... China is poised to reap the substantial benefits of pursuing its interest amorally — what the US did during the cold war." (Kaplan, 2005, p. 62)

The new global realpolitik will attempt to secure oil supplies over Chinese objections:

> "This may well lead to a fundamentally new NATO alliance, which could become a global armada that roams the seven seas ... Since Europe increasingly seeks to avoid conflict and to reduce geopolitics to a series of negotiations and regulatory disputes, an emphasis on sea power would suit it well ... Armies invade; navies make port visits." (ibid)

Kaplan points out that the Dutch, Norwegian, Germans, and Spanish are investing in fast missile- bearing ships and beach assault equipment (ibid). The war that Ahern was so keen to engage his Slattery's mounted foot regiment in, to use the trope of the great Irish engineer and comic Percy French has had unintended consequences:

> "With the invasion of Iraq, the world's suspicion of American hegemony intensified enormously and now China and Russia have expanded their military cooperation." (Schwarz, 2005, p. 28)

China's economic growth depends on continues access to oil. Apart from the Middle East and Sudan, it is encroaching on American interests in

Canada, where oil extraction from shale is continuing at an unprecedented pace, and Venezuela. The response from the US has been to allow TV evangelist Pat Robertson to urge the US government to declare war on Venezuela by assassinating Hugo Chavez.

Khrushchev famously exclaimed to John F. Kennedy that it was the US that was turning Castro into a communist. Robertson's death threat was altered immediately prior to a UN visit by Chavez, who was consulting with Castro as the threat became public. Castro's response was a sarcastic comment that, as only God could forgive Pat Robertson, he was not going to pre-empt the Deity.

Chavez, like the early Castro, is a profoundly ambivalent figure. Castro rejected overtures by the US in the mid-seventies and by the UN non-aligned nations, which he briefly led, only when pressurised by the Soviet Union to engage in and/or support military adventures in Angola and Afghanistan. Chavez has withstood a US supported coup d'état.

> "Despite Chavez's often radical discourse, the government has not engaged in mass expropriations of private fortunes, even agricultural ones, nor plowed huge sums into new collectively owned forms of production. In fact, private property is protected in the new constitution promulgated after Chavez came to power." (Parenti, 2005, p. 17)

Lest it is not obvious, the position of this book is that Ireland should immediately nationalize its copious oil and gas in its territorial waters and continue to promote wind power, as it is successfully starting to do. We are completely out of our league in these matters. Chavez has not yet become a Fidel Castro, except in their shared economic naïveté:

> "In the past four years this internal debt has gone from 2 billion … to more than $27 billion … 60 percent of this debt is held in government bunds … the government is depositing all its oil revenue in the same banks at about 5 percent, then borrowing it back at 14 percent … this is a government for the rich … Last year the Venezuela banks made $1.38 billion in profits, just a bit more than they did the year before." (Parenti, op cit, p. 20)

With a population which is a fraction of Venezuela's, each of Ireland's two major banks until recently made almost double this amount of profit; Anglo-Irish was less a bank than an Enron-type criminal conspiracy against the Irish citizenry. The dear land is even more lucrative than manipulation of government bonds in an oil-rich economy. Holding the country's citizens hostage to international usury benefits a very small class of property owners and indeed bankers. Chavez has been imaginative in his social programs:

> "1.3 million people have learned to read, millions have received medical care and an estimated 35–40 percent of the population now shops at subsidized, government-owned supermarkets. Elementary school enrolment has increased by more than a million." (Parenti, op cit, p. 17)

The formula advocated for Ireland has been tried and found wanting in Latin America:

> "After two decades of the US-promoted Washington census — a cocktail of radical privatisation, open markets, and severe fiscal austerity — Latin America is an economic disaster marked by increasing poverty and inequality." (Ibid, p. 16)

One might extend the period to over three decades, which is the time elapsed since Milton Friedman's Chicago boys began to run Chile under the war criminal and torturer Auguste Pinochet. While Bartholmew "Bertie" Ahern was hardly of the same ilk, his liking for dressing himself and his mistress in military fatigues was indeed noticed.

The state *qua* social contract, exemplified by the hurricane response, has essentially collapsed in the US, and it will take rather more than Sunday school pieties altered by the president to reclaim it; Obama's disingenuous recitation of the uniqueness of the opportunity that America gave him began to grate even before he became elected president.

What of protest there? In the wake of the egregious and disastrously incompetent response to Hurricane Katrina, it was left to black rapper Kanye West to say the obvious; the Bush administration did not care about black people (nor brown, nor poor, he might have added). The rampant racism and classism was amply demonstrated by the fact that he was allowed to utter these words on national TV, as the censors who could have pulled them obviously associated black people with wardrobe malfunctions a la Janet Jackson or unparliamentary terms, qua the Great Bono. Articulately spoken home truths could safely fly.

As the social contract of Roosevelt's New Deal unravelled, the racism incarnated in the infamous southern Jim Crow laws has rekindled. Those who died in New Orleans for lack of a bottle of water were disproportionately black: rebuilding contracts were being refused to local contractors of colour, according to the famously rightwing (and now Murdoch-owned) Wall Street Journal (Dreazen et al, 2005). GW Bush would have had to do rather better than a token black female secretary of state to rubberstamp his Swiftian decisions.

West's courageous and forthright protest enhanced his career as the top US rapper, yet the liberal elite in general seems to have come to the conclusion that, since the eighties proved that the personal is political, one engages in politics by emphasising a personal predeliction.

The response then, to the 2000 coup d'etat has been to promote gay marriage (Heuvel, 2004) as distinct from destroying e–voting machines; to promote the candidacy of Hilary Clinton (Sargent, 2005) instead of Barbara Boxer, the only senator to contest the results of the stolen 2004 presidential election; to spend hours grilling prospective Supreme Court Justice John Roberts on his opinions on abortion, while an environmental catastrophe occurred on the US mainland. US army recruiters have access to domestic phone numbers of school children through the egregious "No Child Left Behind Act". The US environment is threatened daily by such Orwellian fantasies as the Clean Air Act.

The Bush administration seems to have read 1984 and decided O'Brien is the hero; the Democrats cry like babies for legislative incarnation of their pet predilections, while ignoring many outstanding issues of social, radical, environmental, and international justice. The pathetic John Kerry campaign was reprised by Hillary Clinton, who deservedly lost to a relative unknown:

> "In effect, she's taking her husband's small-time centrism … and remaking it in her own image, updating it post 9/11 America with an intense interest in military issues" (Sargent, 2005, p. 13)

Just as Democrats guzzle gas at precisely the unsustainable rate of Republicans, Hillary's solution to the Iraq imbroglio was Lyndon Johnson's "surge" idea; send in more troops, to create a decent interval for a relatively orderly withdrawal. The American economy may stay afloat for as long as the Chinese needs it to and no longer. Fallows (2005), envisages collapse, followed by restriction in civil liberties. The occasional coherent proposal emerging from the deliberations of the American left goes largely unnoticed there drowned out by a sea of righteous squawks, requests to remove rosaries from ovaries, and so on:

> "As in the decades before the great Depression, rising productivity gains made possible by the spread of industrialization and technology and the opening up of new production centers and labour markets have created a glut of capacity, savings, and labour" (Schwenninger, 2005, p. 18)

The toys, gadgets and bric-a-brac we now spend our money on is manufactured much more efficiently, partly by coerced labour, in South East Asia than anywhere else. Ireland cannot possibly compete in any of these markets. Having destroyed its native software industry (see chapter 6), and native music industry (see chapter 7), it needs to reflect on the forces that gave rise to Joyce as to Iona software, to Riverdance as to Riverdeep, in order merely to survive as a producer of anything apart from personal debt.

Schwenninger (ibid) continues:

> "The problem is that we are building a world economy that is too small, too risky and too dependent on American consumption to accommodate both the aspiring middle classes of the developing world and the existing middle classes of the developed world."

She proposes as a solution that instead of; "encouraging emerging economies to develop through the export of manufactured goods, we should champion … domestic consumption … home ownership … public infrastructure … more small and medium-sized businesses." (op cit, p. 20)

Labour standards should be raised worldwide; the solution also takes the pressure off the US to be the very indebted engine of economic growth. Coherent thought from the American left and/or liberals (Chomsky deplores only the latter) is to be encouraged. Perhaps the most astute decision that the Bush regime has made is not to introduce conscription; they calculate they can get enough trailer trash and wetbacks to guard any oil pipelines they need in Iraq, as distinct from its people. The class and race bigotry, and indeed the sheer incompetence of this regime, is now a byword as it fades into history; it is discussed her partly because it looks that /Romney will do precisely the same things.

Middle-class liberals are still largely cocooned, despite falling somewhat in relative income. They are free verbally to protest against American military adventures overseas, which they do from a self-created moral high ground; there is no serious campaign (a la Chomsky in the 1960s) to withhold taxes, or take any personal risks. Safe in the knowledge that the

Democrats will support them in any military adventure they care to engage in, the right point to the existence of the protest as evidence of the existence of the freedoms that killed Iraqis for.

Only a concerted attack on Shibboleths like Roe versus Wade will create a real political conflict in the US. GW Bush got away with being noncommittal about abortion, despite the Christian rhetoric, so it looks as though even the fundamentalist Christian part of his support base are a little more pliable or dispensable than initially seems the case (Famously, divorce rates and sales of Playboy magazine are higher in core republican states than in liberal Massachusetts). The prognosis for this would-be partner of Ireland is not good.

Before discussing Europe, it is appropriate to re-emphasize the fiscal effects of globalisation:

> "To an even greater extent, states are proving too weak to impose rules which regulate the affairs of a particular territory … The world market is extending its irresistible power to control the price of money and currencies on the one hand, and on the other hand to set technical standards." (Malakopf, 1999, p. 146)

Resistance is futile? One wonders. In the late 1990s East Asian crisis, Malaysia resisted, and introduced currency controls. The trope of nation was used against the seemingly irresistible force of international capitalism; the result was that Malaysia was the least badly hit of all the Asian economics. In the past decade, we have seen the dictators of international finances allow a stock market boom that Alan Greenspan was describing "irrational exuberance" as far back as 1996, then set interest rates at record low levels when recession set in subsequent to a prodigious international stock market crash causing in turn a real estate bubble. As this crashes, the cast-iron laws of economics, rather than the set of arbitrary fiats they increasingly resemble, will again be appealed to as an "explanation". Ireland can and must separate itself, at least partly, from these forces; however, it must also rescind certain of the conditions of its membership of the European Union.

5.3 Ireland in the EU

The entry of Ireland into the European Economic Community, as it was at the time, on 1 January 1973, was *de jure* if not *de facto* the end of Irish sovereignty. The Irish overwhelmingly voted for the end of the legislative autonomy of their parliament, and their own constitutional requirement that power was vested in the people of Ireland. The relevant referendum wording, as presented to the people on 10 May 1972, and approved by 83.1%, read as follows;

> "No provision of this constitution invalidates laws enacted, acts done, or measures adopted by the state necessitated by the obligations of membership of the communities or prevents laws enacted, acts by the communities, or institutions thereof, from having the force of law in the state."

(In the spirit of that appeal to punctuation values, "eats shoots and leaves", I have repunctuated the text, which is now Article 29.4.3° of the Irish Constitution).

In the 1930s, the mathematician Kurt Goedel further developed a technique in which statements about the natural numbers could be transformed into statements in the natural numbers. His target was unpacking the famous paradox of Epimenides, the Cretan who states that all Cretans are liars, into a consequential thesis about formal systems in general (As the mathematics teacher and wannabe researcher Eamon de Valera, who is responsible for the 1937 Irish Constitution, was fully aware, the constitution is a formal system). Gödel established that no non-trivial formal system can prove its own consistency; if assumed consistent, it will contain statements that can neither be proven nor disproven in its formal machinery (for example, "This system is wrong"). Article 29.4.3° is the Godelian sentence at the heart of the Irish Constitution; less charitably, it rescinds Irish sovereignty. (See O' Nualláin, 2003, p. 207, for a summary of Goedel's work.)

Some years ago, this writer had the privilege of co-founding the Musicians Union of Ireland (MUI) of which most of the great Irish Musicians of the past 35 years are members; Donal Lenny, Andy Irvine, Christy Moore and indeed Sinéad O'Connor, who has not stormed out on us yet. Due to EU law, it is now illegal for us to attempt to strike a rate for musicians performing at a gig. If the musicians meet before the gig and agree to demand a certain sum, they are in breach of EU competition law and liable to criminal penalty. Let us continue; had the Irish state invested in its national airline, electricity service, or telecommunications infrastructure (when it had such things), it too must give account of its sins to Brussels.

Indeed, Brussels recently stymied further development by Intel in Ireland by demanding trade secrets from Intel before agreeing even to countenance further state subsidy in what has been, despite Intel's chequered legal record vis a vis its rival AMD, an undoubted Irish success story. Ireland cannot set interest rates, police its incredible marine resources, which have by now been over fished by its EU "partners" (famously, the Irish patrol boats disproportionately pursue Irish fishermen), or indeed behave like an independent state in very many ways. How did this come to pass?

Murphy (1986) writes of Ireland's accession to the EEC, and the preceding debate. In 1987, to update Murphy, a TCD economist called Raymond Crotty found that the (Irish) republican Judge Barrington agreed with him that further deepening of the EEC in Ireland was unconstitutional without a referendum. Lest we forget, it should be noted that the EEC and EU were never intended as fully democratic entities; countries, not individuals, are members, and the unelected European Commission has massive power.

It can be argued that criticism of the imperial ambitions of the US can equally be targeted at the EU. O'Hearn is described as arguing:

> "The most important change is in European integration strategies. These have shifted from a primarily US-inspired plan to integrate Europe into global trade, to a project by the European core itself to increase its economic and military power." (Tovey et al, 2003, p. 74)

Crotty's protest at the single European act proved futile; later came the equally centralising Masstricht, Amsterdam and Nice treaties, with the status of the 2012 economic treaty increasingly ambiguous as countries threaten either to attenuate or expand it.

The Maastricht treaty was passed relatively comfortably after being supported by a grand coalition of all the major political parties and trade unions; the same coalition could get Amsterdam passed only by a hair's breadth. The Nice and Lisbon treaties, as mentioned, were initially turned down, as the Irish turned against almost their whole political class. The very survival of that political class, and the bizarre structure of the Irish political system in which the two main parties (Fianna Fáil and fine Gael) play electoral musical chairs in deciding at random which will be left and right wing, is worth examining.

As in many countries, a Civil War shaped the two main parties; the recent transformation of Fianna Fáil into a neoliberal's dream belied their origins as a working-class radical Republican Party. In 1992, after nearly a quarter-century of tumult in the party, Fianna Fáil received their worst general electoral drubbing for some time. Their then leader, erstwhile music "entrepreneur" Albert Reynolds, came under enormous pressure from the Dublin-based wing of the party. (See chapter 7 about the wonderful world of the Irish music industry.)

Luckily for him, the European Community, as it was, stopped in at just that moment with a gift of 8 billion ecu/euro for Ireland. Reynolds was ousted two years later after a truly abominable clerical sexual abuse scandal shook the very juridical foundation of the state. Similarly, Ahern was forced to resign in 2008 for what looked like a relatively trivial set of gifts from cronies; the problem was that two judges (one from the High Court) whom he had recently appointed were to be called up to defend him in public, and confidence in the judicial system was going to suffer. For the first time since independence, Ireland now had an appointed, rather than elected government, in which the upper house of parliament had been rigged by the party now in opposition in the lower house. Certain subsequent legislation, not least the 1997 Universities Act, shows the damage done.

The degree to which membership of the EU has compromised Irish political life will be debated for many years to come. The position taken here is that, if an Anglophone country near all the major centres of consumption cannot make a living, the worst possible thing to do is to bail it out. The inevitable post-colonial malaise and post-famine Roman Catholic frenzy were going to burn themselves out in any case. EU interference in the Irish legislative and political processes is preventing the natural development of the country.

The prospect of certain of the great historical European civilizations — Bulgaria, Lithuania, Poland, Tand so on — attaining full expression in an enlarged Europe is exciting beyond words. Judicious injections of capital and opening of markets will work wonders there. However, the EU insistence hat Ireland act as a whipping-boy for unsecured bondholder – one assume because the ECB uses them to raise capital - raises a question to which we will return:

> "Should we leave the EU?"

Coda: Making economics boring

This writer is a veteran of many forays by applied mathematics into hitherto unexplored areas. A good general rule of thumb is that if the mathematics is particularly complex, the area is not properly modeled. For example, the nascent area of bioinformatics uses a methodology called singular value decomposition, which requires a fair subset of Heisenbereg's insights into physical reality expressed in his "Matrix mechanics"- and much else to boot. Likewise, financial traders use baroque formalisms like Black-Scholes, perhaps the major cause of the LTCM crash. Even the rebranding of subprime as "AAA" had a mathematical model.

Our political-economic system needs to be de-economized, and the economy that remains has to be de-financialized. Glass-Steagal and Sarbanes-Oxley need to be implemented in full, to start with, and punters on stock markets should resemble those on greyhound racing in financial impact. Such initiatives require the action of a state; as of 2011, it is clear that public support will follow if the state can continue to provide certain basic needs. Clearly, any state that attempted to remove itself from the golden horde of speculation would experience a quickening of speculation against its currency. That is a risk that must be taken; luckily, Ireland is self-sufficient in basic foodstuffs many times over.

This initiative would result in an economic status quo in which the 30 years or so of fruitive work that constitute the guts of most of our lives would be honoured in a state currency and banking system that is rock-solid. The move away from a fiat currency into something based on the tangible is a desirable one. A period of improvisation, in which perhaps the Chinese manufacture much of our technology (plus ca change) in exchange for the high-protein food they so crave is on the cards. As a non-colonial power, the Irish have few enemies; Venezuela, to give one example, might extend its fossil fuel largesse beyond Cuba to another revolutionary island.

CHAPTER SIX

SOFTWARE/BOGEARRA: HOW THE IRISH GOVERNMENT BUGGERED UP ITS NATIVE TECH INDUSTRIES

6.1 Myths and Legends of the Silicon Isle

For a brief period, Ireland looked like a software giant in the making. Indeed, it was actually the world's leading exporter of pre-packaged software at one point. This chapter investigates what went wrong, and what other ex-colonies can learn. It argues that the central problem was a lack of intellectual sophistication among key decision-makers; alternatively put, it was the new-found interest in computer software by technically inept senior politicians and their plants in the public service that forced a delicate consensus between civil servants and software entrepreneurs to be destroyed.

Some of the results are frankly hilarious. A previously sophisticated funding mechanism was abandoned for the creation of a digital hub with the promise of 700 companies and initial investment of $130 million. Four years after the announcement, it had four companies and close to zero non-state investment. A much-ballyhooed joint venture with MIT, which cost the State over $50 million, was revealed to involve no substantive commitment of any sort on the MIT side. In particular, MIT refused to accredit any degrees from Medialab Europe, or indeed allow its name to be used; the fact that it chose to send over academics who had been refused tenure itself speaks volumes for the contempt shown to the project. In January, 2005, the project collapsed at a huge loss, both financial and in terms of social capital, to the Irish taxpayer. Unless radical changes are immediately made, the moment has passed for the creation of a viable 21st century Irish software industry.

Of course, the scenario just outlined fits in perfectly with one of the central theses of this book; that there was an attempted political coup in 2004, and that a massive enclosure of the intellectual commons was being attempted. One essential step in the plan to turn Ireland into TNC heaven was to impede development of native initiative. The conspicuously talentless individuals who held the levers of political power saw no difficulty in serving up their talented fellow Irish to this project. This chapter examines how native tech was turned from a world leader into a loss-making laughing-stock. The next chapter examines how the same was done to the hitherto vibrant Irish music industry (It is extraordinary that Ireland had more international successes in the world of international music in the early 1970's before there effectively was any Irish music industry).

The native software industry in Ireland, and with it other initiatives like bio-computing, has reached crisis point. Both the technical standards and governance of Irish universities are utterly inadequate to the task of resurrecting these industries. Nor did the model of importing staff who had been refused tenure at MIT to set up Medialab Europe work. Although the failure of Medialab Europe (MLE) was predictable, and predicted (by the author in the Wall Street Journal of July 5, 2001), aspects of the rationale for its establishment were and remain correct. The fears that Ireland would end up with little other than call centers, low corporate tax rates, and an uncertain future (including massive unemployment) in an expanded Europe where basic costs are lower elsewhere have proven justified. A generation's living standards can be protected only once by passing on the bill in the shape of vastly higher property prices to the next generation, and that has been done.

While there is not a single documented case of a top-down government intervention, including Medialab, having the effect it seeks to have by investing in native software industries, the state can play a role -as in the US - in removing roadblocks to entrepreneurship and innovation. While the Crito institute at UC Irvine argues that the state can do nothing but damage to a national software industry (Dedrick et al., 1998), Peter Evans' (1995) perhaps more sophisticated analysis of the IT industry in Brazil, Korea, and India ("Embedded autonomy: states and industrial transformation") claims that state involvement can lead as a by-product to inward investment. The Irish state can and should also make up for its disastrous decisions of the late 1990's by doing a once-off reallocation of resources.

The generally low ratings achieved by Irish universities, with the exception of TCD, in recent real international surveys like the Shanghai one sit uneasily with the impetus of the 1997 universities act in removing many aspects of what are state universities from the control of state, and vesting frightening concentrations of power in university presidencies. Effectively, what have happened are privatizations without the benefits of exposure to market forces. This is precisely the opposite to Stanford, a private university - and one of the world's finest - that resembles a coalition of small businesses with little top-down control. Thus, in founding Google, the entrepreneurs Larry Page and Sergei Brin capitalized on the world-class educational and technical expertise at Stanford, but were free to remove themselves from its control, and IP claims. The response of Stanford's president, John Hennessy, has been personally to buy Google stock.

The 1997 Universities act has resulted in often ill-equipped university management engaging in truly egregious behaviour to staff and students. This has now been documented by the equality auditors Sean Ruth and Associates, who pointed out that there were high levels of bullying and sexual harassment at Dublin City University (DCU), and attested by Justice Minister Michael McDowell (see Irish Independent 12 April 2005).When these issues have come up in the Dáil, we shall see that the responsible ministers have continued to receive advice that the act should be interpreted in a manner that ensures that Irish universities are totally outside the state's control, and thus will remain international bywords for incompetence and corruption. Simultaneously, the institution of academic tenure, accepted even in private US universities, has been destroyed as management feel free summarily to dismiss permanent university staff, often wrecking world-class labs in the process, and to use the resources of state to submit endless appeals when they lose in court. We shall revisit this is chapter 8.

Were this ruthless behaviour in some way conducive to efficiency and excellence, some kind of case, however ill-motivated, could perhaps be made for it. What has emerged instead is irredeemable mediocrity at best, and a situation where normal academic freedom, a venerable institution in every other Western country, is stifled (Washburn, 2005). Thus, to take one example, a protest at the doubling of the numbers on a computing degree was met with threats of libel action by a university president. Staff were hired to cater for the increase in numbers before the project was abandoned 3 years later at a cost to the state of perhaps E 30 million and many ruined lives among the students. Intriguingly, the decision-makers have since been rewarded with even more of taxpayers' money. Small wonder that Ireland's reputation for technical excellence, hard-won as it was, is going down the tubes.

While the 1997 act is thoroughly overhauled, as will hopefully happen, a new model is necessary. Ireland is currently at an economic crossroads, and would have faced a real estate correction even had international investment continued at the massive 2003 rate. The ratio of native to foreign tech industry is the opposite of Israel's, where there is intelligent state intervention. (Source: Intel's general manager in Ireland). There have been attempts like SFI, loosely based on the NSF in the US, to bring state-of-the-art research to Ireland, but they have excluded the NSF's entrepreneurial wing and in any case are dinosaurs in the era of open science. In parallel with this, entrepreneurship within the universities has been stifled by a management structure that rolls administrative, academic, and technical issues into a single hierarchy. The understandable response of many Irish academics has been to opt for a quiet and civilized, if underachieving existence, in preference to diving into the crucible of dealing with what frankly are often laughably under-equipped administrative structures in order to implement initiatives.

6.2 The 1990's boom/bubble and the autochthonous software success

Ireland's population is over 4 million, the highest since 1880. The workforce is still at approximately twice its historic level, despite current high unemployment, exceeding 2 million in October, 2005. It exports approximately $10 billion in software each year, making it the world's number one. It has been a republic with a written constitution since the late 40's; a gradual transition to full independence begun with the first Dail in the teens of the last century. On the face of things, this seems like outrageous success. Its intellectual history has been benighted by colonialism, as we have discussed, and this perhaps is the Achilles' heel.

Economically, to repeat one of our central themes, personal indebtedness is now so high that the banks had to keep the value of land prohibitively high for their own survival/profitability. The creation of NAMA may be viewed as an attempt to deflate the bubble, gently. The total personal debt exceeds $1 trillion, so entrepreneurship is increasingly rare. The rate of personal borrowing, $6 billion a month as of March 2005 with a steady increase, portended an economic correction, started by the crash of 2008 and concluding in massive house-price realignment.

From the late 1980s, as described by O Riain (2004), a network of software entrepreneurs and civil servants, adapting an old rugby slogan, and exploiting Microsoft's presence in Ireland, began to produce a critical mass of successful software companies. If it moves, fund it; if not, kick it until it moves, and then fund it, went the slogan. The conservative government elected in 1997 and re-elected in 2002 was the first to attempt to put IT, science, and particularly software on an institutional footing.

Why is software important? In short, because of its low environmental impact, high skills base, potentially enormous profit margin, and the healthy intellectual culture it nurtures. Software will always bounce back, and any country that can cultivate and cherish excellence in it will have a jump start. Witness, for example, Germany's SAP and Sweden's Ericsson, both countries that turned down Media Lab. Intriguingly, the Irish government had commissioned a report from a Nordic faculty member at the University of Limerick who had access to the Swedish deliberations on MLE. The facts that he decided against the project, and that his recommendation was overturned, invite the dark explanation we see below; it was, quite simply, a scam.

At some point, Ireland was going to have to outgrow its initial reliance on the presence of Microsoft; on the contrary, Steve Ballmer now visits Ireland and recommends changes in its immigration policies further to quicken Microsoft profits. The author's highest degree is in computer science, and the shoddy quality of Microsoft products has been a byword in the industry for some time. Eventually, Microsoft itself admitted that its software methodologies were antediluvian:

> "Jim Allchin, a senior Microsoft Corp. executive, walked into Bill Gate's office here one day to deliver a bombshell about the next generation of Microsoft Windows 'It's not going to work' … Throughout its history, Microsoft has let thousands of programmers each produce their own piece of program code, then stitched it together into one sprawling program. Now, Mr. Allchin argued, the jig was up. Microsoft needed to start over. Mr. Gates resisted at first …" (Guth, 2005b, p. 1)

But, briefly, resistance was futile. The result was Vista, already something of an industry joke before it was even released, and time has not improved its reputation.

Yet due to Microsoft's and Intel's market share, this very incompetence worked in their favour, as well as that of Dell, the other IT TNC with a massive Irish presence (until they departed for Poland in 2009, one assumes inspired by the hundreds of thousands of Poles who had used Ireland to learn English). So your software is regularly crashing, and you often see the blank screen of death? You obviously now need version 4.2.3.3, which gobbles up so much memory that you will need a new processor (supplied by Intel) and a new computer (supplied by Dell). I have described what if effectively this protection racket elsewhere (2004, p. 104)

Manes et al. (1994) paint an immensely disturbing picture of Microsoft and many of its principals. The coarseness and vulgarity of Ballmer is legendary; his exhortation to "BOGU" (bend over, grease up) when looking for new business sets the tone. A rather revealing video of Ballmer in excited state has done the rounds on the web for some time. An insider's comment is revelatory:

> "But at Microsoft, the immensely likeable Hallman had been seen as an ill fit for months ... Veteran developer Steve Wood put it simply: 'Mike Hallman was a human being'. What you had to be to succeed at the highest levels of Microsoft, he left to the imagination." (Manes et al, p. 434)

The antitrust suits against Microsoft have been going on for some time:

> "A mousemaker worth about as much as Microsoft made in a single day had stared the Software Monolith in the eye and won." (op. cit., pp. 401-402).

There is little that Microsoft will not do to crush competition. Ballmer once teamed up with his old nemesis Palm to attempt to crush the Canadian competitor Blackberry:

> "Microsoft and Palm yesterday penned a deal that will put the Windows Mobile software on Palm's Treo 700." (Guth, 2005a)

(Then, of course, Palm signed a separate deal with Blackberry for the Treo 650!) Microsoft's travails in the US antitrust case were worsened by the fact that, while they had to make the case in court that its Internet and web wings were integrated, at home they were stressing their separation (Bank, 2001, carefully exposes this contradiction).

Intel has recently been chastised in Japan for anti-competitive practices against its rival AMD in Japan, as we alluded to earlier. As for Dell, the slogan used by the workers in its Limerick plant was simply "Dell is hell".

One of the most profound ironies of the much-trumpeted Irish tech boom is that it began to be trumpeted worldwide just exactly when the Irish government began to destroy its native tech industries. The insane MLE initiative ensured that cutting-edge Irish software(s/w) companies were deprived of basic resources, not to mention some kind of acknowledgment by the state. The results can be seen in the analysis of the "Dublin Tech 25" by Mulcahy (2005), an analysis of the top 25 new s/w companies in Dublin which had at that point lost E350 million between them.

As Mulcahy (p. 32) points out:

> "These investments represent a huge leap of faith by both indigenous and overseas venture capital (VC) firms. What VCs hope for is a few home runs to pay for many more duds."

Yet that is not the truly disturbing part; business, properly done, is largely about risk management. Rather, the ephemeral nature of most of the technologies developed by these Irish firms, which are oriented to solve trivial business problems of today at the expense of addressing fundamental technological needs, truly gives pause. (Even less are they oriented to addressing fundamental movements of the human psyche like the desire for totally natural language and gesture interaction with computers). The Irish company Aldiscon developed the world's first text messaging system; Doug Engelbart, fitting the latter category, demonstrated the first mouse and hypermedia system 40 years ago.

Silicon Valley entrepreneurs tend to have a wide range of interests outside computing alone:

> "Last June, when (Sunil) Paul sold his second company, Brightmail, to Symantec for $370 million, he … dedicated himself to politics … he has been training on the trapeze and has thrown himself into the study of pre-Columbian archaeology …" (Rivlin, 2005, p. 69)

Joe Kraus, co-founder of Excite which was sold for $6.7 billion "established an advocacy group in Washington to promote liberal digital-copyright laws" (op. cit. 68)

Their new applications tend to be innovative:

> "This includes Mark Pincus, who helped found Tribe.Net, a social-networking company, in the spring of 2003." (69)

IT applications are so various now that wide experience of the world is vital; and is it not ironic that someone in the supposedly individualistic USA, rather than the supposedly communitarian Ireland, would look for applications involving community like Facebook? Irish software applications show a disturbing lack of imagination, perhaps a consequence of the MLE disaster:

> "CR2 provides channel banking, ATM and card payment solutions to the financial services industry." (Mulcahy, op. cit. p. 33)

The problem is that so do many other companies from much bigger countries:

> "The company had a horrendous time in 2002 and 2003." (ibid)

In the intellectual vacuum that is contemporary Ireland, one tends to reinvent the wheel:

> "O'Donnell had devised an ingenious arithmetic method to scramble credit card numbers so that online purchases could be made more secure." (ibid)

Such schemes are commonplace and only exploitation of quantum states would be an innovation:

> "Bringing it to market has proved challenging." (ibid)

The company in question, Orbiscom, lost E32 million in its last year of trading. So where should Ireland fit? First of all, the cultivation of niche ideas like what text-messaging originally was should be encouraged. Secondly, it should engage itself in open-source.

Open Source (or the related term Free Software) is a concept for the collaborative production of computer software, the most well-known examples of which are the Linux operating system and the popular Apache web server software. This movement has been big enough to make the computer giants take notice, and in some cases, to rework their corporate strategies. But Open Source is now being applied to other kinds of endeavors, from pharmaceutical development to book publishing, as a means of harnessing individual work in communal effort. Though there are different flavors of open source, the root extends from Richard Stallman's GNU public license and free software movement, which emphasizes "free as in freedom", the freedom to use, modify and redistribute the product; with that freedom being transmitted to all future uses of that product. It's a radical notion that still takes a bit of getting used to.

Open Source is possibly the most important new industrial movement for centuries; the primary historical significance of Bill Gates may be that he sparked this reaction to his *modus operandi.* Consider the following alternative history; disgusted as they were with the shoddy quality of mass-produced artifacts, the Luddites decide to poll their resources in a creative manner instead of destroying factories. They arrive at a means of quality control that involves critique by fellow craftsmen.

Globalization touches every realm from trade to culture, increasing the interdependence of everyone in the world, blurring traditional lines, and creating new tensions. The increase in circulation of money and ideas is often to the benefit of the largest multinational corporations, who by definition have less interest in the small scale of individual lives, and who cannot be counted on to have our best interests at heart. These faceless global forces frighten and anger us.

At the same time, rapid technological advances have put the means of production in individual hands. A media company may be a global conglomerate (http://www.viacom.com) or a single Japanese computer consultant (Channel 2 was reportedly Japan's biggest and most popular Web site, started by 24-year old Hiroyuki Nishimura in 1999. More than a million people posted comments on Channel 2 every day, and the site got 600 million page views a month.)

The rapid rise of the PC, computer networks and the "network of networks", the Internet, has created not only a new mass medium, but a fertile environment for fostering the creative commons. The increasingly global infosphere is a place where human collaboration arises naturally and informally, from the ground up. It is also a place where people can easily relate directly to one another rather than to the corporation, the state, the hierarchy.

One group outlined the core principles for the creation of working online communities, and this is a powerful model:

- self-unfolding as the main motivation for production,

- Irrelevance of exchange value, so the focus is on the use value,

- Free cooperation between people,

- International teams.

How can this be applied to the creation of other kinds of knowledge and products in an age where human ingenuity is needed most?

Peer-to-peer is associated with illegal file-sharing, but in fact it describes a networking protocol different from the traditional client-server model. The peer-to-peer paradigm is about direct relationship of "client" to "client" without the mediation of a higher-level server. This is used to drastically amplify means of distribution of files over the Internet, making efficient use of resources, and there are many legal uses. Skype, an archetypal peer-to-peer system where every new user actually added to the computational power of the system, was recently sold for more than $4 billion. As a conceptual model, where can we go, as a society, when we can relate directly - and on a massive scale - to one another? How does the economy of scale provided by the Internet change what communities are - and what they can do?

Rupert Sheldrake has often made a "modest proposal" that 1% of all funding for scientific research be directed towards projects regular people are interested in. But perhaps there are avenues by which civil society may pursue its own goals and projects without mediation, in a self-organizing way.

Can these new models be applied to create new endeavors critical to the survival and well being of the human race in the arts, media, religion, and academia as well as the proven successes in technology?

6.3 The government response; the digital hub and SFI

The failure of Ireland to capitalize on the native talent and choosing instead to plumb for what this author described as "the most horrendous scam I have ever seen" (Wall Street Journal, July 5, 2001) and Science Foundation Ireland is a cautionary tale for other ex-colonies. (Note that since then Anglo-Irish, not to mention Bernie Madoff and subprime, have further eroded this author's innocence) We were never going to be able to compete in low-level software with India and Pakistan; the disastrous and lazy response was to import untenured people from Media Lab as MIT took our money and formally distanced itself from the project. Science Foundation Ireland (SFI) is a colossally expensive attempt to parley blue-sky research into commercial gain without an intervening entrepreneurial ethos and as such is doomed to failure.

Case Study 1: The Digital Hub

Cost ???. The auditor and Comptroller General, John Purcell, could not even hazard a guess at what the eventual cost beyond $200 million or so was going to be. MediaLab alone cost at least $50 million and its promise to raise $130 million by its own devices was soon declared "irrelevant" by its chief operations officer. It certainly never came to pass. When the digital hub body was set up, there was no thinking whatsoever about what the products to emerge were. There seemed to be a focus on covering up after its predecessor organisation Digital Media Development Limited (which once gave the responsible minister and its technical owner less than 24 hours' notice of a meeting).

Let us look at some sections from the Digital hub Bill:

AN BILLE UM GHNI OMHAIREACHT FORBARTHA DON MHOL DIGITEACH, 2002

DIGITAL HUB DEVELOPMENT AGENCY BILL, 2002

Membership of Agency and term of office of members.

[No. 3b of 2002] Development plan.

8 (b) formulate strategies to encourage individuals and enterprises engaged in digital content and related activities to locate in the digital hub;

Comment: This, as we have seen, has been a dreadful failure.

> (2) The Agency shall have all such powers as are necessary or expedient for the performance of its functions.

(7) Where an agreement or arrangement was entered into by Digital Media Development Limited on a date before the establishment day and was entered into in good faith, then the agreement or arrangement, as the case may be, shall have effect and be taken to have had effect when the agreement or arrangement was entered into.

The above fit in well with the ethos of giving its owner less than 24 hours' notice of a meeting. The following is an excerpt from the equally vague SFI bill:

AN BILLE UM FHORBAIRT TIONSCAIL (FONDUIREACHT EOLAIOCHTA EIREANN), 2002

INDUSTRIAL DEVELOPMENT (SCIENCE FOUNDATION IRELAND) BILL, 2002

(2) The Foundation shall have all such powers as are necessary for or incidental to the performance of its functions under this Act.

(3) In this section "strategic areas of scientific endeavour" includes (a) information and communications technologies, (b) biotechnology, and such other areas that concern economic and social benefit, long-term industrial competitiveness as may be prescribed from time to time by the Minister.

The restriction of science to these areas, and lack of reference to the Impact on society, should give pause. Criticism by the chief state Scientist in Ireland, inter alia, focussed on the fiat by which IT and biotech were imposed; he was publicly humiliated and forced to resign shortly afterward. The official reason for his demission, that his was a fictitious "bought" PhD had been well-known for some time so it is possible that he was appointed to this position precisely because they knew they could get rid of him anytime.

So far, this body has spent almost all of its €billions budget, including €11 million to take a photonics research group from the Corning Research Centre in Ipswich that the British had closed. The VC situation in Ireland as I write is close to its worst ever.

6.4 The New Magdalene Laundries: Universities as Corporations

The problem can be stated thus; the lack of intellectual history and an inappropriately competitive zero-sum culture in areas in which the national interest should be in question. In the course of a sequence of decisions related to compensation for those physically and/or sexually abused in state institutions that led to the resignation of Justice Laffoy from the commissions dealing with this matter, the minister for education, Mr. Dempsey, declared open season on students and staff in the universities. As we have seen, this came home to roost in a report on DCU in 2005 that specifically referred to abusive behavior there in precisely the time frame since the minister's set of dictates below, and the 2006 death of a young professor who had undergone an illegal disciplinary procedure. On December 18, 2002, Mr. Dempsey answered a number of questions requiring an interpretation of the 1997 universities act in the Dail. Paul Gogarty TD and others received a consistent line from Mr. Dempsey in this and other Q&A sessions; Irish universities are autonomous and independent, and neither he nor the higher education authority have any direct control over them. Therefore, the universities do not need to account to the people of the state, in whom power is vested by our constitution, as to how they spend taxpayers' money. It is fair to say that the minister continued to give this response to Gogarty, even when confronted with what frankly seemed like egregious behaviour, as the December 18 Dail record shows.

Mr. Dempsey promised the provision of a "code of practice" for the universities, in the context of anxieties expressed by Union of Students of Ireland (Sunday Tribune, June 22, 2003). Whether this would make the 1997 act constitutional even if delivered is of course a moot point. I have described the chain of events elsewhere (2004, 8-13 and on the "tenure' blog: chapter 8 finishes this discussion). Remarkably, in what logicians refer to as a self-referential event, the Dail record stresses the mysterious cancellation of a subject called science and society, the teaching of which is surely the least that universities funded to do science owe us. As it happens, Dempsey's replies are incorrect, as he was advised by the universities to apply section 14 of the act, dealing with academic freedom, to the conduct of universities as a whole, in contradiction of the provisions of the act which allow him to intervene by appointing a high court judge to visit and report on suspect universities.

Dublin City University (DCU), whose independence of the state has been declared to the point where it refuses to disclose its finances to the higher Education authority (HEA), the relevant statutory body, once appointed a high court judge as its chancellor. Its President then accused her publicly of incompetence; she died, prematurely, soon afterward. The behaviour in question by university management is, of course, unspeakable, and yet no action has been taken by the government. Therefore, in this time of deepening debt in Ireland, monies given by the state to the universities are irredeemable, nor do the universities have to account for their use, or for any of their behaviour. We revisit this theme in chapter 8.

Let us focus on what might usefully be done for science, in order to have it serve the public interest. Harold Varmus, the outgoing head of the national institute for health (NIH) in the United States, has recently argued that the current system of academic careerism is itself rather less than perfect for the pursuit of human knowledge. What he recommended for the US is a national science website, in which all state-funded research has to be published in the first instance. As Varmus had the infamous NIH/Institut Pasteur scandal to deal with, wherein both claimed precedence for the discovery of HIV as the cause of AIDs, he should be listened to (Crewdson, 2002). So far there is some compliance with Varmus' suggestion. Ireland is not currently, and never will be a major player in science. The massive sums being invested in such institutions as SFI and MediaLab need to be re-examined in the context of cutbacks to the arts, many of which we are undoubtedly good at, and the disaster where our health services used to be. The last thing we can afford right now is another open wound in the public finances.

6.5 Gigantism and its Discontents: Ireland of the Call Centres

A large percentage of the I.T. jobs that are regularly announced by ministers during the "Celtic Tiger" glory years were in actual fact jobs in call centres. In fact, of 1997's famous bounty, fully 2100 fell into this category (see *Irish Times*, 23/12/97), if one includes related work like claim-processing. These jobs require multi-lingual people to use a small subset of their vocabulary and language skills in order to answer an oft-repeated set of technical support questions. Wages and job satisfaction are low. Employee turnover is high; it is no wonder that this sector has been dubbed "the salt-mines of the computer industry". 1997 seems to be the period when the rot set in; currently, India trains thousands of its citizens to do these jobs working night shifts and affecting names like "John Smith".

At present one of the arguments used by policy-makers to justify the targeting of the teleservices sector is that it gives multinational companies a foot-hold in Ireland and that further inward investment may follow. IBM (who located a new facility in Blanchardstown after a favourable experience with the establishment of a call centre there) was cited as the paradigmatic example here; in May 2005, they decided to locate such a centre in Asia, much to the Taoiseach's displeasure and anxiety.

In fact call centres are probably one of the most mobile forms of industry that exist. A new call centre can be established in a country within months (less than 90 days in IBM's case) and can move on just as quickly. American Airline's call centre in Dublin was established after it decided to shut down 4 smaller call centres based in the U.S. Just as these kinds of organisations can move into this country quickly they can step out again just as fast. With the continuing spread of American culture across the globe, Ireland's position as an English-speaking country where American multinationals would face minimal problems integrating with the local economy/potential workforce is not as valuable a card as it used to be. Increasingly, US managers who have been exposed to Europe are perceiving that "setting up a base in Europe" means setting it up on the Continent and not in some geographically remote English-speaking island. They want to be "at the centre of the action". Furthermore, our poor linguistic skills (even among graduates) further emphasises to foreign companies that we are on "the edge of Europe".

6.6 Some Proposed Solutions

We are now in a stronger position than ever to insist that incoming companies bring in an R+D division to qualify for tax breaks. The occasional spectacular success is insufficient. Moreover, the main thrust of our strategy should be toward encouraging indigenous start-ups, even if what they originally do is outsourcing for multinationals as is often currently the case. In order that a pool of leading edge indigenous software companies is developed, those currently engaged in research in our Universities must be actively encouraged and aided to move their research from the academic laboratory to the industrial one. The only effective way to achieve this is to put in place an agency which actively seeks potential start-up companies and serves as a conduit through which some of the current international trickle of venture and seed capital available for IT sector start-ups may be funnelled into companies which are Irish by birth and therefore more likely to remain. (The alternative, of courses, would be the libertarian move of getting the state completely out of technology. Even that would work better than the current set-up).

O Riain (2004) describes an informal version of benevolent state action that flourished in the 1990's; it needs to be formalised, if possible; if not, the state should simply withdraw completely from this area. As a service to humanity, Ireland could also become *the* open-source nation. To date the government has been short-sighted in that it has sought the employment which the IT industry can support - by attracting multinationals - a strategy which has and will continue to have some adverse consequences; as all short-sighted policies do. Instead we should be concentrating on attracting the venture capital and fostering an ethos of entrepreneurship coupled with innovation: the same eclectic mix which instigated the information revolution in the first place. The addiction to gigantism needs to be gotten rid of; smaller companies famously create more employment, and will certainly stay longer. Finally, like many other EU countries, Ireland has been hindered as much as helped by such EU initiatives as Esprit and Framework. After having brought this to the attention of the officials involved here to no avail, several of us have either given up or pursue our research mainly in North America. This in itself gives pause; we need to take cognizance of the level of funding for scientific research in Ireland versus what the U.S. (or India, through its institute of technology) invests.

Of course, there is a more radical alternative, which is quite simply to refuse to compete in this area at all. The macho restructuring of Irish universities by their presidents looks likely to yield nothing except industrial relations disasters. The economic emergency that they allude to is most of all caused by the negligence of the current government in allowing house prices to rise unimpeded. In the meantime, not a single major new Irish writer or musician has emerged in the decade of so-called boom. The decade to follow of fighting off IMF intervention may be more culturally productive.

Finally, as we have seen, Ireland can define itself as a place for open source ideas. We can start with science, and here is another modest proposal;

6.7 Open Science Ireland

Literally billions of Euro have been spent on science in Ireland over the past decade. This spending is based on two absurd premises. One is that academics used to the privileges of their positions throw all caution to the winds, give up their jobs, and attempt to commercialise discoveries made in the lab; the second is that corporations feel a need to give back. On the contrary, even in the unlikely event of discovery in the kind of hackneyed science favoured by SFI funding, academics will of course hang on to their comfy tenured positions and try and find a middleman. The exploitation of their discoveries will then most likely be handed over to the R&D division of a giant corporation. Experience elsewhere has shown that the taxpayer will end up paying three times for SFI and its cognates; once through the direct taxes used to fund the lavish salaries at universities in Ireland, again for the SFI projects themselves, and finally in royalties exacted by the corporations in any products developed. To add insult to injury, the acting head of SFI responsible for this enormous budget from mid-2006 to early 2007 is someone with no scientific training or commercial experience.

Since 1997, we have had the spectacle of perhaps the least scientifically qualified government cabinet in Europe trumpeting the virtue of science to the Irish public. We are told that gargantuan spending in science is necessary to keep Ireland from the dark ages, and the failure of the policy as attested in a 2005 ESRI report prompts demands for even more spending. The spectacular failure of Medialab is just the tip of the iceberg.

There is another way, one that does justice to the authentic thirst for scientific truth that motivates Irish people as it motivates people all over the world. We are fully aware of the pressure on scientists to publish in narrow fields, and to sign away their copyright to the likes of Pergamon and Elsevier. To adapt Pearse – The fools! They have spent all our money on a forlorn quest to develop new gadgets and left us with the big, interesting questions, the ones that impelled Einstein to say that a human being who has lost the ability to wonder is already half-dead. Let us look at a few such from some of the sciences:

PHYSICS

Do the Copenhagen and ontological interpretations of wave-function breakdown reflect different psychological dispositions, or are they in principle formally distinguishable?

Why is there so little progress to a grand unified theory that string theory is starting to be derided?

BIOLOGY

Why was Darwinian evolutionary theory accepted even before there was a plausible theory of genetics and is this premature acceptance underlying the intelligent design debate?

Does the very limited success of the human genome project imply that we need a new theory of symbol systems in nature, encompassing gene expression all the way to natural language?

COMPUTER SCIENCE

Why can we not parse any complete natural language after a half-century of trying?

Will quantum computing change our notion of computability?

PSYCHOLOGY

Is consciousness best regarded as a property of the cosmos, or an epiphenomenon of mental processing?

Does this also go for emotion?

EDITORIAL POLICY

Openscience Ireland will be peer-reviewed, with reviewers in turn evaluated by their peers in a weighting system before a final decision to publish or not is taken. However, scientists from anywhere who have managed to maintain copyright of their peer-reviewed material can publish it. No copyright transfer to the publishers of Openscience Ireland is countenanced in either case.

An analogous set of considerations for the arts and humanities might include;

Music

Most of the western "classical" repertoire up to Schoenberg; a careful selection after that of musics actually based on some folk knowledge like jazz. Most of other musical cultures seem not to have had a formalist like Schoenberg, and they can be embraced. Avoidance of the crass.

Painting/Sculpture; Dada is here a similar dividing point, and trends like pop art (Warhol etc) can be looked at sociologically, not aesthetically. Impressionism and its aftermath seem to speak most powerfully.

Cinema; It should be noted that this, unlike the other arts, developed in a technology of mechanical reproduction and the trash here is greater

Theater; The demands of the genre means that most everything is valid, to some extent

Architecture; likewise, there are massive demands by the medium and here the "enemy" tends to be more statist/corporatist, whether an Egyptian or communist potentate

Arts and crafts; have nothing that is neither useful nor beautiful.

6.8 Two recent commentators

Garvin (2004) is concerned with establishing how deluded old Ireland was before the onset of technical education and transnational capital. In other words, a country that essentially was debt-free was inferior to one in which personal debt was €315 billion (in 2004; it has now risen enormously) and state debt projected at well over €200 billion, with a current account shortfall of over €20 billion expected every year for the foreseeable future.

Garvin recruits Senator WB Yeats, speaking in 1926, to the cause as one focus of Garvin's book is going to be how vastly superior technical education is to a classical one:

> "For two or three centuries people thought that their various religious systems were more important than the child. In the modern world the tendency is to think of the nation…there is a tendency to subordinate the child to the idea of the nation." (In Garvin, 2004, p. xi)

Garvin ignores the fact that Yeats had recently undergone a conversion to Fascism:

> "Yeats's political speeches of this period are not pleasant reading. On August 2, 1924, he spoke with cautious satisfaction at a public banquet of the curtailment of liberty which he foresaw: We do not believe that war is passing away … a great popular leader (Mussolini) had said to an applauding multitude, 'We will trample upon the decomposing body of the Goddess of Liberty.'" (Ellmann, 1978, p. 248-9)

The subtitle of Garvin's book is "Why was Ireland so poor for so long?" as distinct from "How did Ireland manage to run over a trillion dollars in debt without producing anything that was not there in 1995, destroying its software and music industries, renouncing a historically valid claim on its north-east corner, bringing in a half-million immigrants in a bizarre attempt at multiculturalism, and deluging its populace with pornography?" As a historian, Garvin makes some valid points:

> "The political split of 1921 seriously demoralized Sinn Féin and led to a much-documented but not quite measurable culture of cynicism and disappointment." (p. 4)

Indeed; it could also be argued that the brutality of the Civil War allowed Fianna Fail to posture as anti-establishment even after over a half century in power. The continuing imbroglio over NI allowed it room openly to interfere with the legal process right up to 2002 and, as we will indicate in the final chapter, beyond this.

Garvin (p. 31) correctly points out that the "Irish state was born between 1850 and 1870, when the Catholic Church was reorganized, the Dublin administration was modernized ... and the mass of the population became literate and English-speaking." The Irish revolution unfortunately failed to restructure this state. This thesis is corroborated by Coakley (2008, 29) who argues that, after 1922, "the control bureaucracy continued with little change". Indeed, post the act of Union, 19th century Ireland witnessed a concentration of power in the executive, in the absence of a domestic elected assembly

Garvin's haste to identify the root problem of the putative Irish crisis as educational reaches apotheosis toward the end of his monograph (pp. 210-214). He excoriates Newman;

> "The nation that there were 'high ideas' which had little connection with the mechanical arts is Platonic and aristocratic." (p. 210)

Garvin misses the point entirely; the bubble in Ireland's economy from 1997 to 2007 was almost entirely an artifact of the availability of credit in international financial markets. In actual fact, native tech and manufacturing contracted during this period. While there is nothing as significant in Irish scientific history as Newton and his rivals (described ably in Clark et al, 2001), we have seen that Mac Cnaimhin (1966) did not lack for exemplars of Irish scientific genius. It is is this context that we should read;

> "Here we have the real root of the fatal innocence about science and the link between scientific theory and practical application...which actually shocked the OECD team in the early 1960s." (p. 211)

By his own admission, Garvin is a neophyte in economics and the innocence is his downfall. (Let us acknowledge, also, that the very existence of political "science" is controversial) Practical applications of computing technology typically take a part of civil society like social networking, the humanities Garvin's brave now Ireland is to repudiate, and implements it in systems like Facebook, MySpace, and Youtube.

The remainder of Garvin's argument is equally specious. Above all, he seeks solace in Mancur Olson's work, from the quantitative end of political science. Garvin interprets this as proving that social change may not happen because "free riders" do not participate in the political process, even though it be at their own cost not to do so. However, here as elsewhere, Garvin is naïve; we shall see a much more realistic analysis in David McWilliam's work. Aumann (2000a, p. 35) summarizes;

> "The 'competitive price of a vote' is an idea that appears … in voting for 'non-exclusive' public goods … the 'price of a vote' is next to nothing, and so the vote becomes insignificant."

Aumann gives an example; if a populace is divided into those who prefer public libraries and public TV, there is so little to be gained for voting in state investment in either that it is hardly worth one's while:

> "In a voting game with nonexclusive public goods, each voter will enjoy the public goods eventually produced no matter how he votes. He is a free rider … he sells his vote for whatever it will fetch, producing cutthroat competition which drives its market value down to zero." (Aumann, 2000b, p. 350)

Nonexclusive goods we can also term non-rival resources (2005). This does not at all hold when we are dealing with exclusive resources or "exclusive public goods." What Garvin assumedly meant was the phenomenon of blocking coalitions:

> "In the convention example any coalition with more than one-third of the members is blocking." (Aumann, 200a, p. 31)

There are in fact many results from game theory that apply to Ireland, which has two main parties (now fine Gael and Sinn Fein) and many smaller ones:

> "Let us next consider a parliament with two large parties and many small ones. Suppose, for example, that each of the large parties has one-third of the seats … it would be foolish for the small parties to form a 'common front.'" (ibid, p. 34)

Garvin also fails to mention the many incursions on personal freedom that even the initial healthy economic recovery from 1992 to 1997 was built on; social partnership agreements that effectively neutralized unions; closed shop agreements in the public service with no recourse for a bullied or fired public servant. The clash between individual republican citizens and a corporatist state will surely eventually produce a Kundera-esque literature (with hopefully less controversy than Kundera's alleged spying career excited).

David McWilliams (2006) is perhaps Ireland's most prominent public "intellectual", with a firm hold on the reality that financial realities as pathological as modern Ireland's have created massive cultural shifts. While his book and TV series "The Pope's Children" was subtitled "Ireland's new elite," the reality is that the generation born in the baby boom following the Pope's visit in 1979 is "all grunt, no power. This is most evident in the housing market" (p. 113). The transfer of wealth from young to middle-aged, he argues, is unprecedented (ibid). He comments on a "demographic civil war" wherein "those in their fifties represent only 11% of the population yet they dominate business, the law, the media and politics" (p. 112).

McWilliams book is largely a compilation of his journalism with some connecting text and profundity is not his métier. However, he begins in fevered style with discourse about the expectocracy:

> "The new Irish dream can best be summed up by 'I want to trade up.'"

In many ways, the Irish behave precisely as one would expect from a nouveau colony; 14% of houses have Sony Playstations, and video rental is twice Britain's (ibid). "The ninety-six packages offered to Irish and English punters are exactly the same" (p. 188), and "87% of us admit to drinking a bottle or more of wine on a Friday night" (p. 269).

Though we can take it that the latter figure is nonsense, this statistic is a little more significant as it seems. As McWilliams elsewhere puts it "years ago, the posh entertained at home ... it wasn't in competition with the pub" (p. 268). So dinner parties were for the upwardly mobile, and the rest of us socialized in that great leveler of inequality, the pub. This public space ethos in civil society extended to sports ground terraces, to public promenades, and its apotheosis in the electoral booth was a natural continuation. Unlike in the U.S., and indeed most European countries, kids under ten could stay in pubs, often playing music with musicians 70 years their senior, until midnight. Pub sessions were one of the great preservers of Irish music. One of the reasons for the demise of the socializing nexus that pubs were in the past is quite simply financial; people cannot afford to go out: "Bank of Ireland and AiB make more profit per customer than any bank in Europe" (p. 103). Neither gives anything back, apart from token support of already extant social events. They should have been the first to pay when the squeeze hit.

The Pope's Children, or Kell's Angels as he describes them after the town many miles from Dublin from which many commute are "the first Irish generation for centuries who are able to actually live (sic) in the same country as their parents" (p. 203). Well, no, actually; they too now have to leave. Moreover, in the most profound depths of the economic depressions of the 1970's or 1980's, as now, one could go on the dole, take some casual work, and afford a house in the countryside within a few years. Food and drink were also so cheap that the unemployed had in real terms a higher standard of living than many Kell's angels living in their own country, but at huge alienation from its culture as from themselves as they deal with choked-up roads, crippling mortgages, and a dreadful public health system in a new country that they did not vote for.

McWilliams (p. 203) eventually superimposes some ethical concerns, "the common ground for all these forces is that we are losing some core values that make us Irish." He argues that hope is at hand in resolution of a Classical debate; "the patriot versus cosmopolitan debate has dominated our national thinking since independence." McWilliams, whose German is fluent, makes elementary mistakes in his Gaelic (p. 224), but poignantly asks;

> "When exactly did Irish and reference to Celtic mythology infect the language of business and marketing?" (p. 224).

A precise date is impossible; however, perhaps 65 years after British withdrawal, the forces conserving the music and language began to feel confident enough about their survival to allow their commodification. Around the same time, the Gaelic games association abandoned the ban on their players engaging in soccer and rugby, and for the same reasons. Gaelic ways are returning, as they did post the Norman pyrrhic victory over the Bruces.

McWilliams comments further on these trends:

> "Irish traditional music has never been more popular in the face of massive saturation … pagan Irish names are now de rigeur."

The resurgence of this culture is frankly our best hope for the future in Ireland.

Let us now look at the state's attempted destruction of Irish artistic culture.

CHAPTER SEVEN

AISLING GHEAR/BITTER VISION: THE SECOND IRISH REVOLUTION?

7.1 Et 2, Bono; the destruction of the Irish music industry

Globalization is many things, some of which are beneficial, but we use the word here to point out to a combination of economic neo-liberalism and an insistence on the removal of protectionist measures by sovereign states. Neoliberalism, in turn, is exemplified in the state dedicating itself to creating a market; the EU is a classical neoliberal project in that its primary goal is th creation of a unified market. The word "Neoliberalism" has experienced a semantic shift since it was coined; it now connotes also an economization of life and a financialization of the economy. As a result, billions of people throughout the world currently have their lives compromised by the use of baroque mathematical models in trading houses over the past ten years, with mistakes being made for which we have to pay. That compromises the notion that Neoliberalism is some way a beneficial way to organize society; in Ireland, the Catholic Church did a rather better job when it was in charge. Ireland can do better still.

Paradoxically, in view of the avowed cosmopolitanism of many anti-globalizers, a key weapon used recently by both Malaysia and the United States to counteract globalizing forces like the UN and the World Bank is nationalism.

A cynical take on the Ireland of the past ten years is Orwellian in inspiration; massive levels of debt are viewed as economic success, acquiescence to the most debased impulses of American neocons is viewed as internationalism, and the destruction of the civil society structures that supported the highest achievements of Irish culture is viewed as progress. We have been looking at contemporary Ireland through the prism supplied by these themes. This led us to consider whether there has not been a successful attempt by transnational corporations to adapt the thought-crime ethos of traditional Irish Catholicism to suit their own ends. We consider here a similar period of Irish history, astutely identified by O'Faoláin (1941) as the beginning of globalization, through the eyes of the poetic class dispossessed by the Tudor and Cromwellian settlements. Their humour, defiance and assertion of identity may prove an invaluable resource when the IMF comes to chastise the profligate Irish in the next few years.

This chapter begins with a set of meditations that draws together themes from the previous chapters. As we noted, one of the primary targets of the Bertiestate was the native tech industry; we proceed to discuss another, the native music industry.

Music is and always has been an essential element in Irish republicanism:

> "No revolutionary movement is complete without its poetic expression. If such a movement has caught hold of the imagination of the masses they will seek a vent in song for the aspirations, fears and hopes, the loves and hatreds engendered by the struggle. Until the movement is marked by the joyous, defiant singing of revolutionary songs, it lacks one of the most distinctive marks of a popular revolution movement: it is the dogma of the few and not the faith of the multitude". (James Connolly, 1907; this an be found on the wall of the Starry Plough pub in Berkeley)

The 1916 rebellion was commemorated in many ballads, both good and bad; James Connolly himself inspired at least two great songs. The "Foggy Foggy Dew", previously a love-song, lost one "foggy" to become an elegy for the dead of the rebellion. David Lloyd, in Castle, 2001, writes eloquently about this invention of tradition.

No major Irish group has broken through since 1995, the beginning of the so-called boom. Even minor successes like Damien Rice and the Thrills are the exception that proves the rule in that they moved stateside for success. Remarkably, the supposedly stagnant years of Catholic repression and economic gloom immediately beforehand gave us, in admittedly subjective order of increasing quality, U2, the Cranberries, the Corrs, Sinéad O'Connor, the Pogues, and Moving Hearts, not to mention countless others. (Let us note that U2, whom I personally deplore, are indeed saintly compared to their British competitors, as described in Cole 1992, inter alia)

Perhaps not coincidentally, 1996 was the year that IMRO was given an effective monopoly in Ireland (McCann, 2005). The emphasis in the Irish music business changed to aiding exports of CD's by non-Irish artists, and so Ireland joined the top ten of music exporting countries in the world.

IMRO has facilitated, both explicitly and implicitly, an effective enclosure of the music commons; its connection with Rupert Murdoch through its illegal role in collecting dues for Sky TV gives pause. Musicians who join IMRO are asked to sign an indenture assigning copyright of all their works, past, present, and future, to IMRO. They do not realize that they are giving up ownership; it is highly likely that there is no “meeting of minds” here, and that the assignment is illegal. Venues are effectively fined for putting on live quality music.

IMRO’s lawyers, Matheson Ormsby Prentice, chaired by “Sir” Tony O’Reilly, add to the lack of accountability in IMRO by aggressively attacking musicians who dare question the often illegal re-assignments of copyright that IMRO performs. Ireland’s greatest ethnic musician, Dónal Lunny, said as much as he resigned from the IMRO board after they tried to force him to sign a self-incriminating document. Lunny’s material, 700 of the greatest contemporary pieces of Irish music, are now registered with an American rights agency. Likewise for those of Melanie O’Reilly (www.mistletoemusic.com) and Ireland’s greatest poet, Nuala ní Dhómhnaill. As all this is happening, Ireland’s performance in classical music as in sport is simultaneously deteriorating.

The Irish state has protected IMRO. One of IMRO’s pet bands was the appalling Westlife, whom they funded. In 2003, a police inquiry into IMRO of three years’ duration was mysteriously aborted after IMRO leaked confidential documents from the public prosecutor’s office to O’Reilly’s Sunday Independent. It turned out that the ex-chair of IMRO, a government bagman, was being protected for copyright theft. He has also been in charge of the Irish presence at music trade fairs like Midem through Enterprise Ireland. The state thus colluded with criminals in stealing from what is now a lost generation of Irish musicians; the matter was eventually resolves in a US Federal court, with Ireland’s corporate enforcement head found in the discovery process to have given evidence for the copyright violators, who lost the case,

The loss of Irish music to the world, both by these means and the more direct one of issuing a licence for public domain Celtic/Irish music, is a catastrophe. We may not be as good at swimming and show-jumping as we seem, but music was different up to recently. The state has openly protected criminals also by allowing them violate company law. They are allowed steal from Irish musicians by trading illegally from dissolved companies.

Record Services, a CD distribution company set up by U2's manager Paul McGuinness with others (including, according to Ireland's music mag Hot Press, U2 themselves) is a case in point. Musicians who just put their life savings into a recording give it to Record Services for distribution. When they found they are not getting paid, they made inquiries. Tough luck; the company was dissolved in 2000. However, McGuinness owns a very solvent parent called Rathgordon.

Pour encourager les autres, and faced with a tricky lawsuit in London, U2 invited Bertie Ahern on stage with them in summer, 2005, and then won a victory against their erstwhile stylist in the circuit court in Dublin. Fresh from proving to the Dublin court's satisfaction that he thought of wearing a Stetson all by himself, Bono went back to save the world made shortly after in Live 8. Bono and U2 have always been purely establishment figures in Ireland, as indeed elsewhere, when one looks at their record.

Ahern's persistent and self-admitted interference in the criminal justice system is perhaps the most corrosive current threat to Irish democracy. The Bertiestate applied the rule of law differentially; only dissenters were subject to it.

The next few sections are a snapshot of Ireland, circum 2005. It was the author's last broadcast as there were many complaints about the "politics". Two years later, Bertie suggested that those who criticized his policies should "commit suicide".

7.2 Ireland in the world reprise

The recent revelation that Ireland, an avowedly neutral country, is allowing its airports to be used as refuelling stopovers for planes carrying Guantanamo Bay hostages as for those carrying Iraq occupation troops exemplifies the spirit of a transformed state. In this brief section, we will investigate how acquiescence to the international neoliberal/neoconservative agenda has wounded Irish culture. It is necessary first of all to consider how far the facilitation of the CIA's "rendition" plane, the Boeing 737 with a serial number N313P, diverges from the impetus that caused the creation of the Irish state in the first place.

Ireland's independence came about essentially as a chain-reaction from the decision of the renowned socialist theoretician, James Connolly, to put his theories into practice by starting a revolution in 1916. Had the civil war not happened, it is possible that the nascent Irish state of the 1920s would have been a great deal more radical than it actually was. We might indeed have sustained the alternative legal system that existed during the lifetime of the first Dail and prevented the current embarrassment of wigs, gowns and would-be Rumpoles of the Bailey who cannot say "th" in the 4 courts, the Irish omphalos of jurisprudence.

As it was, the infant Irish state felt confident enough in itself to support the first ever land claim by Native Canadians at the League of Nations and, thirty years later, to sponsor the nuclear non-proliferation treaty. Textbooks were written in Gaelic and many families attempted total revival of the language. With respect to this latter, there is a Seán Og O hAilpín, proud of his heritage, for every Hugo Hamilton.

Fredricksburg was one of the early battles in the American civil war. One of the key engagements was at Marye's heights between a group of confederate Irish and Meagher's regiment for the union side. The Irish slaughtered each other with gusto; until recently, uncompromising physical courage was part of every Irish man's ego ideal. The sequence has been brilliantly staged in Maxwell's film "Gods and Generals". It should perhaps be shown on national TV every time Ireland contemplates joining a military alliance.

In signalling its willingness to join the Iraq war effort, Ireland joined forces with a country whose highest legal officer has authorised torture to be used. In assenting to the EU constitution, it would have buried the last traces of its neutrality. We have never shown much ability at global realpolitik, and the childish hope that conforming to the worst American impulses will somehow make us richer and more modern urgently needs to be re-examined.

7.3 Early 21st century Irish artistic culture; failed gangsta movies, Westlife, and chicklit

As everyone knows, "The Commitments" was an enormous hit both as book and movie. It radically empowered many working-class Dubliners who found their accents, earthy language, and penchant for Anglo-American culture being affirmed worldwide. Since then has come a rather precipitous fall from those dizzy heights. In the mid-90s, someone had the bright idea to examine the lives of the truly earthy and foul-mouthed of Dublin's denizens; the criminals. The result was a set of movies celebrating vicious Dublin criminals that unsurprisingly no-one wanted to see; The General, its Hollywood remake Ordinary Decent Criminal, Veronica Guerin, and so on. Every city has its subworld of filthy sociopaths, and the healthy human reaction is to avoid it. After his ordeal in "Ordinary Decent Criminal", Kevin Spacey wisely went "Beyond the Sea" with Bobby Darin's gentle and meaningful life. Even autobiography has not been spared; Pp 3-5 of Sheridan (1999) has loving descriptions of farts, the author's father doing epically malodorous craps, and grease on the hair.

The last decade has witnessed a remarkable redefinition of official Irish culture in several other art forms. The marriage of our prime minister's daughter to a member of Westlife was in a sense every bit as dynastic as that of Richard II of England to Isabelle of France. A new dispensation is at hand, a system that guarantees the prevention of future Planxties and Thin Lizzies by a glut of government-sponsored boy and girl bands. Our TV screens fill with music represented as sporting events, with Pop Idol type events plugged even more than in the US, and taxes are imposed with the State's blessing on any venue that dares to stage live music by real musicians. The reaction of these real musicians in forming the Musician's Union is to be praised.

Some years ago, a French academic coined the term "auto-exoticism" to refer to Ireland's concept of itself. We sell a very ordinary stout as the national drink; we go like children cap in hand to seek derogations from certain of the provisions of international treaties that we have signed; we produce sub Julie Burchill examinations of the female experience in Anglo-Saxon society and have the temerity to applaud their Irishness. In the meantime, the punitive cost of living insures that many artistically gifted individuals either give up completely or emigrate to countries in which they are accorded some dignity as artists as well as a realistic chance to cover their costs. That a decade of so-called economic boom has done immense damage to certain of the only arts at which Ireland undoubtedly excelled must surely give pause?

7.4 How financial debt became the new repressive Catholicism

In Japan, interest rates were close to zero for more than a decade. We are living in the Golden Age of usury; tons of cash, and utter reluctance by the banks to invest it productively. That is one reason that Irish house prices are so high; foreign banks need more profits. In Japan, the first novels are beginning to appear that examine the effects of debt on the core of the individuals' being. Just as Milan Kundera created scenes whereby the communist state intervened in the relationship between the individual's body and mind, perhaps by the provision of sexual blackmail, so are sensitive Japanese writers examine how inheritable debt shapes the individual. Though as yet we do not have inheritable debt in Ireland, neither do we have bankruptcy protections. Even without Chapter 7 protections, Americans are still much better off than us.

It is possible that we are headed to a new global era in which the struggle against the consequences of debt after the roller-coaster economy of the last quarter-century will be a major cultural theme. We could argue that just as Catholicism taught alienation from one's sexuality, and Buddhism taught alienation from the core of one's subjectivity, the new repression will feature the fear of an indigent life on the streets, forever and ever. Only leaps of faith can save one; the sacrifice of one's bargaining power in the serial union/management partnership agreements, the acceptance that Arthur Griffith's economic nationalism was really about the right to work for transnational corporations, and a final surrender of the will in buying a semi-detached house for five times what one knows it is worth.

James Joyce's revolt against religion and nation, though brilliant in its execution, was no more than the assertion of reason and the goodness of life that had been done in the face of Catholic repression centuries before him. What is unique about our contemporaries' rebellion is that it must be done in the face of facts, or at least the science of economics. Projections show that house prices will grow for ever, that free trade will halt more wars, and indeed that you will end up out on the streets if you do not conform. Facts show that we are no more than a bunch of neurons, so forget about the life of the spirit. It will be interesting to see the holes that free and integrated people find in these arguments.

7.5 Intellectual life; why do the Irish often act against their own best interests?

Politically, the major achievement of the 1997-2007 government, by dint of the impenetrable Good Friday agreement, may be seen to represent acquiescence to the British claim on the North-East of Ireland as somehow conforming to standard republican narratives. Though this has in the short run bought an uneasy peace, it is not what the Irish people voted for. A treaty between two countries should not involve the capacity of one of them to suspend any provisions of the treaty when it wishes to do so, particularly if that provision is the keystone of democracy, a functioning parliament.

Looking at it from the British point of view, it is easy to see the sequence of negotiation and implementation of the agreement as a complete and bloodless victory. The Irish response was to launch a round of internecine political warfare with the scapegoating of Sinn Féin for all the failings of the agreement. It is now evident that the Irish people should have withdrawn from the agreement at the first unilateral suspension of the assembly by the British , and in particular that the Irish state did not have the right to give up a territorial claim on the basis of a treaty that was not going to be honoured. As things stand, the legality of the British action must be formally challenged in an appropriate legal forum.

Yet nobody is talking about this in the frenzy of bloodletting and the cut and thrust of allegation that constitutes our politics. An outgoing European cultural attaché here made the comment that it was the absence of ideas that made Irish politics so boring. It is likewise the absence of a respect for technically accomplished abstract thought that prohibits us from creating appropriate national institutions to reflect the cultural patterns of the finer aspects of what we create as a nation. Likewise, the absence of a respect for norms makes us turn the justice system into a scapegoating system.

So, what can be done? We probably have to wait until the property market officially collapses and recent buyers experience negative equity. Until then, much of the vision of the country - what the French call L'Imaginaire - has been consumed by seeing as infinitely valuable tiny tracts of land in an almost deserted island. This frenzy over, official Irish life may begin to consider issues like citizenship, human rights, and — above all — how to pass bankruptcy legislation that will take the burden of this steroid-puffed economy from the generation under 30

7.6 Magdalenism; the chronic abuse of power in our state institutions

In the recent Irish comedy "Intermission", starring Colin Farrell and Colm Meany, there are numerous scenes where a hapless employee is confronted by a bullying manager, and two where a full-fledged disciplinary procedure, in which the employee is unrepresented either by a lawyer or a union official, ends in a sacking. In our newly secularised country, our often poorly trained human resources staff truly hold the keys of heaven and hell. If one wants to own a house, procreate, or indeed eat and keep any kind of roof over one's head, one better stay on their good side. This is all the more the case due to a little known provision of our great partnership agreements; your colleagues cannot go on strike for you as an individual who just got sacked. Just how and why the unions allowed this violation of basic human rights to take hold surely merits some examination, particularly as management can appeal unfavourable rulings all the way to the Supreme Court, and use state resources to do so in the public sphere, which is the only realm in which there is strong union membership, while the unions refuse to participate in any courts higher than the Circuit court for these cases,

In any case, the general Irish impulse that gave us the Magdalene laundries seems alive and well. We have seen that the 1997 Universities act has been interpreted in the Dáil as allowing University managements to do anything they want to staff and students. As none of our universities is accredited by international standards, and as they are in general fifth-rate, this is dangerous indeed. So what must be done?

First of all, we need to reconsider the role of the state itself. The partnership agreements are perhaps a paradigmatic example of a inappropriate extension of the state into organised labour, a crucial part of civil society. It is easy indeed for union officials who compromise with management to find jobs on state boards. What we in Ireland must do is radically reconsider the role of the state. Given the rampant corruption and economic incompetence that has characterised the Irish state, it is meet to start the ball rolling with one question. Would we really have been worse off since 1920 under rule from England, where a great number of Irish people live in any case?

7.7 Aisling Ghéar; the poetic response to the Tudors and Cromwell

We define globalization for the purposes of this book as a claim-jump by economic interests on the resources and apparatus of diverse countries. One predictable consequence of this, felt very directly and expressed very articulately by the dispossessed Gaelic poets, is a stripping away of all privileges accorded to artists working in an ethnic genre. Of course, 17th century Ireland was hardly going to look like a modern nation-state even without the Tudor conquests, but as the poets themselves found out, if they neglected to define themselves as Irish, the invader would do that for them. The occasional attempt to ingratiate themselves with their new English lords by, for example, celebrating a cattle-raid on Shane O Neill fell on deaf ears. The less extreme case of Aodhán O Rathaille is more typical. He praised a local planter named Warner thus:

"Ceannasach séimh glan sughach
Do bhí san mbaile gheal aosta chlamhail
Flaith nar bh'fann roimh dheoraidhe"

Warner's wisdom and hospitality is praised. On the other hand biting satire is apparent in "Amhráin Sheagháin Chláraigh mhic Dhómhnaill" on the death of Colonel Dawson of Aherlow and Daithí O Bruadair's broadside is vicious:

"Gach ardmhac uabhair uasamh agus
Do dháil i mbuaidh's I n-uanaibh geala a ghnaoi
Geadh lanfhada uaidh sean
Luascadh a dhearc dom dhroim
Ar sráid da thuar is luath mo hata díom."

Even the feel of their glare on his back is excoriated. There is an awareness of the massive environmental changes being wrought also in such poems as "Seán O Dhuibhir an Ghleanna". The technical mastery of the music in this song indicates the culmination of the tradition that Geraldus Cambriensis, against his own deepest impulses, so admired. O Rathaille, snubbed and humiliated by his historical patrons, the Brown family, began the poetic tradition of the personification of Ireland as a woman waiting chastely for her redeemer, in the poem “Mac an Cheannaí”, which supplied a template for, inter alia, “The Bold Fenian Men”.

O Rathaille and O Bruadair targeted the new Seánin (little John) class of his time, jumped up acolytes to the new masters. Like all truly egregious theft, the dispossession needed a strong legal framework to support it, beginning with the notorious “Tanistry” case. O Rathaille brilliantly and hilariously parodied the pompous style of these writs in his “Whereas” poems which sparked a genre. These macaronic poems, which are parodic legal writs, juxtapose the punitive and self-serving mannerisms of English legal fiat with mocking Gaelic text (see O Tuama et al. Eds. 1981, pp. 146-149).

It may be a human universal to eschatologize after military defeat. Native North Americans did so with their "Ghost Dance"; the German romantic philosophers like Hegel, Schelling and Schiller produced similar spiral views of history that, it can be argued, arose from the German experience of military defeat at the hands of the French. In Ireland, the poets like Piaras Mac Gearailt rendered verses that are almost Koranic. Nature itself is seen as in revolution while Ireland awaits its Caesar:

> "Tá lasadh sa gréin gach lá go neoin
> Ní taise don ré, ni théann faoi néall."

Thus, Isaiah-like, both sun and moon shine continually in the song "Rosc Catha na Mumhan". "Róisín Dubh", translated in spirited style by James Clarence Mangan, Ireland's poet maudit, is similar in intent to "Mac an Cheannaí":

> "Da mbeadh seisreach agam do threabhainn in aghaidh na gnoc
> 'S dheantainn soisgheal i lar an Aifrinn dom Róisín Dhubh
> Bhearfainn pog don chailin og a bhearfaidh a h-oige dhom
> 'S dheanfainn cleas ar chul an leasa dom le mo Róisín Dhubh".

The poet would blaspheme at mass by preaching his own gospel about his Dark Rosaleen. Roisin Dubh, when processed through the psyche of the 19th century poete maudit and Trinity librarian James Clarence Mangan, becomes transformed:

> "The Erne shall run with redundance of blood
> The earth shall rock beneath our tread" ...

The redeemer, when he came, was a disappointment. It is the bad fortune of many who seek a Messiah to find one. Brendán O Buachalla's massive "Aisling Ghéar" studies the precise effect of the vision poem on Jacobitism. The Jacobite parliament of 1689, it became clear, would not rescind Poyning's Law, and Ireland was to remain subject to the crown, if not to the English Parliament. Though Old English and some Gaelic Catholics were reinstated, the plan merely was for a different oligarchy.

It would be foolish to understate the brutality of the Cromwellian campaign. The massacres are an exemplification; however, the massive deportation of Irish children to work on sugar plantations, and perhaps much worse, in the West Indies is well documented. It is very much to the credit of O Rathaille and his contemporaries that they rose to satire. They did so, of course, outside any received structures of the state, and that emphasis on civil society is a leitmotif of current anti-neo-liberalism.

Indeed, it could be argued that the major current contribution of Ireland to world culture derives from precisely the ability to preserve relatively sophisticated forms of culture, from whatever origin, in civil society, safe from any arm of State. "Irish" reels are, for example, very often Scottish; the "Lads of Laois" is actually the "Lads of Leith" (the port of Edinburgh). "Irish" dancing is influenced hugely by other forms, including French. Yet institutions arose, like the Irish music session, which have proven resilient enough to modernity to flourish. Paradoxically then, the major threat to these forms would be an Irish state which has assimilated them and abuses them. It is with great regret that we will demonstrate later that this is in fact the case.

7.7.1 Joyce's Hibernian home project

Ulysses is deeply confusing for many new readers. There are lists, logical nonsequiturs, and many breaks with the novelistic tradition. This is all quite deliberate; part of Joyce's project is to subvert the linearity of the novel, and its correlate in classical epistemology, as we saw in chapter 2. His work is often more akin to Talmudic writing and uses the Irish trope of dindsenachas:

> "the most improbable stories in early Irish literature have topographical precision". (Tymoczko, 1994, 156)

But there is a deeper level;

> "In Portrait (of the artist), the esthetic emotion... is therefore static. The mind is arrested and raised above desire and loathing" (Tymoczko, 1994, 205).

This can be recognised as the beginning of his later interest in the pure awareness of Advaita. Again, Joyce is after very big game indeed;

> "Through his mythic architectonics...Joyce offers his observations about Ireland...for the mind is seized, arrested by eternal verities about Ireland...and in fact life in general" (ibid.)

The architectonics have mysteriously been missed by many critics:

> "most of the links between Ulysses and Irish literature are elementary" (ibid., 2). In fact, "neither Gilbert nor his successors could see the significance of the information Joyce had provided" (ibid. 12)

Nor was Joyce trying to be provincial:

> "Joyce's use of the Irish framework from the 'Book of invasions' is part and parcel of his insistence that Ireland must be European if Ireland is to be renewed" (50)

And so, using tropes from that book, Bloom is Jewish, echoing the notion in mediaeval Irish thought as the Irish as the lost tribe of Israel; Molly comes from Spain, and so on. Molly is also the Sovereignty:

> "The most distinctive Irish goddess is the sovereignty ...with the rightful kiss was thought to result in the fertility and prosperity of the land" (96-97).

Joyce also uses the Voyage of Bran in Penelope (218-220). a description of Ireland coming from the voyage of Bran:

> "a beautiful land where music and poetry are in the air, where love and sexuality exist without sin, where sectarian differences cause no conflict" (328)

We discussed above Joyce's take on consciousness, and its interrelation with the postcolonial, poststructuralist interpretation of Descartes. We can be said, yet again, to be attempting to be contemporaries of Joyce. Ireland is not a possession for us, not to be apprehended through focal consciousness a la the citizen. It is to be lived in, exulted in, enjoyed, in a way that transcends classical western epistemologies. Joyce can be read as an articulate and brilliant synthesizer of his Irish literary predecessors, and a writer of the modern colonial dispossession. And yet even all this may be just scratching the surface.

While the workaday implications of Bloom's peregrinations have been worked perhaps to death, more fundamental themes are perhaps thus discernible in Joyce. For example, the attack on coloniality may be perceived as being mediated through an attack on space and time itself, particularly after the "Nighttown" episode. On a more prosaic level, the occasional cartographic inaccuracies in Ulysses may perhaps be a reaction to the ordinance survey.

Yet the attack in Joyce's last two great works may be more fundamental still. The Citizen in "Cyclops" is secure in his identity as coextensive to, and identical with, the island of Ireland. After Nighttown, it can perhaps be argued that this distinction of subject and object will no longer be possible. In fact, a new way of experiencing Ireland is being proposed; one that counters classical western epistemological tenets. And so, the Bhagavad gita is evoked in lined like "I am the dreamery creamery butter"

Yet many will recognise this as referring also to the song of Amergin. So was Joseph Campbell correct in finding tantric echoes in the Wake? Or is the material linking Joyce to the medieval Gaelic sagas mere fantasy? The answers would seem to be "Yes" and "No".

7.8 Case Study; the attempted privatisation of Irish Music

Proceedings from the Senate, the Irish upper House, on June 18, 1998:

Coghlan "While I know the Minister of State means well, he must safeguard those who are in the right and that, of course, is what he intends to do. I was heartened by the eloquent contribution of Senator Ó Murchú. I am delighted he is here as a safe and loyal custodian of that tradition and those rights. He is a careful watchdog and I salute his success in standing up to IMRO (the Irish Music Rights Organisation)"

"This discussion reminds me of the debate on biodiversity and the way many large food, technology and chemical companies in the northern hemisphere are appropriating rights to natural materials, substances and properties which have been used in many countries in the southern hemisphere for generations. We are aware of the difficulties presented by that issue. The appropriation of traditional music is an analogous matter. I do not want a situation where we must try to undo damage to traditional music similar to the type of damage that is being done to traditional peoples in Africa, Asia and Latin America under patenting and copyright legislation. It is a salutary lesson. I thank the Minister for his attention to the remarks made about this matter. I urge him to engage without delay in contacts with the performance rights organisation and to consult Members before the next Bill is introduced."

Ms. Cox: "The law is there to protect people who are right. No one who is doing something within the law will be prosecuted. The Bill is an attempt to protect the intellectual property rights of the people who are entitled to that protection."

Mr. Mooney: "This is not a debate about IMRO versus Comhaltas Ceoltóirí Éireann or traditional musicians. The comments expressed have nothing to do with this. It is most unfair to all the legitimate and genuine composers and publishers who have attempted to make a living in Ireland to suggest that the actions of IMRO on behalf of its members are tainted to any degree. Senator Gallagher's suggestion that there is a link between biodiversity policies in Africa and intellectual property rights in Ireland is a quantum leap of gigantic proportions."

Labhras O Murchu

"*Earlier I quoted three cases regarding IMRO. They have not been retracted, there has been no apology and they are a matter of record. I restate them for the record of the House. Fleadh Cheoil na hÉireann, the national festival of Irish traditional music, received a demand virtually seeking a licence for playing that music, as did our two cultural centres in Counties Meath and Clare. That was the thin end of the wedge. We made it clear to IMRO that if it wished to create a battleground we would resist it vigorously. That was the only reason IMRO backed off. We cannot ignore the facts*".

Remarkably, the recent Hollywood blockbuster "PS I love you" (based on a book "written" by the prime minister's daughter, and funded massively by the Irish state) showed some of the first fruits of this privatization. The Scottish piper Robert white claimed to have written the late Clare piper Willie Clancy's "The South wind", which he plays in the movie. A glimpse at his website reveals this is no accident; he lists Clancy as one of his influences.

In "The New Rulers of the World", John Pilger argues that current states are essentially tools of corporate interests. Though this may be an overstatement, the fact remains that the most effective responses to globalization outside raw nationalism have sought refuge in civil society. Battling the police in Seattle and Genoa was brave, but creating Linux was more effective. Setting up a "Smack a Spice Girl" website sends a message about the crass commercialization of music, but running a jazz club without state subsidy makes a difference. The annual protests at UC Berkeley ritualize previous victories over corporate takeover of education, but setting up truly independent colleges and scientific websites pre-empt the possibility that all human intellectual culture be subverted for commercial gain.

We have already witnessed proceedings from the Seanad of Ireland in 1998. O Murchu secretly signed the very document that he is praised here for rejecting as described in Anthony McCann's (2005) Ph.D. thesis and weblog (beyondthecommons.org). As leader of Comhalltas Ceoltoiri Eireann, then, O Murchú set a precedent in allowing the private company IMRO to issue a licence for the performance of Irish traditional music. As much of this music is not in fact Irish in origin, this is a truly international cultural problem. Perhaps a dozen questions were asked in the Dail about this and related breaches of copyright and company law; It is clear that the rule of law does not apply to culture objectified as IP, if what has become a permanent government decrees otherwise.

Therefore, Ireland may achieve the ultimate victory of globalization; a debasement of an authentic national impulse in favour of neo-liberalism. We can perhaps expect a cultural desert, as O Rathaille's Seanin class continue in perpetuo as the ruling class. We re-examine some of these themes, including the attempted privatization of public domain music, in the next chapter.

7.9 Conclusions and tentative prognostications

The Irish economy, per unit of gross national income per capita (GNIPC), borrowed the equivalent of the entire American personal debt mountain every 7 months or so from 2004 until its effective collapse in 2008. The US worried about a $2.1 trillion total personal debt; the Irish, with an economy about one hundredth the size, borrow more than this gnipc almost twice a year, and this is going up about 25% a month. The collapse of the Irish economy is no longer in question; the only issues that remain relate to precisely how severe this collapse is going to be, and what sector will suffer the most.

One likely scenario is the Argentinean one, where the currency was pegged to that of a foreign country. In that circumstance, the banks were allowed to export money, and personal savings evaporated. We have seen that one possible escape is through passing the debt burden on to the banks by the introduction in Ireland of the chapter 7 type bankruptcy legislation which the Bush administration, under pressure from financial institutions, rescinded. This could of course cause Ireland's expulsion from the WTO, and on the face of things looks like a highly unlikely turn of events. However, the country is running out of wriggle room, and let us not forget the progress from the greasy till to terrible beauties being born is a very short space of years.

Aung San Suu Kyi, scholar of Burmese history, successful democratic politician, political activist and Nobel peace laureate, speaks of the positive influence that Irish home rulers had on Burmese Nationalism. For long historical periods, the Irish have been colonial dupes as much as rebels. Yet the examples of the Rossport Five, the Tara Skryne campaign, the musicians' union, and the successful campaign against e-voting and removal of tenure we have come across in this book all give hope that Aung's faith in the Irish is not misplaced, a hope incarnated in her 2012 visit to Dublin.

The ineptitude of the neo-liberal/neo-conservative 1997-2007 government in imitating the Queen of Tarts by imprisoning and firing dissenters summarily has actually helped stoke protest. Mary Kelly, a middle-aged mother, beat on a US warplane at Shannon airport and was subjected to the rigors of the Irish criminal justice system. She is now a convicted felon for attempting to save the lives of innocent Iraqis.

Revolution is for the moment primarily personal or postmodern (to use that hackneyed term); full political expression will come later. The Open Source free software movement, extended to media, politics, medicine, literature, and much else means that there is much food for the body and soul available free of charge in the commons. One can live a full creative life with minimal participation in the debtor's prison that the Irish state has become.

Real political change, as distinct from the election of a powerless supposedly social democratic government, requires a true national movement, one that would inspire the world as Aung and her peers were inspired to liberate themselves. Such a movement would make explicit what is an unspoken in our contemporary Irish psyche; the immense personal debt has the ontological status of the sin idea that the Catholic Church used to imprison the Irish. (The argument of this book is that the impetus of the "nation" concept may be sufficient to relegate the debt to the realm of the theological). Insofar as a person has overspent, she should be allowed bankruptcy protection. Insofar as, initially at least, the debt is owed by Irish people to Irish banks for Irish houses built on Irish land, it is an issue that the state can with good conscience encroach on.

The dictator Fidel Castro is aware of the joke that lauds the three victories of his revolution, health, education, and sport and adds the three failures; breakfast, dinner, and tea. Yet Cuba scores highly on many indices of human development; the outgoing President of the World Bank praised its achievements in health and education. Cuba has 2% of Latin American's population and 11% of its higher-level students. Without, in any way sacrificing its democracy, Ireland can build a much more decent life for its people. If Cuba can run parallel national and convertible peso systems, so can the far more technologically advanced Ireland. If Cuba can allow the dollars and Euro as well as a native currency, so can Ireland.

The alternative is the continued debasement of national culture. While one can as an individual still live a decent life in Ireland due to the 2004 victory over the coup plot, the country is still politically dominated by real estate interest and bank interest. It will remain so regardless of which parties are in government, rather than in power, post 2009. Cry, the dear land!

CHAPTER EIGHT

MANIFESTO FOR A NEW IRELAND: ACTIONS REQUIRED

8.1 Introduction

This book began with two cautionary tales; a further two, echoes from my own experience, in which the state, putting it rather gently, played a morally ambivalent role formed many of this author's views. Specifically, the attack on academic tenure in Ireland – described below - and the destruction of the native music industry, which Melanie O'Reilly discusses in the "Ireland in crisis" conference proceedings (in preparation) had a devastating effect on my life. The incidents have served to allow several of us to preserve a certain distance and intensity of alienation from the Irish state. A short meditation on the legacy of P. "Bertie" Ahern follows. We then come to a set of prescriptions for how Ireland can be returned to something like a natural shape.

That particularly Irish experience labeled by the great Breandán Ó hEithir "a slow swim in a sewer" in the past has been exemplified, perhaps, by the Patrick Kavanagh libel trial, where a lyric poet/acid social commentator was forced for nearly a week on the witness stand to justify rhetoric in the language of the pedant, and pay for poetic metaphor in the coinage of the drudge (Walsh, 2010). The poet, Patrick Kavanagh, collapsed during the trial, and underwent cancer surgery immediately afterward. His persecutor, John A Costello, then became Prime minister. A further example was the De Valera family's campaign to turn their Irish Press newspaper company into hard cash, at the huge cost of losing a daily Irish newspaper (O'Brien, 2001)

The end-point proposed is one in which the Irish people live in harmony with their land with a lifestyle that is sustainable in financial, political, social, and environmental terms. The surrender to globalized corporatism which quickened since 1997 has resulted in disaster. It would seem to be the case that a state that would nationalize its natural resources and assert a national currency ring-fenced from the roulette wheel of the international financial markets, would be more stable. Throughout this book are diverse proposals about how to implement this, including an only partially convertible local currency for real estate. Above all, Ireland needs to establish more social equality, without an absurdly overpaid public sector, and real opportunity for Irish people of initiative.

The more radical proposals here may themselves seem anodyne in the context of the upheavals of the second decade of the 21st century. This book anticipates a dance macabre as the previously monolithic Irish establishment fragments into mutually antagonistic interest groups. It is now clear that the task of the unions will have to change from suppressing workers' rights and accepting government largesse to fighting for rights. In the process, a new breed of union leader will emerge.

At a guess, the state's GDP will contract until 2015 if the IMF/ECB rule is continued. While this will involve attenuation of some essential services, an 80:20 rule will hold. Essentially, cut state funding by 80% for 20% decrease in services. There are many state institutions, like SFI and the HEA, whose total demise would be salutary and far superior civil society mechanisms would take their place immediately.

Unemployment will continue at epidemic levels well after 2014, the end of the "troika" period and probably beyond; those irredentists who argued that the creation of the Irish statelet was simply a device to continue the British genocide of the Irish are finally being vindicated, as tens of thousands of clearly unhappy young Irish are emigrating, to have their Irish homes occupied by foreigners. In Berkeley, the visiting young Irish have caused a change in the city codes to prevent their "parties"; Perth, Australia, has issued similar fatwas. Costs in Ireland are simply far too high, and the euro prohibits inflating one's way out of a recession, or devaluing against the pound. Decreasing salaries is inevitable, and this will start in the public sector, initially causing much industrial unrest, including the first real strikes for decades. To repeat; real union leaders may even emerge in the private sector.

NAMA involves taxpayer guarantee of the banks. Yet property prices need to decrease, particularly in the commercial sector. This will decrease the value of NAMA's assets, and this dread momentum is inexorable. Given the dynamics that exist, radical solutions will increasingly become respectable.

For example, perhaps we should leave the euro, after allowing euro holders to take their money out, if they wish. The catch; the state will insist that they change it back into the local currency at an exchange rate it sets in order to buy property. In conjunction, renege on foreign debt, making a once-off offer, and nationalize all natural resources.

On the highest level, what is in question here is a battle for the Irish state. The current crisis is of sufficient urgency to facilitate a new vision, one that allows Ireland contribute the lessons from its ancient culture and colonial past to the world. Paradoxically, it is unlikely that Ireland could ever have been wrested from the current set of corporatist criminals who govern it without the freezing of the international money markets in 2008.

Allowing the Irish state to attenuate to the point that it largely consists of simple and inexpensive mechanisms to assert the rule of law (or even better, real justice) is by no means worse than the alternatives its people are about to experience. It may be less traumatic to do this quickly rather than allow a potentially bloody decade as people's material expectations forcibly are lowered. That constitutes the main argument of section 8.1. Let's first have an interlude

Interlude; Toes in the sewer; a devout meditation in memory of P. "Bertie" Ahern

A devout meditation on P. "Bertie" Ahern follows the classic work on Eichmann by Thomas Merton, where he points out that the Israeli psychiatrists who examined him indeed pronounced Eichmann sane; it is the anti-war contingent who probably would fail a sanity test. Ahern is a profoundly important figure, if unconsciously so; he followed Reagan in reflecting a dark urge within his country's body politic with great agility as circumstances changed. Being empty and uneducated helped both men; the only book Ahern pretended to show engagement with was Putnam's antinomial treatment of civil society. For Ahern, " civil society " was initially about being polite and occasionally finishing a sentence; when its political ramifications were pointed out to him , he used it to restrict those aspects of Irish society beyond state control (and thus his party's control, following De Valera) to Gaelic Athletics, the Church and soccer. (He would interfere from time to time with all three).

It is argued here that Ahern represents the end of the 26-county Irish state in very many senses. Economically, he further integrated the state into the casino that is third millennium globalized corporatism, and presided over the running up of insurmountable levels of personal and later state debt. All this from the standing start of his election in 1997, with sound public and private finances. In the meantime, he and his cronies profited hugely.

Culturally, he followed the path trailblazed by the mid-twentieth century FBI's campaign against Pete Seeger et al in attacking the folk music industry and, incidentally, destroying the native rock industry. Again, his own intimates flourished; in particular, both his daughters became pop icons, one benefiting from Murdoch's famed largesse in awarding book contracts to the influential and the other, after a rather feeble attempt at becoming a pop star, marrying a decidedly manufactured one. With the decision to plough ahead with the destruction of Tara/Skryne, perhaps the most mythologically resonant site in neolithic history, Ahern revealed his links with the neocon plans for declaring year zero in Iraq with the destruction of its heritage therefore inevitable.

Industrially, Ahern managed to destroy much of Ireland's native technology, with a truly deranged project involving MIT Medialab rejects failing abysmally. The attempt to set up a native science authority (Science Foundation Ireland) headed up by a refugee from Biosphere 2 resulted in further monies being thrown at already overpaid university staff who, in their infinitely polite manner, thanked him and continued in their cosseted existences with nary a penny or moment of their own being risked. Future heads were to include, in 2006, an academic with neither scientific training nor industrial experience; in the meantime, a chief science advisor to the nation was found to have a bought Ph.D. It is fair to label this initiative "Biosphere Dublin".

At the end of the Ahern era Ireland was part of the Lisbon EU, a cosignatory of the Good Friday agreement and everything suggested by the WTO; Bertie never saw an international treaty he didn't like. Only mass protest prevented his entry into the Iraq war; he did not fear special rendition. Finally, before becoming PM, he sold off all Ireland's fossil fuel resources for a song to multinationals in a deal which still confounds any objective observation.

Yet none of these achievements approach, in the inversion of their logic as in the damage to the health of the state, his retellings of the nationalist republican and religious narratives, consideration of reinstating which will conclude this book. Some biographical details are relevant. Ahern's father Con was the last irredentist to be released in the southern province of Munster in 1924; 27 years later P "Bertie" came into this world. Certain tensions between father and son were relieved somewhat by Bertie's friendship with a Mr Holohan of 1 Glenarm ave, Drumcondra, Dublin, father of the composer Michael, and secretary of the local political "cumann". Bertie learned his psephology from this master; while his later claim to have had accountancy training is of course less than truthful, he did indeed learn what a pie chart is, and how to get elected.

To further explain that Ahern senior eventually landed a plum job as the gardener at the Catholic "All Hallows" seminary would be a cheap shot, perhaps, were it not for the fact that Bertie named the house whose purchase destroyed him "All Hallows". The family lived in northside Dublin, where criminality is not unknown, as the novels of Roddy Doyle - himself like Bertie from the petit bourgeois class there - celebrate.

So we end with a young man immersed in the twin narratives of Irish nationalism and very possibly enduring rather painful renditions of them before he fled away to his substitute father, His other main outlet was soccer; his lack of engagement with any of the pillars of Irish culture – sport, language, music, history - is rather famous, as his is lack of a university education, despite his claims to the contrary.

And extremely convenient, as it turns out. To be innocent of Locke, Rousseau, the French and American revolutions, and the enlightenment allows the notion of republicanism to be cashed out simply as the fact that he and his cronies, who lived close to the graves of Irish republicans, were doing well financially. Furthermore, he could claim genetic republicanism down the Y chromosome. In fact, he could begin to regard "Irishness' as a franchise to be handed out by him and his cronies; the rest of us were enemies of the state. Surely it is significant that, in his swansong appearance in front of US Congress, he brought over as his retinue some "developers' and party hacks (who proceeded to misbehave in egregious fashion at the hotel, causing a secret service visit) with nary a poet or other cultural icon in sight?

Consequently, it is not at all surprising that he could spent his last two days in office opening a centre to celebrate the Anglo-Dutch victory over the combined French and Irish at the Battle of the Boyne, not forty miles from his desecrations at Tara, and then visiting the graves of the dead of 1916 in Arbour hill. What he learned from his father and Mr Holohan, perhaps, was rather simple; as long as Fine Gael, who had imprisoned his father, were out of office, the eschaton of Irish republicanism had been reached.

Indeed, the truly cynical would see a rather darker dynamic. The IRA ceasefire of 1997 was landed in Bertie's lap as he entered office; all was already over but the shouting. Bertie's achievement was to integrate succumbing to British interpretation of the 1998 “Good Friday” agreement, and eventually succumbing to British interpretation of the whole sweep of Irish history, as part of the “republican” narrative of his party, Fianna Fail. To say that this would be inconceivable to the real founder of Fianna fail, the hunger-striker-unto-death Terence MacSwiney, would be quite an understatement. Indeed, neither MacSwiney's sisters nor his wife were able to accept, even in their everyday business dealings, the existence of a partitionist Irish state.

Yet Bertie was able, masterfully, to declare crises in the “peace process” at will whenever, as in 2006, his utterly dishonest financial dealings came to light. The solution to the crisis was always to make Ireland just a little more British; a close election could indeed be won by a well-timed invite to address the Houses of Commons and Lords; British studies at home and internationally started to receive Irish taxpayers' money to reinterpret Irish history. Bertie's republicanism, for reasons that should by now be clear, remained unshaken through all this. (That Gerry Adam's also remained unmoved is a similar story, which this writer does not want to spoil; however, think of Gerry as Ireland's Condoleeza Rice, about a tenth as clever as he thinks he is, to orient yourself).

This interpretation can be applied also to Bertie's Catholicism. To continue to receive communion while living publicly in adultery invites three interpretations;

1. Bertie remained chaste with this woman, to whom he diverted so many national, personal, and party resources;
2. He is a breathtaking moral hypocrite;
3. He reconstructs all these moral dilemmas into simply what suits him.

As an individual Bertie was of course entitled to take option 3; as a prime minister, it is one of the reasons that under his leadership – or, better put, lack thereof – the country squandered all its moral resources, as well as political, artistic, and financial.

So Brian Cowen would now appeal to a republican ethos that has been attenuated close to non-existence; call on a tech sector that did not exist any longer; and, finally, perhaps seek Keynesian solutions at a time when the tax take was near equal to personal borrowing. Only when the evictions start would the people wake up; conveniently, it was found in 2009 that a legal loophole prevented most evictions.

8.2 Manifesto for a new Ireland; a plan for action

8.2.1 The status quo

It is surely self-evident that a state should exist for the welfare of its citizens. The U.S. A. uncontroversially identifies this welfare with "life, liberty and the pursuit of happiness". The Irish state now exists apparently to serve neoliberal ideals, even if this service can be performed only at the cost of its citizens. As this service continues, EU policy dictates that an economic depression will in turn continue to tighten its grip on Ireland as all liquidity in the state is to be used to pay down debt that has for the most part been imposed in the country in a way that stretches conventional financial practice beyond breaking point.

These neoliberal ideals have been extended to justify an attack on many ancient and well-functioning aspects of Irish civil society. For example, EU competition law was used, with the collusion of the head of Ireland's largest union, to prevent musicians from negotiating a living wage for their services through their own union. Ireland is by some accounts the most regulated country in the world, making it a nightmare for anyone outside the elite (who continue to enjoy impunity) to set up a profitable business. In fact, this state's policies are simultaneously causing Irish citizens to emigrate to find work and increasing the number of non-Irish at work in Ireland. The attack on the culture has forever prevented proper excavation of the huge monument surrounding Tara, while native industries like the music business are clearly suffering as young people consequently suffer a state-imposed identity crisis.

A century ago, Durkheim completed his landmark work on alienation and suicide. Remarkably, he comments on the Irish low suicide rate; the life of a peasant was miserable, but clearly it did not cause him to bring the moment to its crisis. That is no longer the case, as the possibility of "family annihilators" aka "going postal" has become a real one with a rate exceeding that in the USA as the state presses further for the magic of "individualization".

Yet the changes being sought in Irish society by the state were greater still, and only stiff resistance stopped them. Electronic voting was clearly drawn up in a way designed to destroy democracy, and was abandoned only after fierce struggle. I have written about this in Californian Progress Report. (In fact, it may be the case that Sinn Fein were invited into southern Irish politics only because it was thought e-voting could control them). Given the Prime Minister's wish that academics who disagreed with him like Morgan Kelly, an economist at UCD, should "commit suicide", the attack on academic freedom discussed below - fought off only with great sacrifice by a few academics tarnished and targeted by the state – now looks sinister in the extreme, particularly as it was combined with increasing business incursion into the universities. The great reservoir of human culture that is called "Irish" music (involving both English and Scottish components) was privatized in 1998, and the legal status of this has not been challenged.

In fact, the Ahern era manifested a much more complex process of state encroachment than most realize. Essentially, the mechanism involved first padding the public service with functionaries without a discernible function; a classic example is the health service, where the job of allocating beds, heretofore 30 minutes each day for senior medical staff, was assigned to a triumvirate of full-time admin. More warm bodies – in the offices if not the hospital beds where they seem to grow cold with alarming speed- strengthens the state. More regulatory agents to check whether a farmer driving home along a deserted road has had more than one pint, likewise adds to the state's power; the unions were co-opted as a mechanism to ensure that state salaries are now, along with the debt, an insurmountable burden for the producers in the society.

Along with neoliberalism, the state preaches what is essentially moral nihilism. Its unwillingness to prosecute its own, and the hangers-on in the self-appointed elite, has meant that it consistently wears a scarlet letter. To cater for the existence of a moral sense, it takes on board every "liberal" notion current in world affairs, be it gay marriage, "multiculturalism", or the worst of pop culture, and gives it the imprimatur of an institution that claims charter from moral giants like Terence MacSwiney. While entities like gay marriage and "multiculturalism" might have a different resonance in Berkeley, involving ineluctable personal freedom, in Ireland they have simply been used as tools further to entrench a self-designated elite/intelligentsia by legitimating them as somehow possessed of an international perspective – however much the evidence suggests otherwise.

Even the above is mild compared to what was revealed by the crash of 2008; to adapt Warren Buffet, we finally got to see who was naked. It is clear that a massive transfer of funds had been implemented, overnight billionaires had been minted, and - for reasons that have never been made clear – the international financiers who bet on these would-be masters of the universe did not have to worry in the slightest, as it is clear that a deal had been done that the default was for the citizenry to pay them back.

Ironically, therein lies the opportunity. While the state can keep going for a few years on an ECB life-support machine, it can do so only by selling the family silver, and imposing further cuts on essential services. Now is the time to draw up an alternative for when the tipping point is reached, and the Irish will be prepared to take a risk on themselves as opposed to dependence on institutions which do not have their best interests at heart.

It must be understood that the Irish state is an ethnic project, one that seeks the full self-expression of the Irish (which includes the Anglo-Irish who have contributed so much) as the Indian state does for the Indians, as the French republic does for its people, and so on. In our case, we have not been allowed have a period of classical culture, where patronage could allow refined production, since medieval times. We need to build on the resources of civil society that still exist – and revive those whose death we can remember – to recover the period a score years ago when it became clear that scores of generations had worked incessantly, risking opprobrium, ridicule and worse, to preserve many superb achievements of

Irish and indeed ancient aspects of Indo-European culture in the fabric of civil society.

The laxity on social, political, intellectual, moral, and artistic matters preached by the Irish establishment – perhaps the only instance where they practice what they preach – urgently requires public rebuttal in debate and action. First of all, complicated issues have to be teased out in a patient and respectful way. The main ascesis here is intellectual; it is the realization that hype does not change reality. The lesson from the Bertie Ahern era should not be the nonsense about what now look like piddling sums going through various accounts; it is rather that an attempt to avoid intellectual engagement by prematurely turning complex issues into political issues.

So, to take one example, in our history we have had William Rowan Hamilton, George Berkeley, Eriugena, and James Joyce. What they all shared was a self-aware sense of themselves as being Irish (epitomized by the name Eriugena, "of Ireland"), and genius. None of them could have survived in contemporary Ireland; the principal state mechanism is to disempower Irish people of talent, and import willing foreigners to produce an inferior version at great taxpayers' expense of what the Irish person was doing as a gift to his country. That requires serious discussion, as state agencies for science and tech multiply like rabbits. Briefly, there has been a pro-active attempt - in which the attack on tenure was one aspect – not to hire Irish academics as permanent staff at universities, but to create very expensive adjunct positions instead, often filled by charlatans like Edward de Bono at great expense to the state.

A decade (or far less in this case) is far too speedy to go from a ban on contraception (which existed in 1990) to an age of 17 for consent for all sexual acts (well before 2000). A generation (or far less, yet again) is too speedy to go from the state's cheating to introduce divorce and – when the same government gets back -to try and impose gay marriage. Like the closure of the Irish embassy to the Vatican, a diplomatic mission that reflects an alliance of great intensity, this drive came from nowhere, and it did not reflect public sentiment, as expressed in the poor performance of the openly gay Senator David Norris is his run for the Irish presidency. A decade is a risibly small period to "progress" from a narrative that placed the Irish on an island that they had been attested to inhabit for ten millennia to announcing that any immigrant could enjoy rights forbidden the natives.

A contemporary Irish artist faces penury, as well as a caterwaul from the noise machine in Dublin, as she starts to create work that we as Irish can be proud of internationally. The attempt to create a genuine Irish jazz form in the Gaelic language has met with heaps of scorn from the critics as well as state-organized theft from the artists in international trade fairs. A police investigation into what is effective a sacrosanct music rights agency was aborted – presumably by political fiat – when it was established that the chair of IMRO, and eminence gris of the Irish delegation at Enterprise Ireland trade stands, had been stealing the copyrights entrusted to him.

We found several limitations to the Irish state's competence as the Ahern government turned it into a toxic vehicle that in turn spread itself throughout the whole of society and saw its role as buttressing the privilege of a few. The Irish state cannot do technology; in that it is not unique. What it refused to do was precisely its only proper role; that of providing an appropriate regulatory structure to protect the innovations of those involved in technology, particularly Irish such. The Irish state cannot regulate universities any more than it could industrial schools; while Trinity should survive, in any case market forces on foot of disruptive educational technologies might force the state out of this game. The state needs to focus on courts, roads, and the services that Irish people are willing to provide each other in a manner that reflects their sense of being part of one nation. Historically, this has worked for aspects of education and health – by no means all.

8.2.2 Actions required

This is divided into Plan A and Plan B. Plan A involves attempting to get the EU and ECB to behave reasonably. If necessary, Ireland should be willing to abandon its anomalous corporate tax status (with exotica like the "double Irish" scam) to avoid paying down this unjustly-imposed debt. In either case, the rule of law (or, better still, real justice) must be re-established in Ireland – as distinct from the current situation wherein gargantuan law firms are employed by the establishment to deploy law as an instrument to buttress the privileges of a minority.

This leads us to a discussion of the nature of power itself in Ireland. The classical irredentist Republican move has been to claim that the state is illegitimate, because of the aftermath of the flawed dissolution of the second Dail. While this argument has some merit, it is in this writer's opinion too facile; an elaboration that argues that the state in turn fell into the clutches of theocrats and equally fundamentalist neoliberals as soon as it lost its sense of guiding the destiny of the Irish people to full self-expression seems better. In either case, there does not seem to be anything privileged about the current disposition of power in Irish society.

It could in fact reasonably be argued that the current state is just one of many possible usurpations of the changes wrought by the tremendous events of a century ago. In fact, the major arguments against wholesale armed rebellion are possibly pragmatic; it would be unlikely to succeed, and voting still has some consequences.

Where laws are honored more in the breach than the observance, they should be dispensed with. The fact that Ireland routinely violates EU environmental codes suggests we should get our own. In other cases, the fantastical apparatus that makes it so hard to set up a business in Ireland needs to be abandoned; the high minimum wage encourages "black work" by illegal immigrants. Similarly, the state should allow strikes for single dismissals, and refuse to allow its resources be used against individuals in an unfair way in civil matters, however lucrative this has been for lawyers.

All these are of course tweaks; yet it involves rescinding about 75% of laws passed in the past decade. The goal of the society has to be a decency in which human beings can carry on the activities appropriate to their stage in life - be it learning, working, or reflection - without the obsessive incursions of a power-mad state. That in turn requires that the state should explicitly repudiate its habit of finding some totalizing idea – be it clericalism or neoliberalism – and simply applying it blindly instead of looking at the merits of a situation before making decisions. An amended constitution should incarnate ideas even beyond "life liberty and the pursuit of happiness" to reflect Terrence MacSwiney's titanic vision of Ireland as a means of self-realization for its people, and this self-realization as sacred.

Specifically, this means the end of all state-subsidized apparatus that deals with strategy in a way not monitored by the citizenry. It also means the end of the various state-subsidized industries that have come into existence like that "protecting" the rights of immigrants. This will save the taxpayer a lot of money, and a lot of grief.

Unfortunately, while there is no question that Ireland should continue to comply with international refugee norms, it became a very soft touch from

1997 on with Nigerian women arriving at Dublin Airport over 8 months pregnant and claiming refugee status with no medical history. The resulting children were automatically Irish citizens; even now, at a time of massive emigration of the Irish from their country, tens of thousands of work permits are handed out – including massive amounts to non-Europeans.

All state activities need to be subjected to citizen's monitoring. Fortunately, the Internet provides a tool whereby any mature deliberations can immediately be broadcast. Stricter FoI rules would mean that bureaucrats could not attain the cachet and power that they currently have as their deliberations would be subject to monitoring. It is not a bad idea to restrict secrecy to issues that can be kept in non-written form in the heads of leaders. As soon as it gets written down, it should belong to everyone; the Wikileaks revelations of what was really going on were salutary.

So far, then, we have discussed a revolution in power in Ireland, insofar as this power is administered by "law". Obviously, the current massive salaries being paid to often incompetent and venal functionaries of the state need to be reduced to put them in line with earnings of people of their ability in the private sector – a considerable reduction, and one that the EU supports, as it happens. Coupled with that is a principle of subsidiarity with decisions being made at the most local possible level. In fact, it could be argued that the 1998 agreement caters for the possibility that other parts of the country may want to secede – another way to keep centralized power in Dublin honest.

Where there is a clear illegal break with centuries of practice, it should be reversed. A classic example is the privatization of folk music. Likewise, the organization that implemented this privatization - IMRO – is probably unreformable, and needs to be replaced, and properly investigated. Music is a vital part of Irish society, and the opportunity exists to introduce a collection agency that will charge venues only if they are demonstrably playing Anglo-American pap.

Irish industry will recover immediately once the state removes its boot from the throat of the producing class, with tax used to pay an ever-burgeoning civil service. For example, workers in agriculture have felt diminished by nonsense emanating from a government department of innovation – as if farmers and other business people don't constantly innovate! Paradoxically, this usurpation of the new by the state has effectively killed off the last of the native software industry, as it was perhaps intended to do. Instead of importing garbage like Facebook, the state might wonder why Ireland's many brilliant engineers are so frustrated, and get out of their way.

All of this is Plan A and its proposals apply also to Plan B. Unlike B, Plan A assumes that a deal can be cut with the EU; the issues of EU legislation can be catered for by noting that often the state has inflicted on its people an overly-radical interpretation of EU directives. However, should the EU decide not to play ball, the stage is set for a more radical alternative.

This more radical alternative will yet be nowhere near as radical as the changes wrought by the Ahern governments. To do so, we would have to do a root-and-branch overhaul. Since our opponents will accuse us of this root-and-branch overhaul in any case, let's take a look at the details.

The dirty little secret is that, even in the event of the worst possible exit from the euro zone, much of the ordinary fabric of social and economic life will go on as before. Farmers will produce food. Teachers will teach, and parents will bring their kids to school. In the case of universities, the great bulk of the work will as ever be done by the students, whose gift of some of the best years of their lives to learning might better be reflected in beneficial shares in the university than imposition of fees. Musicians will get together and make music for similarly convened audiences. The desolate scenario being conjured up by EU integrationists reflects more the current catastrophe than the dystopia they envisage. It is indeed true that the "double Irish" and other accounting scams developed by firms like KPMG to allow Silicon Valley firms to avoid tax by booking their profits between Ireland and the Caymans will disappear; they will not be missed, either in Ireland or the USA.

The state can play a vital role in endorsing a currency in which prices are couched. This writer agrees with the Austrian economists on one point; price has a vital social role in telling us where things fit in a society. The last decade has seen a worldwide frenzy of "cash for trash", with (super) governmental agencies – both in the USA and the EU – paying inflated prices for bad investments, often made by criminals. A too little known fact is that one result was that Ireland now has the largest property company in the world, the state agency called NAMA that bought up the junk property funded by the banks at the height of the bubble. This included failed developments from China to the UISA, as well as Ireland.

As already stated, we don't have to go quite this far; but a true revolution would involve serious thought about the stages of human life, and interventions the state should and should not make to allow humans fulfill their potential. Children need a vast amount of protection and formation; adolescents need guidance as they enter an often dangerous world, coupled with the recent sense that they are often substantially wiser in the ways of technology and its impact on social life than their parents; adults need a sense that the money that they earn to pay their mortgage is not being sucked up into some kind of casino, often driven by ideological garbage. Since our banks are essentially nationalized, it is a short step to state guarantee of sound money.

Nuriel Roubini (Roubini et al, 2010) among others, predicted the 2008 crash and proposed a set of solutions; the first is that organizations like Citibank that are "too big to fail" should be broken up; he also insists on much higher capital reserve requirements in banks. Until these desiderata are acted on, Ireland would be much better off away from the international financial system, which is prone to moral hazard and will almost certainly fail again in our lifetime. What I'm recommending, then, is the possibility of relative economic isolation - at least until the international system is fixed - rigorous enforcement of corporate law by the state, an emphasis on belonging to a community and to a nation, and deployment of the propaganda tools most recently used for neoliberalism to foster an ethos stressing the real purposes of human existence, and allowing both civil society and the state to contribute to it.

Plan B starts from the assumption that, if Nice and Lisbon can be voted on twice, so can they be voted on a third time. Indeed, Maastricht and the original crazy accession treaty – which essentially handed over all power to the EEC – should be fair game. These steps could be used as negotiating tools with our European friends as we look for a better debt deal. If they decide to call our bluff, things get interesting. Being exiled from world markets would also allow us undo the illegal transfer of natural resources to companies like shell and Statoil. It would enable us to patrol our huge fisheries in a law-enforcement role in which that Irish people in the USA have proven competent. The fact that there are about 100 million people of Irish ethnicity worldwide, all proud to be from a country with a non-exploiting past, will become salient as our moral ascendancy over our neighbors becomes clear.

Should we get expelled from the EU – impossible according to current legislation, though apparently Lisbon allows one to leave - the fact is that the carrying capacity of our island can easily support our population. We cannot – but never could – support a frivolous bunch of parasites in the cities e-mailing strategy documents to each other while working scams, and welfare scroungers from all over the world. Using modern technology, it is well within the capacity of our island to produce the minimum energy required to avoid infant mortality, as Cuba does; to provide food and shelter; to give access to information through telecommunication; and above all to restore people's self-respect in Ireland.

The censorship that has made us ashamed of ourselves is subtle; we need to pay back debts we didn't accrue as this makes us members of an elite club, and any counter-argument is from backwoods men outside that club. Yet that club is precisely the one that exploits workers all over the world and exterminates species daily; that substitutes pap for culture; that funnels workers' money to financial service operatives who have notorious personal lives.

Ireland can do better.

8.3 Sewerswim; Barrytown University

Emboldened by the early Garvin (2004) school of thought on Irish culture and economic development, a program of building 3rd level technical colleges was embarked on in the 1970s. While these would correspond roughly to a techie equivalent of Clark Kerr's community colleges, the later National Institutes for Higher Education (NIHEs) map roughly onto his state universities (à la SFSU). An NIHE was started in Limerick, directed by Ed Walsh; in the late 1970s, one was proposed for North Dublin under Danny O'Hare. Myriad shenanigans later, it occupied the site of the *ancien* Albert agricultural College at the centre of Fianna Fail criminality.

O'Hare was a perennial Fianna Failer: he had directed two technical colleges, and later chaired the expert skills group for the Irish state. One burning issue was to transform NIHE Limerick into David Lodge's "University of Limerick". As both colleges were self-consciously technical, that was going to be difficult. But not impossible, particularly as Thatcher has made universities of the polytechs in the 1980's. A committee was assembled under the chairmanship of a Mr. Michael

Gleeson. The investigation was done, Mr. Gleeson accepted a job at the designated Dublin City University (DCU) and the report was issued, in that order. Accreditation is famously a private deal between consenting adults, and is always politically labile. Nevertheless, Mr Gleeson's accepting the DCU job before parliament had considered the accreditation report was surely *de trop*.

Mr. Gleeson's tenure as secretary of DCU was a short one, and he quickly left for the same job at Trinity College. Unconstrained, O'Hare began to implement his vision for the place. A reliable and sympathetic human resource director, whose hobby was parachute jumping, was in his job replaced by a female admin assistant as he emigrated to Australia. Gleeson's replacement was from the nearby second-level vocational school. We academic staff hardly noticed; practically all have good memories of this period as, in conjunction with our students and with great effort on the part of teaching and technical staff, we were creating something world-class in Ireland with minimal resources.

Irish learning was praised even by the Venerable Bede, who commented on its excellence as on its hospitality to foreign students. In the 2004 edition of my "Being human", it is described how generations of development was thrown away in the name of "autonomous statutory responsibilities", a phrase used by successive Irish Ministers for education to disclaim any accountability by the universities. Specifically, all the provisions of the 1908 national university act and the 1997 universities act – including the appointment of "visitors", typically high Court Judges, to test adherence with the law – were subject to a prior test within these self-same institutions to check that they were ok. It was similar to Nixon's firing the prosecutor assigned to investigate Watergate, except that this new dispensation was to be permanent. The resulting legal imbroglio has directly cost the Irish taxpayer millions in legal fees, indirectly much more as staff opted not to commit to these colleges, and ruined many lives both of staff and students

It was the pleasure of this writer to create the first undergraduate degree of the new DCU university, and en route to establish the precedents for accreditation of such degrees. While DCU's own accreditation is suspect, the reception given our degree document by several of the best universities in the subject (computational linguistics) on the European mainland was very positive. The universities included Nancy 2, Bielefeld, Saarbrucken, and Goteborg. It helped matters a great deal that such an interdisciplinary degree could be proposed in a new environment without a history of clashes between departments. Yet.

The computer applications department had lifted itself by its own bootstraps to world-class levels. Our teaching, and administration load, which included teaching hours all weekday nights and Saturday mornings, was a whole number multiple of any I have seen since. I was not untypical in teaching a full load without teaching assistants, running a degree program, and doing a Ph.D. all at the same time.

Our computing students went out on work experience their third year. Almost uniquely for Ireland, all 70 or so of them got jobs both then and after they qualified. When we needed extra equipment, which was often, we paid for it ourselves, or got the boss's secretary to use her only skill: that of forging his signature. It was the perfect environment for a computing department and, had it continued thus, with a slightly expanded budget and staff cohort, would by now be world-famous for all the right reasons. Our students were aware of the efforts being made on their behalf, and responded in kind with goodwill, humour, and diligence. DCU was producing many brilliantly maverick computing graduates, the type of people who go on to work for Anonymous or Wikileaks, as well as the corporate drones it aimed to produce

My own career plateaued rather early. Certain misgivings that I had expressed about the fact that Ireland's representative in our area at European meetings, by his own admission, know nothing about the subject got back to O'Hare. My own boss induced a structure clash by utterly incompetent teaching on my degree, with the result that the excellent students that we hosted failed in droves in his subject, and in no other. His response was to tell me in summer 1992 I had resigned as Chair, and that he had replaced me. As of 2007, the degree no longer existed, at heaven knows what cost to the taxpayer.

The lower standard symbolic systems program at Stanford, on which I have also taught, goes from strength to strength with students gaining employment at a vast range of jobs, as I planned for our degree. If at first you don't succeed, etc. From 1993 to 1996, I worked at the National Research Council, Canada, where we developed new human computer interface technologies.

My return to DCU was not exactly a public holiday, and it quickly became clear not only that I was there on sufferance, but that once again I would have to buy equipment from my own pocket, and similarly, pay my own conference travel. Within three years, I had a stellar group of students, whose peers were told by the head of department not to talk with them. Stanford entered into an NDA with us, which I duly registered at DCU president's office. We ran two annual conferences from 1992 to 1999, each of which was offered book publication. The response from management was obstruction, attempts to set us up on various spurious charges (of not teaching, and so on). All my graduate students have gone on to magnificent careers, with an abiding hatred for DCU and for Irish bureaucracy.

It had occurred to several administrators, including my boss, that if we could put 70 through a year, why not 150? So we took in 150 and 70 or so got through. The number became known as Moynihan's Constant, after a departmental professor. Since we could not do 150, surely 300 was possible? My cavils about this within the department went unheard, so I broadcast them in my capacity as Green Party science and technology director. We were threatened with a lawsuit, and a year later I was informed that I had again resigned, this time from my job. Of the initial 305 in 1999, fewer than 90 got through in 2001. While I am no Hellenist – in fact, for all I know the event may not even properly belong to the Hellenic period – I am reliably informed that the attrition rate of the 300 resembles that in Thermopylae.

The context of much of what went on in Ireland – which is described at great and perhaps excruciating length in my "tenure" blog – was above all an attempt to destroy academic tenure in Ireland as happened in Britain in the 1980's and 1990's. Specifically, Thatcher decided to rescind the "permanency" part of tenure for new staff, and then her successors continued to extirpate the "freedom from redundancy" part by ruining the life of Edgar Page, a lecturer in Hull University. Page was eventually removed from his tenure on a technicality, causing many ructions as academics went so far as to boycott Hull; DCU then had inflicted on them the head of Hull's law department, one Ferdinand von Prondzynski, as their chief officer in 2000 after at least two others had demurred after being offered the job.

The father of Ferdinand von Prondzynski, like Hitler's special ops director Otto Skorzeny, settled in the Irish midlands after WW2. Ferdinand's public statements about his agenda were clear; the Irish were to become an ethnic minority on their island, to be replaced largely by Chinese (he chose to reveal this at commencement); universities were to be moved out of education and into the government trade department; students were to be deprived of the opportunity to choose their own career path. He was helped greatly by the 1997 act proposing the role of a "chief officer" who essentially had dictatorial power in the university.

In fact, it could be argued that his is a test case for quite how arbitrary the Irish state sees its legitimation. The doctrine of "autonomous statutory responsibilities" meant that there was effectively to be no accountability whatsoever. In my conference proceedings (in preparation) this is further explored. Yet once the state had decided to dispense with tenure, which arguably is its via media with the scholars with whom it shares a society, it really does look as if there are no barriers to what it can do with staff and students alike. The transcript of the Paul Cahill versus DCU High Court case does indeed indicate that DCU felt it had a right summarily to dismiss any staff member; "summarily " in both senses as without cause and without right of reply. The Supreme Court agreed with the Irish High Court that this violated certain inalienable rights. Yet DCU's response was to replace this illegal disciplinary statute with one that contained exactly the same trapdoor.

We seem trapped in the antinomial world of Bush/Cheney, shock and awe, and yet the closed-shop union at DCT (SIPTU) refused even to allow staff to ballot on the statute until 2012, when SIPTU had lost its closed shop due to staff discontent with it and no longer had any teeth. So it stands at the time of writing; personally, I like to think of it as the reduction ad absurdum of the social contract of the first Irish republic. By 2012, it was in any case clear that the online offerings of Stanford, MIT et al were going to dominate tertiary education, and that the Irish state was in an uphill battle to gain any traction in this new world, game the world university rankings as it might.

It is utterly impossible to fight removal from a state job in Ireland. The union cannot strike for an individual dismissal; as was the case during the heroic action of union train drivers in the war of independence in refusing to carry British military personnel and equipment (Costello 2003), it has decided to accept individual dismissals. The preliminary vote to strike on my case was 150-0, as management had crossed a grievance procedure with an illegal disciplinary procedure; no matter.

Four meetings of the labour relations commission later, I was ordered reinstated. Management refused to do so. Evidence was produced in Parliament to show my students had been threatened, offered bribes of extra marks to give evidence against me and bullied; no matter. (All of this can be found in my 2004 book) The minister for labour affairs was given the same evidence, and further documents proving fraud on the part of the university authorities; he refused to act. The theft of my research funds that formed part of the initial grievance procedure was brought up in Parliament, and police abandoned the investigation. The Irish business and employer's commission refused further to represent DCU; DCU's response was to use state money to hire a barrister. SIPTU refuses to hire barristers, and seem to believe that their negotiators can take them on. They cannot, and SIPTU has no business pretending to represent people. Equality of representation is a universal legal desideratum.

DCU computing could have been world-class. What seems to have happened is that the resources we requested depended on assent to management by a Fianna Faíl (FF) nominee. Since FF are tech illiterates, they are unlikely to hire anyone competent. The problem boils down to this: technological innovation is done by individuals, often of a maverick disposition, or small groups. The response of the Irish state is to form ever more unwieldy and huge organisations to manage this process. It is inevitably a disaster.

There was no way Paul Cahill and I were ever going to win a clear-cut victory about tenure, once the state had decided to engage in litigation. All that we could do was ensure that we did enough of a delaying action to prevent the state irrevocably closing off this area of intellectual freedom. Shades of the Battle of the bulge, where the Americans delayed the first surge; or indeed Iwo Jima, where the doomed Japanese were issuing a lesson about what the Japanese mainland was gong to be like. The state has since then tried to rectify matters but SIPTU has lost so many members at DCU that it is no longer whoring itself at the same low price.

Fortunately, the Irish state, like the Irish people, now has no money. The incompetents they paid to do their bidding from 1997 to now will, in many cases, renounce what was a temporary attack of Irishness, and go back to where they came from. That will hopefully bring back into focus what has always been the case: a 4% inhabited land, and a cultural crossroads of great potential. It seems a priori the case that the state should offer only accreditation, facilities and the legal protections it currently refuses to offer students. It is too corrupt to do university education, and independent colleges should be asked to tender to offer education on the facilities. Elsewhere (2004, Pp. 8-13) I give further details and outline the alternative structures.

Yet my 2004 book has been superceded by recent initiatives from the great American universities; EDx from MIT-Harvard and coursera.org from Stanford-Berkeley-Princeton (it has been commented that, sans the last, it would have resembled the West-East rap wars of the 1990's). By the time this book of being read, there will be tens of millions of the world's best students enrolled in one or the other of these colleges, and a new "super-accreditation", to distinguish the certificates issued from the mundane regional bodies, will surely follow. It's game over for the Irish university system, and they will not be missed; why submit one's kids or oneself t abuse when they can do better courses at home?

Finally, the name "Barrytown University" of course comes from Roddie Doyle's variation on Kilbarrack, the real-life location for his novels. Think of Jimmy Rabbitte in an academic gown, or Doyle's other characters swapping the Van for a gown, and you are close.

There was a final tragedy in the farce turned Gothic drama that is DCU. Joshua Howarth, a brilliant organic chemist, first faced disciplinary charges there in the late 1990's. Being foreign, he did not realise that one cannot win against the Irish state, and attempted to fight the charges at the High Court. As it turns out, the statute used against him was later found illegal, due to my victory, and rescinded. The stress eventually got to Josh, who killed himself in his early forties in 2006, having previously settled his case, and leaving a broken marriage with three kids.

Again, none of the Irish media were willing to cover this case; the garbage Daily Mail and Sunday Independent gave grotesque versions of my case, and the Irish times was so biased and inaccurate that it was sued both by myself and Paul Cahill, and issues an apology. . Since the disciplinary statute used against him Howarth has been adjudged to be flagrantly illegal, and certified so in a high Court judgement in 2007, in that it was a deliberate attempt to circumvent provisions in the 1997 universities act, it can be argued that his death is a felony murder.

DCU finally went to the Irish Supreme Court to assert what they saw as their right summarily to dismiss any employee, including senior tenured professors. Such an assertion was treated with the contempt that it deserved by the Supreme Court, and the taxpayer has had to pay at least $3 million in legal fees.

My case dragged on from 2002 to 2010 without ever emerging from the employment appeals tribunal (EAT), the lowest court empowered to deal with it. Welcome, again, to the crazy world of Irish jurisprudence; I returned, at my own cost, twice to Ireland from the USA between 2003 and 2004 to attend hearings of DCU's appeal. I had informed all parties involved in 2003 that I was taking a high court action in parallel to deal with sundry items of criminality outside the EAT's scope, including bribery of my students. In 2004, the EAT announced that this parallel process meant they had to suspend proceedings, as there was an overlap. In 2009, I fired SIPTU, and brought in a legal team. The EAT, violating its own written procedures, had allowed DCU yet another deferral. This time, the newspaper coverage focussed on the fact I had raised the issue in a blog of Ferdinand von Prodzynski's father, and his role in WW2. It was conceded by von Prodzynski *fils* that his father was a director of Dyckerhof cement, which was forced to pay compensation to slave labour victims after a hearing in federal court in 1998.

On Jan 26 2010, my legal team told the EAT that they were in error in suspending proceedings as the provision had been rescinded. The EAT explained that it was the non-overlapping material that was the problem – and indeed there was a precedent in law. Pressed by my team for the precedent, they again reversed themselves, and admitted there was none. On hearing this in August 2010, I withdrew my life savings from the Bank of Ireland, transferred them to France, and fled there.

In 2009, I decided to make sure that there was media coverage of this attempt to destroy tenure, so that at least the previous "*Nacht und Nebel*" tactics could be countered. . It was predictable, perhaps, that the gutter media would seize on the "NazI" element. What was not predictable was the Irish Times taking a line that was so grotesquely unfair that it has so far had to issue a retraction, and an apology, and is still being sued along with Prondzynski.

It should not surprise readers of this book that the Irish establishment debauched itself so thoroughly in an effort to destroy academic tenure. It has not succeeded; I won the case, there is yet another appeal, and we will soon be resuming hostilities in the circuit court.

8.4 Decolonising Ireland — Further Modest Proposals

In world affairs, we are at an interesting historical juncture. There was an African-American in the white House. The US colonial effort in Iraq, which had the overwhelming support of US public and elected representatives until gas prices went up, has failed. The suspension of habeas corpus, elevation to respectability of torture, tearing up of the Geneva Conventions, and imposition of an Orwellian "Patriot Act" that imposed draconian limitations on traditional American freedoms, has yielded nothing except a destabilised middle east. Nothing that is, unless you had shares in Halliburton or any of the major oil companies. The new world order dreamed up by the current chief of the World Bank and his PNAC colleagues will never come to be. Indeed, the questioning of US state involvement in 9/11 has quickened, and it is likely that Bush, Cheney, and Rumsfeld will join Kissinger (and the late Pinochet) on the list of people least likely to fly to Europe (for fear of arrest on crimes against humanity).

The neocon tendencies of the Ahern Irish government were arrested by its electoral trouncing in 2004; they were reinstated in modified form by its unexpectedly good showing in the general election of 2007, and again given pause by the forced demission of Ahern and world economic crash, both in 2008, and the further midterm electoral drubbing in 2009. This has afforded us a breathing-space to review their agenda as its implementation is delayed, essentially to optimise Ireland as transnational heaven, a European Delaware for American companies who were to benefit there from low corporate tax. Education at all levels was to be replete with capitalist ideology, and its goal was the production of compliant, appropriately skilled and "transferable" employees, as specified in the OECD report. In the meantime, the leadership and their cronies were to become unimaginably rich. The 2011 elections produced a government which is sleepwalking; if it really tackled any of the criminality of its predecessor, it would become immensely popular. But why have the name without the game? Many of us suspect the same shenanigans are afoot.

A Berlusconi/Bush type "state of business" patrimonial system, implemented by the bureaucracy of the state, with resources assigned to those close to power was to be intensified I the Ahern plan, with privatisations of everything that could yield a profit. Already, the health service was partly privatised with sociopathic results, and the privatisation of the telecommunications system has contributed to Ireland's tech collapse, with Eircom having the nerve to ask the state for €200 million to help introduce broadband. The New Ireland was to be implemented with utter disregard for the rule of law: a murderous edge tinged the state's activities. Finally, Northern Ireland was gradually to be assimilated into a classic corporatist state with the attenuation of parliamentary democracy that we have already seen in the 26 counties. This was perhaps trumped by the MI5 HQ idea; now the idea was that Ireland as a whole island was to be moved back into the British sphere of influence.

Ironically, some of this agenda could have been implemented through the 1997 state, when Ahern came to power. The unions had been domesticated, and public employees signed what is less a contract than an indenture. The acceptance of "economic analysis" (read neoliberal boosting) as national culture had already taken hold, and its grip was inevitably going to be tightened as a bubble followed a boom. Let us be clear: there is nothing wrong, a priori, with economists replacing artists on the ramparts of national culture except that artists are in general better with money than economists, since they have to be to survive, and have no theoretical baggage. Conversely, economists in the media spotlight get in touch with an artistic side of their nature, and begin to unleash fantastical speculations. Finally, the draconian Irish libel laws and fearsome size of the big law firms forbid anybody writing or saying anything that might shock the self-appointed elites.

The viewpoint of this book is that the bureaucracy of the Irish state is terminally corrupt and, at its worst, is essentially a criminal conspiracy against the Irish people. However, are Bernadette Sands McKevitt and Ruairi Ó Brádaigh correct in saying it is illegitimate? The Irish people, in voting for the GFA with its withdrawal of the territorial claim on NI, had no idea that any of its provisions could be withdrawn at any time by the British (Costello, 2003). They voted for partition in 1922 and against it in 1937.

Had e-voting been introduced, the state would have lost its litmus test of consent by the governed. While Ó Brádaigh (until he "retired", accusing the Adams cohort of treason for decommissioning) et al perform the needed service of keeping the state honest that Sinn Féin used to do, their military strategy is nothing short of insane. The recent attack on the

Massarreene barracks was less a full-frontal assault than a symbolic gesture, with the plan being to force the British army back on the streets. Thirty years of resourceful combat by many in the PIRA (tose not working for the Brits) resulted in nothing other than a withdrawal of its sovereignty claim by the 26-county state and the manufacture of an assembly in which the extremists on both sides begotten by the conflict would be forced to talk to each other with the British and Irish governments holding their hands.

The British, as we have seen, were happy to use NI as a training ground, and had their outdated cryptographic, telecommunications, and spy capacities modernised for them by the IRA. (Indeed it is possible that the IRA's use of a weather channel frequency for detonation of bombs that we have noted was a key turning point, as the Brits could no longer detonate the IRA bombs remotely by emitting signals at random). While shooting at the army in NI is possibly satisfying, only large-scale attacks on commercial targets in Britain have any impact. Post 9/11, and the GW Bush prohibition on American funds, it is highly unlikely that we will see another large-scale Irish military campaign in our lifetimes .Indeed, the "real" IRA seem to have recognized that they will not be able to get the British to withdraw by military means; however there are currently upwards of a thousand IRA volunteers.

The Irish people should be given another opportunity to vote for the abandonment of the claim on NI. They would do so, perhaps. That would destroy Ó Brádaigh's successors final claim to legitimacy. The succession has not been smooth, as the 2012 shooting dead in Dublin of the IRA activist Liam Kelly makes clear. In the meantime, the state should make it understood that with Sinn Fein and the DUP now forced to talk with one another, all deals with the British were forced on them by asymmetry of powers due to genocide. Moreover, there should be an insistence on British schoolchildren learning the facts of their genocidal forebears, and a campaign similar to the one that Armenia is currently waging against Turkey to declare an Gorta mór and the Cromwellian campaigns acts of genocide.

So much for the "national question". There are more pressing issues relating to the neocon Parnassus that Ahern was trying to push on us. The modulation of the collapse of the banking system affords an opportunity to introduce some sanity into Irish affairs. True real-estate values, as indicated by the rental market, are perhaps double what they were in 1995.

However, over half a million housing units have been built since 2001, and many have not entered the market. From 2008, the question was no longer if or when the banking system will collapse; the issue has become how to control the collapse in the manner that Tipler (1994) attempts to modulate the cosmic big crunch, but hopefully with more effect.

McWilliams (2006) argued that the introduction of Irish "banking bonds" underwritten by the state was the solution, and this is effectively what happened with the same disastrous effect as his success in guaranteeing debts owed to all bondholders of these bonds. As he is a former central bank employee, who correctly points out the King Canute inefficacy of the Irish Central bank post the Euro, he was listened to. We wished to avoid the Argentinian debacle (see Naomi Klein's documentary "The Take") with money physically being taken by truck and under cover of darkness by foreign creditors, and a generation losing its bank deposits.

The argument used to be that the Irish $500 billion debt was dwarved by a $1 trillion housing value. When house prices decreased by more than 50%, the country was in very serious debt. So, McWilliams argued, prop up the banks, which have had the highest profits in the EU (ibid) and contributed nothing culturally by guaranteeing all deposits. Alternatively put, make Irish citizens pay for the banks' cupidity and ignorance through the NAMA/Anglo Irish process, which is closer to what happened.

It is doubtful that this current dispensation will even work, unless the state introduces legislation that will prohibit a new housing bubble. For example, it might set up a proper banking regulatory authority that prohibits mortgages of over twice a worker's salary, and of greater than twenty years. It is also highly unlikely that the international financial institutions that have loaned to Ireland will go away without their pound of flesh. Otherwise, every nouveau rich state will be encouraged to create a housing bubble with foreign borrowing, thus creating a demographic war between a filthy rich middle-aged set and their frantically pressurised sons and daughters. The influx of cash has not been used to create new industry.

Two things could be predicted about the collapse, which this author predicted at many fora in American Universities from 2004: it would cause a lot of suffering, and it would result in state intervention in real estate, as it has done. An alternative path, which this book has broached, would be partly to withdraw from the euro, and introduce a non-convertible currency that caters for property and food essentials. In the manner of Argentina's Kirchner, the state could make a single "take it or leave it" offer to foreign creditors. While Ireland's good standing in the EU, WTO, and so on could be deeply compromised, a partial solution might be implemented through the provision of low corporation tax "export processing zones" for transnationals with a convertible currency/euro/dollar economy. Irish employees could convert their earnings to the non-convertible form, and the tax revenue used to pay off international debt.

Now we come to the part many will find unpalatable; all work permits awarded to immigrants without a previous long-term commitment to the country since 2000 should be rescinded, unless the immigrants can prove their skills are essential. The thousands of Polish and Chinese bar attendants and shop assistants that make social life such a chore in Ireland clearly do not qualify. Should this get us kicked out of the EU, so much the better.

Let us now proceed to the main thrust of this book's final chapter. It is argued that Ireland's economic collapse heralds an opportunity. Before, during, and after the collapse, the Gaelic language, music, sport, and culture will continue to gain strength. The process of the collapse can be used to instil a moral national vision as some degree of economic isolationism becomes necessary, and the strength of the state can ensure that it takes. While its economy is utterly out of control, and has been for some time, the state can continue to combat the rampant criminality (Williams 2006), insist on high standards in education in a way that OECD reports cannot comprehend, destroy political interference in law enforcement, including that of corporate law, and — ironically — liberate the Irish citizen in doing so by introducing first amendment type legislation, a rescission of "social" partnership to allow real trades unions, and a proper system of representation to allow citizens to deal with the state on a more equal footing.

In this context, judges should be elected as in much of the US, and similarly elected rights commissioners given an extended mandate. It should replace the theocratic preamble of the constitution with one like that of the constitution of India:

> "We, the people of India, having solemnly resolved to constitute India into a sovereign socialist secular democratic republic and to secure to all its citizens:
> Justice, social, economic and political;
> Liberty of thought, expression, belief, faith and worship;
> Equality of status and of opportunity;
> And to promote among them all
> Fraternity assuring the dignity of the individual and the unity and integrity of the nation"

Coupled with this should be a renationalisation of the health services, telecom services, and national airline. For what McWilliams (2006) correctly predicted is a nationalisation of the banks but so much done on the banks' terms and on such a scale that it amounts to takeover by the banks of the state. The banks need not necessarily have been nationalised; if they could withstand the financial shock by standing on their own two feet, well and good. If they could not, and particularly given their role in their own demise, and lack of contribution to Irish society, they should pay for the consequences.

What the bubble of 1997-2007 amounted to was essentially a generation's declaring the eschaton, the end of time, and abstaining from farther work, or moral engagement. A proper implementation of the law will divert the Irish moral impulse into proper channels; much of the current nihilism/materialism and bad taste derives from the amorality and cynicism of the Catholic Church.

We can quickly graft together a national religion, should such be necessary. With tongue somewhat in cheek, and referring the reader to the discussion earlier in this book, I offer the phoneticised "Slí na fírinne", the way of truth.

8.4.1. Slee na feerinne; an ancient and contemporary Gaelic spiritual path

The metaphysics, mythology and language of the Irish, from their first recorded writings, together with cutting-edge contemporary neuroscience, affords us an opportunity to revolutionize our conceptual systems, and indeed way of life. In particular, it gives us cues to root our identities at the most fundamental level in a more veridical experience of selfhood as pure subjectivity, and so feel less inclined to seek environmentally toxic and socially pathological ways of proving our existence to ourselves when societal pressures impinge on us.

The creative power present in the cosmos, currently explained (away) by the anthropic principle (see my 2012 paper), was called "nyart" by the Gaels. They conceived god as immanent in nature, including themselves; Brahman is the same as Atman; the observer just before wave-function breakdown is identical with the wave-function itself, nowhere and everywhere. We have seen this theme being echoed in Joyce. This is exemplified in the song of Amergin, the first human arrival on the island of Ireland from whom the Gaels claimed ancestry. His song is epiphany, and also Bhagavad-gita style theophany:

> "I am wind on sea, I am an ocean wave … I am an ox of seven fights … I am a tear of the sun"

As in classical Indian thought, the "I am" is identified with the nyart of nature. Even later Hiberno-Christian thought, including present-day Hiberno-Catholic writings, stressed that one central goal of the spiritual path was to amplify the experience of God in nature in oneself.

There is much political sociology in Irish mythology, even if it is adulterated by later Christian interpolation. The nadir of the latter can be read in the "Exodus to Connacht", comparing the transplanted Cromwellian Irish to displaced Israelites, and Sean O Conaill's "Tuireamh na hEireann", a psalm-like complaint against a Semitic transcendent God from the same period.

Some centuries later, some Irish like the fiercely anti-clerical Fenians calmly looked at the facts of their colonisation, revolted against it, and became an example of freedom and courage to the colonised world. Among the pieces that have come down to us relatively intact is the "Battle of Allen", which describes the inevitably disastrous effects of a war conducted contrary to the rule of law. This urgent and contemporary theme is given geophysical and cosmic significance in the "Tain bo Cuailgne" (Tawn bo coolnya). The Tain also features the "reestra", rage, of the Ulster hero Setanta as he combats perceived injustice with great skill and courage. The reestra of the decolonialising Irish resonated throughout the world. In particular, the hunger strike to death of Terence MacSwiney, a potential pillar of the Irish bourgeoisie who had everything to live for, done explicitly in the name of self-authentication, revealed the colonial order for the murderous and parasitic entity we all currently know it to be.

We can ourselves interpolate a post-christian spirituality using Gaelic words. We can use the two forms of "to be" in the Irish to contrast Taw, the activity of the inauthentic self, to "Is", true authentic presence. This realisation, "layergas", which can be achieved through any authentically engaged human activity, including and perhaps especially political struggle, invites the person to "Moknov", contemplation. In this, she can see the deceptive workings of Intinn, mind, while remaining rooted in "Is". She achieves "Seersha", freedom, which stays with her through all her daily activities, as she continues to identify Bealtaine, Samhain, the hunting of the wren/humanity giving back to nature, and the engagement with artistic culture and literacy that the current neoliberal world order is trying to destroy in Ireland (with the help of the corporatist state) as elsewhere.

Of course, Joyce shows us the path here with a truly incarnated, non-dualistic, way of living on our island, the antidote to colonialism, as he himself predicted. Likewise, the emanationist perspective of Erigena – according to Schopenhauer the inspiration for Hegel – shows the Irish leading European thought. Indeed, Rudolph Otto claims that the Rhenish mystics, exemplified by Eckhart, took their cue from this great Irish forebear. The resources of the land itself show that it was regarded by our forebears as itself a sacred space, and we need to refocus on their precise geological and cartographic intuitions.

Let us be clear about a few issues; please see my 2012 paper on this subject as what follows is rather laconic. The first is that we are making a distinction between the search for truth as pursued in the academy, which is rigorous and free inquiry into objective reality, with only a tiny aspect of subjective experience being catered to in analysis of sensorimotor consciousness and that in the "real world". The latter perspective accepts the achievements of the academy but paradoxically has both a humbler starting-point and a higher aim. Its starting-point if the Lifeworld we all – academics and laypeople alike – share in modern society. The bigger game it pursues is neither more or less that a compelling experience of Being itself, infusing every aspect of daily life, and urging us as human beings to ever greater heights of self-integration, refinement of emotion, reclusive ability and that selflessness from which comes not just mere "charity" but contact with the Real.

At times there will be conflict with the academy, particularly as the latter enters one of its all-too-frequent manias. In the past century, ontological behaviorism rejected the existence of mind, and of course consciousness; in response, and quickening in the 1990's, neuroscientists provided fanciful mapping of subjective dispositions to cerebral locations, the majority of which were simply fraudulent. An ontology is necessary, as indeed is a set of irrevocable moral imperatives to maintain distinctions and societal achievements, and preserve nature.

We use a Gaelic term and call this "On Shlee", the path. In the first instance, there are clear desiderata for people living a normal daily existence As it incarnates itself in this quotidian existence, it involves that type of presence in our dealings with others that classically has been called humility; Where one is pursuing an ethical end like the presentation to the public of music that is finer than the average, it is acceptable to use environmental resources at the same rate as one's competitors. In general, however, one should strive to minimize one's footprint, recycle everything possible, all the while asserting our rights as human beings for full self-expression through the arts and sciences. Indeed, political issues like universal electoral suffrage, ecological maintenance, representation by the individual on an equal basis to the state in disputes, an appropriate currency, equality of opportunity for all, and private property are political issues of such urgency that their assertion is itself a spiritual path as one reclaims the correct relationship of part to whole in society.

The cosmology includes the following: It is dangerous to map perennial life-affirming intuitions of the absolute onto one's contemporary science. Science is by its nature subject to refutation. Yet the primordial REALITY, Brahman, godhead, inspires stillness and reverence in much the same way as physicists currently revere their ultimate reality – this time approached by mathematics.

Brahman/Godhead unmanifest can be thought of as the equally fugitive quantum vacuum Nous, the ordering force in reality, can indeed be conceived of as scientific law. The "unseen energies of god" may be the dark energy…or not The meditative state may be able to sustain quantum coherence, with its postulated supercomputational powers. The refined types of energy in the body may be conceived of as Nadh-stored; versus those dormant in fact cells (see our 2011 paper).

The final issue is how life consonant with the principles would be led. In society, the moral imperatives to rationality, compassion, creativity and environmental conservation should be clear from the above. However, there is surely space for a place in which the life is led as a vocation, with three prayer meetings a day for a group, celibate or not, who maintain themselves with ethical work. In classical fashion, they can offer a satsang – or whatever service is appropriate - to those in the "real world" who are interested.

To be specific, this involves a community of respect; it is unlikely that aggressive music like rap or heavy metal has a place, however valuable the catharsis they produce in fragmented societies; there must be work for everybody, even if that begins living off the scraps industrial society has left behind by using freeware products; total commitment to open-ended scientific and artistic creation is encouraged.

I leave it up to professionals to work out how to implement this vision in terms of the conventional accoutrements of religion – cult, cosmos, ceremony, community, and cross-currents. Suffice to say that present-day science, for all its shortcomings, does give us an active proof of the mystery of our existence in a cosmos that inexplicably begets order.

8.5 Conclusion

Remarkably, the 2008 crash of the Irish economy is perhaps the luckiest break Ireland has had for some time. An extremely corrupt self-appointed power "elite' with a dogmatic attachment to the Washington consensus - as to lining their own pockets – might have otherwise been impossible to dislodge. There is now an opportunity to implement a new vision of a nation-state including the enormous and multi-talented Diaspora. This is particularly the case as the state in its current configuration adds precisely nothing to the lives of its citizens, who would be better off as a 51st state of the USA.

Conversely, the brand "Ireland" is possibly the strongest international brand that exists, with a resonance to ex-colonies and ex-colonial states alike. Those who may not admire the toughness of the Irish people, exemplified in their climb up US society (English, 2005), like the culture and missionary work, and vice versa. What has happened since 1997 is the incursion of the state into aspects of civil society like music and tech, using taxpayers' money and lining the pockets of individuals close to power, with destructive results, as we have seen in chapters 6 and 7.

The obliteration of organizations like IMRO and SFI will free up much capital and energy. The active search for new systems of national administration will add dynamism to a weary body politic. A system both federal and ward-based, with proper subsidiarization, will empower people at every level. The exposure of much modern economics for the nonsense that it is allows creation of sound money. Once we have a sense of how much the economic activity of the country really is worth internationally, we can refloat the currency, backed by algorithms which assess that beautiful new term "moneyness" – ie how much CDO's etc really are worth.

A few more obvious points. First of all, Ireland is the country of the Irish, both resident there and those in its Diaspora who want to make contact (like the Argentinian contingent). It is not a neoliberal experiment, a British colony, or a European export zone. Secondly, our sovereignty allows us to rescind the Lisbon and Nice treaties - as we almost certainly must – and to delete all colonial hangovers, starting with the absurd "Royal" prefixed to many "National" institutions.

Back to basics; the Irish civil service is undoubtedly top-heavy, with the prime minister's staff bigger than its British equivalent during the Ahern/Blair era. The prospect of being paid mainly in non-convertible "punts" would get rid of quite a few of them; the prospect of moving to parts of the country that would benefit from a civil service department seemed to cause quite a lot of perhaps necessary distress. Civil servants dealing directly with the public for 20 hours or more a week are wholly necessary, be they doctors, IT specialists, nurses, teachers, or postal workers; those formulating strategies in technology have just led to disaster after disaster. The tax load of the hard-working citizen can greatly be lightened by a strategic cull. As already pointed out, academics who teach historical revisionism should be free to do so, but not at the expense of the Irish taxpayer.

An intensification of the sense of Irishness should continue. The Nobel Laureate John Hume's proposal for certificates of Irish nationality, as distinct from citizenship, to be given to ethnically or provably cultural Irish abroad should be followed up beyond the 2010 proposal to offer shopping deals and the token awrds to celebrities that we have witnessed.

Willingness to pay for their own DNA tests to establish a genetic link would be the start of the process of Hibernicisation. As Hume pointed it, this could reverse the effects of British genocide by adding tens of millions to the country. Coupled with this should come a promotion of Irish culture, as distinct from the current doses of Catholicism and British revisionism, by our foreign affairs staff.

Let us be clear; these changes are by no means as radical as what will inevitably happen as the debt needs to be paid back. If we Irish feel we can keep our quaint little capital, built in the eighteenth century by English adventurers (if using Irish labour), as it is, in the face of hundreds of billions of personal debt to be repaid by this real estate, we are deluded. Life in Ireland must be de-economized, and the economy itself definancialized.

State funding of science, beyond college salaries, should be discontinued. Ireland should introduce radical environmental legislation, building on its tremendous start in windpower. Infant mortality, the best index of caloric quality of life as it indicates an ability to survive, can be kept at the required abysmal rate at an energy use of 100 Gigajoules per person (Historically, during the great achievements of human culture, use has been a small fraction of that). Let us recall also that most commodities are now informational, require small amounts of energy, and are available in free versions; for example, Open Office (on which this book was written) is as good as Microsoft's Office. We should expect no less of ourselves. The final aim is that Ireland should again become a beacon to the colonised in the world, be they the Chinese with their 200 riots a day suppressed by draconian authorities, the British with their post-Blairite Big Brother state, or the Americans with their unelected war president of 2000-2008.

If we leave the Euro and make a single "take it or leave it" offer for our debt a la Argentina, nationalize all resources, then we can watch a competent set of politicians take over as the EU recedes. If we break away from the Euro, allowing anyone who wishes to take their euro out if they do not want to convert into the punts necessary to buy state-owned resources in Ireland.

Secondly, plan B would involve a Moldavia-type situation of returning to a larger cash economy basis. This author would not cry a tear if financial "services" in Ireland died today. To be clear; restricting the import of winter kiwis, as of Serbian sex slaves, would not harm anyone. After what would frankly be a purgative 3-5 years, with the incompetents at the top in Ireland weeded out, we might be perhaps to re-engage with the globalized corporatist "community" again. If during the purge, we also lost our Anglo-Saxon legal system, and scientific/economic wunderkinden imports, so much the better.

What is envisaged is a non-violent revolution in Ireland; as repeatedly stated here, the magnitude of change will be less than that during the Ahern years. This writer, like Fanon, believes colonial states to be massively violent entities which may need to be forcibly resisted; yet we have managed to maintain a relatively transparent voting system in Ireland, and violence is unnecessary. Like Fanon (in the 1977 Evergreen/Random House edition, p 204) and Chomsky's mentor Rocker (Barsky, 2007) this writer also believes nationalism to be potentially destructive unless rooted in celebration of a sense of place and a profound humanism. These are both part of Irish cultural nationalism.

8.5.1 Cometh the IMF

On Easter Monday, 24 April 1916, the socialist writer James Connolly ordered an armed group to march down Dame Street in Dublin in what became a citizens' occupation of Dublin city centre. As Connolly hoped, the shockwave launched by the doomed uprising kindled fires of revolution throughout the colonies during all of the 20th century.

On November 18th 2010, a small unescorted group of IMF technocrats walked down Dame Street, home of their goal in the Irish Central Bank, to articulate the re-colonisation of Ireland. This book has attempted to explain the lack of public protest by the Irish in the face of a grim future. In particular, the author argues that the IMF move simply cemented in place a deal done long ago between globalized corporatism and Irish catholic nationalism. Almost all sectors of Irish civil society that might have offered resistance, including Connolly's Labour movement, had long ago been bought off or destroyed. The single significant exception – academic economists – were publicly encouraged to " commit suicide" by Ireland's prime minister in 2007, and academic freedom has been saved ironically by what were, in effect, kamikaze tactics as described above.

This book began with mention of enormous numbers of google hits suggesting that Ireland was at risk of default, with the pace of such suggestions quickening the business week beginning Nov 15, 2010. On 15th November, 2010 Olli Rehn, EU Commissioner for Economic and Monetary Affairs, fresh from a visit to Ireland, suggested that there was enormous pressure for Ireland to accept a bailout, confirming the rather informal methodology used by this author. Default by Ireland would have meant that the foreign banks, many German, who stupidly loaned to a clique around Bertie Ahern might never be repaid; the IMF takeover means that the E70 billion bill is passed on to the Irish taxpayer along with the tab all the preceding apparent ECB largesse.

The book ends by envisaging a future for Ireland with an attenuated relationship with forces of globalized "capitalism", including the EU. A de-economization of life and – in turn – a de-financialization of the economy are to be coupled with a re-emphasis on cultural and indeed genetic belonging for the resident and diasporic Irish. The IMF may indeed have been allowed to investigate aspects of the banking scam that our law enforcement have been prohibited from looking at; in fact, they may be the only mechanism that can destroy the enormous power wielded by the Irish establishment through a grotesquely over-paid public service. The fact that the unions do their evil in the name of James Connolly surely gives pause? Similarly, the IMF will do us a service by reducing the ridiculously high social welfare benefits that have probably helped greatly in maintaining the status quo by pacifying a source of protest,

Ireland is not an idea, or a test-tube for economic experiments; it has a place which had a relatively stable ethnic culture for close to ten thousand years. In the late 1990's, it looked very much as though a major breakthrough was about to occur, with this ex-colony becoming a world player in the arts, due primarily to its care in nurturing its ancestral culture; in technology and economics, due to a well-attested concern with scholarship; and as beacon for world peace, due to the generosity implicit in giving up what previously was an irredentist if utterly justifiable land-claim. To achieve so mightily in these fields would have been the best possible example for fellow ex-colonies. The argument of this book is that what instead happened was a new colonialism.

The arts were debauched, to a dizzying extent because of Ahern's concern that his daughters would join the jet-set. The technology-driven boom was turned into an unspeakable property scam, for which the 2007 government expected the Irish people to pay - for several generations. The state's encroachment on civil society resulted in Golems like SFI, Medialab, various “social partnership” apparati and “enterprise boards” or “innovation Ireland” stalking the land and repressing the native creative, risk-taking impulses of the Irish people. Massive immigration was encouraged, ensuring new racial problems to complement those in the North-East corner of the island.

All things considered – and it is fair to say that this book has indeed looked at a large range of sociopolitical, technological, artistic, economic and other issues – this author believes that Ireland needs an interlude from globalized corporatism. A country is not a project; it is often life itself for those who live there.

8.6 Epilogue; apocalypse or asymptote?

On the face of things, Ireland entered the financial crisis of the late aughts with a socio-economic system ideally oriented to meltdown just in time for Mayan apocalypse 2012. The civil service had been bloated with highly-paid functionaries with little to do other than administer the neoliberal gospel. In gross terms, of the 300,000+ plus who work in the Irish public service, considerably less than half have any discernible dealings with the public. Civil society had been attenuated, with stalwarts of Irish social life like the pub coming under attack to the point that 1 out of 8 was going out of business as of late 2011.

Regulations had mushroomed to the point that is it well-nigh impossible, even before one pays the inflated Irish salaries in already inflated Euro, to get through a single day in a business without violating the myriad Irish and European laws that apply. Areas in which real Irish genius might have flourished like software and music had been carefully obliterated, as this book documents. The country was optimized for inward investment that was no more, and control had been established at myriad checkpoints at all levels of the state to ensure there was no competition.

The bonds that had been so irresponsibly issued by the banks broke the shamrock's back. Already over 70% of Irish legislation originated in the EU; now both monetary and fiscal policies were to be sourced there. The scenario is clear; a permanent recession with any froth generated by the occasional success being slurped up by Brussels.

That is the asymptotic version, which sees Ireland, metaphorically speaking, vanishing beneath the waves. It is a relatively gentle death and, for those who voted for Bertie Ahern, perhaps ore than they deserve. Yet it leaves a huge Diaspora without a place to call home, and rids the earth of a genuinely interesting ethnicity. The Irish citizenry voted on a set of sweeping fiscal unification provisions in Mat 31 2012 while the French and Germans visibly argued about whether the text was to be changed regardless of how the Irish voted; at this point we are so far away from the MacSwiney vision of autonomy that something urgently needs to be done.

The alternative is apocalypse, for which the state has rehearsed with the heavy-handed security at the queen's visit in 2011. The viewpoint of this book is that the colonization started in the late 1990's, with a dividing up of the spoils in Irish society and a deliberate destruction of academic freedom and other forms of self-expression. In fact, 2008 may be the best thing to happen to us. I write in a spirit of hope; the solutions proposed throughout this book, while allowing the Irish citizenry and diaspora to re-examine every critical demarche from the dissolution of the second Dail right up to the Lisbon referendum, are far less radical in their consequences that the frightening flirtation with corporatism that has visibly failed, and been seen to fail.

The era of consensus on the Irish national narrative now seems in the distant past. It involved an ethnic identity, a territorial claim, an ancient language – indeed, a religion with a "special place" established in the constitution. The excesses committed in the name of this narrative fill the pages of a fair percentage of the confessional literature of the twentieth century. They included a disempowerment of women surely as complete as could be implemented without removing the voting franchise, a philistinism celebrated by the official state, and a mediocrity affecting a remarkable swathe of the country's intellectual and cultural life.

The new narrative emerged during an unexpectedly brief period of prosperity. Where there had been a sense heretofore that Irish people could act effectively because they were rooted in a place and in a culture, all such predication was now to be reduced to considerations of monetary reward. Effective people got paid more; there was no sense in which one worked over one's pay grade for the good of the country. All references to ethnicity were to be eschewed; indeed, it made sense in the new dispensation to import hundreds of thousands of foreign workers even as Irish people had to emigrate due to unemployment. No foreign alliance was to be rejected; indeed, the British were encouraged to construct a large MI5 HQ on the island in which they had long before professed no strategic interest. The result was a disempowerment of the native ethnic Irish surely as complete as could be implemented without removing the voting franchise, a philistinism celebrated by the official state, and a mediocrity affecting a remarkable swathe of the country's intellectual and cultural life.

There is no question of returning to the first narrative; yet the second has failed, and spectacularly so. To base everything on money is rare even for good businesses; for a country it means that all the other human purposes that the modern state has accumulated over the years – self realization in a plethora of cultural outlets, social stability, a hierarchy of value with the unselfish and refined at the top, and much more – have now been negated in the name of an overarching impulse that has reveled itself to be no more than the greed of a few, who simply appropriated sufficient aspects of the first narrative to themselves to seem continuous with tradition as they effectively destroyed the country.

The monetary sums involved in the appropriation are cosmic, and we will not see such money again in our lifetimes in Ireland. We can however insist that nothing of the sort happens again; that we belong to the country, and it to us, in a way not open to others who are not willing to learn the culture; that Ireland is a project in which the self realization of many is mediated through ancient civil society institutions like our music, which must again become inviolate; and that we are capable of being at least the equal of all other nationalities – as distinct from a recidivist beggar – if we are allowed to be ourselves.

So let's consider the ethnic narrative to start with. We have material dating from over a millennium ago from Irish people facing the same existential crisis. The result is literature like the “book of Invasions” which places us on this island as surely as the Pentateuch bases the Jews in Israel, and a great deal more surely than the highly successful Book of Mormon evokes the spirit of its land, with which we share much. We have DNA evidence that has been twisted to suggest all kinds of absurdities, particularly as the 1998 British-Irish agreement was in its early years, but which will almost certainly show a huge amount of genetic isolation.

We have writers of a caliber that need not be evoked here. The celebration of place in the dindsenchas is as sure an inspiration for Joyce as Homer;

this needs to be re-stressed. The survival of ancient aspects of Indo-European culture in Ireland needs to be lifted out of its backward valence

Then we can celebrate belonging to a country that has never invaded another, that has no enemies, and that has achieved a vast amount in fields from science to law. The last will be my final point; it can perhaps be argued that the Anglo-Saxon system does not work for Ireland, As of 2012, the current chief justice is open to its supercession. As we are forced to recreate our country over the coming decades, we should not fear to go there where the state has exerted its authority so unjustly and incompetently for decades.

It is important not to overcomplicate matters. While we began the discussion of the decolonial turn with sophisticated analysis of Mignolo, mentions of Foucault's "biopower" and guesses at how think-tanks might have decided to re-engineer subjectivity to turn the natives back into subalterns, the fact is that Ireland in 2012 resembles nothing so much as a colony from the glory days of the same 19th century European empires, inventors of modern colonization, who are now insisting, together with the USA which has also featured so prominently here, that Ireland pay back money that she really does not owe,. Very simply, there has been no progress on the deals that were announced to assuage the burden of debt imposed on the citizenry through the improvidence of international capital. What is left is the Sisyphean task of paying back debts for which the productive surplus cannot even handle the interest. It is essentially slavery, with a self-appointed native elite administering the new dispensation.

This would be less suspicious, had there not been a palpable attempt to destroy much of an ancient civil society, including its highest achievements in the arts and technology. The means used were criminal in the extreme, with law being used as an instrument to buttress a state of affairs already decided upon; there was no concept of justice. In this, the native kleptocracy colluded with their new overlords. This chapter introduces plan A and Plan B as paths out of this, with the latter likely only if there is political violence.

This book advocates new visions of law, property and privacy consistent with the forthcoming century. It suggests also that whatever new institutions emerge in Ireland must be managed in a far more open fashion; indeed, perhaps managed by a rotating staff to prevent the cabals and vicious corruption that destroyed the first republic. The good news is, as this book makes clear, the moral, intellectual, historical and cultural resources – considered in the broadest sense – available to us as Irish people are massive.

Now we come to the punchline of this book. The reader may be surprised at the range of topics, from religion to economics to the universities to software, for which the author seeks reform. She may also wonder at the unresolved nature of much of the discussion here. My response is that the lack of resolution is deliberate; the themes require the emergence of a discernible national will to give them coherence. Ireland functioned best under what looks in retrospect as moral absolutism, but was simply a nation being itself. What we have seen for the past 15 years or so is the disaster that happens when the nation is overcome by globalizing "whatever" trends. We need a vision of the starkness that inspired MacSwiney and the others who won us that first brief independence. This time, it will be less Roman Catholic, and more aware that 90% of the Irish people live off the island.

We need a country to which we belong.

2005-2012

The Cistercian monasteries of Roscrea and Moone, Ireland; Berkeley, USA; Dublin; Edinburgh, Scotland.

REFERENCES

Abate, T. (2005). "Housing, Hedge Funds Spur Bubble Worries", *San Francisco Chronicle Business*, May 22, 2005, p. 86.

Allen, K. (2000). *The Celtic Tigers: The Myth of Social Partnership in Ireland.* Manchester: Manchester University Press.

Alterman, E. (2005). "Bush's War on the Press", *The Nation*, May 9, 2005, pp. 11–20.

Anderson, B. (1991) *Imagined Communities*. London: Verso

Aron, R. (1965). *Main Currents in Sociological Thought.* New York: Penguin.

Arts Council of Ireland (2004). "Towards a Policy for the Traditional Arts" Merrion Square, Dudlin 2, Ireland ISBN 1-904291-09-0.

Asch, R., ed. (1993). *Three Nations: A Common History*. Bochum

Aumann, R. (2000a). *Collected Papers Vol. 1*, MIT Press.

—. (2000b). *Collected Papers Vol. 2*, MIT Press.

Baker, K. (2009) "Barack Hoover Obama" *Harper's magazine* July 2009

Bank, D. (2001) *Breaking windows* NY: Free Press

Bayley, E. (1981). *Joe McCarthy and the Press*. Madison: University of Wisconsin Press.

Behe, M. (1996). *Darwin's Black Box*. New York: Touchstone.

Berlin, I. (1991e). "Nationalism: Past Neglect and Present Power" in I. Berlin *Against the Current: Essays on the History of Ideas.* H. Hardy, eds. Oxford: Oxford University Press, pp. 335-355.

—. (1991f). "European Unity and Its Vicissitudes" in I. Berlin *Against the Current: Essays on the History of Ideas.* H. Hardy, eds. Oxford: Oxford University Press, pp. 175-206.

—. (1991g). "The Bent Twig: On the Rise of Nationalism" in I. Berlin *Against the Current: Essays on the History of Ideas.* H. Hardy, eds. Oxford: Oxford University Press, pp. 238-261.

—. (1996a). "Kant as an Unfamiliar Source of Nationalism" in I. Berlin *The Sense of Reality: Studies in Ideas and Their History.* H. Hardy, eds. London: Chatto and Windus, pp. 232-248.

Berresford Ellis, Peter (1988). *Hell or Connaught!* Belfast: Blackstaff.

Brennan, C. (2006). "ESRI Warns Economy Could Be on Unsustainable Path". *Irish Times,* 21 December 2006, p. 1.

Brisard, J-C, and G. Dasquie (2002) *Forbidden Truth.* New York: Thunder's mouth/Nation books

Cahill, Thomas (1996). *How the Irish Saved Civilization.* Anchor.

Cahill, J. (2009) "The end of neoliberalism?" *Z magazine*, Jan 2009, Pp 35-38

Campbell, J. (1949) *Hero with a thousand faces* NY: Pantheon

—. (1968). *Creative Mythology*. London: Penguin.

Carroll, C. (2001). "Custom and Law in the Philosophy of Suarez and in The Histories of O'Sullivan Beare, Cétinn and ? Cleirigh". In Thomas O'Connor (ed), *The Irish in Europe 1580–1815*. Dublin, p. 65–78.

Carroll, J. (2001). *Constantine's Sword.* New York: Houghton Mifflin.

Castle, G., ed. (2001). *Postcolonial Discourses*. Oxford: Blackwell.

Chang, H-S (2008) Bad Samaritans. NY: Bloomsbury.

Charles, D. (2001). *Lords of the Harvest.* Cambridge, MA: Perseus.

Cheah, P. (2006). "The Limits of Thinking in Decolonial Strategies", *UC Berkeley Townsend Newsletter*, November/December 2006, pp. 9-11.

Clark, D. and S. Clark (2001) *Newton's Tyranny* NY: Freeman

Clarke, R. (2004). *Against All Enemies.* London: Simon and Schuster Free Press.

Clifford, M. and S. Coleman (2009) *Bertie Ahern and the Drumcondra Mafia* Hodder.

Coakley, J. (2004) "The foundations of statehood" In Coakley, J. and Michael Gallagher (eds.) (2004). Pp 4-35

Coakley, J. and Michael *Gallagher* (eds.) (2004). *Politics in the Republic of Ireland*. Routledge.

Cole, R. (with R. Turbo) (1992) *Stairway to Heaven.* NY: Harper Collins

Coleman, M. (20045 b). "Report Finds High Levels of Financial Illiteracy", *Irish Times*, 20 September, p.1.

—. (2005). "ECB Chief Praises Ireland as Model for Growth", *Irish Times*, 21 September 2005, p.1.

Coll, S. (2004) *Ghost Wars* NY: Penguin

Coogan, T. (2000). *De Valera.* London: Random House.

Cooper, M. (2009) *Who runs Ireland*? Dublin: Penguin

Costello, F. (2003). *The Irish Revolution and Its Aftermath.* Dublin: Irish Academic Press.

Crewdson, J. (2002). *Science Fictions: A Scientific Mystery, a Massive Cover-up, and the Dark Legacy of Robert Gallo.* NY: Little, Brown.

Cullison, A. (2004). "Inside al-Qaeda's Hard Drive", *Atlantic Monthly*, September, 2004, pp. 55–70.

Cunningham, B. (2000). *The World of Geoffrey Keating.* Dublin: Four courts press

Cushman (1990). "Why the Self is Empty", *American Psychology,* 45(5), pp. 599-611.
Darwin, C. (1968) (1859). *The Origin of Species.* Middlesex: Penguin.
Day, Seán (2003). "What Synesthesia Is (and Is Not)". In McKevitt et al, eds. 2002, pp.171-180.
De Paor, L., ed. (1986). *Milestones in Irish History*. Cork: The Mercier Press.
Dedrick, J. and Ken Kraemer (1998). *Asia's Computer Challenge.* NY: Oxford University Press.
Diamond, J. (1998). *Guns, Germs, and Steel.* London: Vintage.
Donoghue, D. (1986). *We Irish.* New York: Knopf.
Dopsch, H and R. Jeffinger, eds. (1984). *Virgil von Salzburg: Missionar und Gelehrter.* Salzburger: Landesregierung.
Dreazon, Y. and J. Opdyke (2005). "Minorities say Katrina Work Flows to Others", *WSJ*, Friday, September 2005, B1, p.1.
Dreider, W. (2009) "Memo to Investigators: dig deep" *The nation* 229(13) Oct 26 2009
Duddy, T. (2002). *A History of Irish Thought.* London: Routledge.
Durkheim, E. (1995) *The elementary forms of religious life*. NY: Free Press
Eagleton, T. (2005) "Ireland and colonialism" In McDonough, T. (ed.) (2005) *Was Ireland a colony?* Dublin: Irish academic press Pp. 326-333
Ellis, D. S. (1999). "More Irish than the Irish Themselves", *History of Ireland*, Vol. 7, No1, 22–26.
Ellman, R. (1977). "The consciousness of Joyce" New York: OUP.
—. (1978). *Yeats.* New York: Norton.
—. (1965) "James Joyce" New York: Oup
English, T. (2005) *Paddywhacked* NY: Harper Collins
Evans, P. (1995). *Embedded Autonomy: States and Industrial Transformation.* Princeton, NJ: Princeton University Press.
Fallows, J. (2005). "Countdown to a Meltdown", *Atlantic Monthly*, July/August 2005, p. 51–68.
Fanning (1986). "Partition". In de Paor, ed., p. 128–137.
Ferguson, N. (2006). "Empire Falls", *Vanity Fair*, October 2006, pp. 222-230.
Ferriter, D. (2004) *The transformation of Ireland* New York: Overlook
Freeman, W., S. O'Nuallain and J Rodriguez(2008) "Simulating cortical background electrocortigram at rest with filtered noise" *Journal of integrated neuroscience*,7 (3)Page: 337 - 344 Sept 2008
Gandhi, L. (1998) *Postcolonial Theory* New York: Columbia

Garvin, T. (2004). *Preventing the Future.* Dublin: Gill & MacMillan.

Gibbon E. (1963). *The Decline and Fall of the Roman Empire*. New York: Dell.

Grant, J. (2008) "Is the Medicine worse than the illness?" *WSJ,* Dec 20-21 2008, W1 section

Grey, S. (2007) *Ghost Plane* New York: St. Martin's Press

Guth, R. (2005a). "Microsoft, Palm Unite to Fight Blackberry", *Wall St. Journal,* Sept. 27, 2005, B1, B10.

—. (2005b). "Battling Google", *Wall St. Journal,* Sept. 23, 2005, A1, A14.

Hamilton, H. (2003). *The Speckled People.* London: Harper Perennial.

Harnden, T. (2000). *Bandit Country.* London: Coronet

Heuvel, Katrina Van Den (2005). "Schiavo as Prologue," editorial, *The Nation,* 18 April 2005, P. 3.

Heuvel, Katrina Van Den, ed. (2004). "Can Marriage be Saved?", *The Nation*, p. 16–49.

Holton, K. (2005). *Revivalist Folklore Performance in Portugal.* Bloomington: Indiana University Press.

Holtzman, E. (2005). "Torture and Accountability," *The Nation*, July 18/25, 2005, pp 20–24.

Humphreys, J. (2005). "Ireland Ranked as Second Wealthiest Country", *Irish Times,* September 8, 2005, p. 1.

Huntington, S. (1996). *The Class of Civilisations*. London: Simon and Schuster.

Ignatiev, Noel (1996). *How the Irish Became White.* London: Routledge.

Ip, G. (2005). "Fed Keeps Focus on Inflation and Raises Rate", *Wall Street Journal,* Vol. CCXLVI, No. 58, 21 September 2005.

Joyce, J. (1966). *Finnegan's Wake*. New York: The Viking Press.

—. (1986). *Ulysses: The Corrected Text.* New York: Random House.

Juhasz, A. (2006) *The Bush Agenda*. New York: Harper Collins

Kaletsky. A (2010) "The Benefits of the Bust" Extarct from "*Capitalism 4.0*", Perseus. In WSJ, W3, June 19-20

Kaplan, R. (2005). "How We Would fight China", *Atlantic Monthly,* June 2005, p. 49–64

Kinealy, C. (2005) "Was Ireland a colony? - the evidence of the great famine". In McDonough, T. (ed.) (2005) *Was Ireland a colony?* Dublin: Irish academic press Pp. 48-65

Kinney, J. (2004) *The Inner west.* NY: Penguin

Kinsella, T., ed. (1989). *The Oxford Book of Irish Verse.* OUP.

Klein, N. (2005). "Torture's Dirty Secret: It Works", *The Nation,* May 30, 2005, p. 10.

—. (2007) *The shock doctrine* NY Picador

Krakauer, J. (2003) *Under the Banner of Heaven* NY: Doubleday
Krugman, P. (2009) *The return of depression economics* NY: Norton
—. (2010)"Myths of austerity" NY times, op-ed, July 2
Kurlansky, M. (2007) *Non-violence* London: Vintage
Laing, R.D. (1967). *The Divided Self.* Middlesex: Penguin.
—. (1990). *The Self and Others.* Middlesex: Penguin.
Landes, C. (1998). *The Wealth and Poverty of Nations.* NY: Norton
Langewiesche, W. (2004). "Welcome to the Green Zone", *Atlantic Monthly,* November 2004, pp. 60–88.
—. (2007) *The Atomic Bazaar* NY: Farrar, Strauss and giroux
Le Carre John. (2001). *The Constant Gardener.* New York: Simon and Schuster.
Lee, J (1985). *Ireland 1912–1985*. Cambridge, England Cup.
Levy, Ariel (2005). *Female Chauvinist Pigs.* Free Press
Lewis, M. (1989) *Liar's Poker.* Kent: Hodder and Stoughton
—. (2008a) "Inside Wall Street's Black Hole" *Conde Nast Portfolio* March 2008, Pp. 130-133
—. (2008b) "The End" *Conde Nast Portfolio* Dec 2008-Jan 2009 P 114 Ff
—. (2009) "Wall Street on the Tundra: How Iceland went Pfft" *Vanity Fair*, April 2009, P 140 Ff
Lindsay, R. (1979) *The Falcon and the Snowman* NY: Simon and Schuster
Litton, H. (1998). *Irish Rebellions 1798–1916.* Dublin: Wolfhound Press.
Lodge, D. (1984). *Small World.* London: Penguin
Loewenberg, J., ed. (1957). *Hegel Selections.* New York: Charles Scribner's Sons.
Lowenstein, R. (2005). "See a Bubble?", *New York Times Magazine*, June 5, 2005, pp 19–22.
MacCnaimhin, Séamus (1966). *Eireannaigh San Eolaiocht.* Dun Dealgan: Magowan.
McDonough, T. (ed.) (2005) *Was Ireland a colony?* Dublin: Irish academic press
MacPhilemy, S (1998) *The Committee* Colorado: Robert Rinehart
MacSwiney, T. (2004) *Principles of freedom*. Ebook #13132, Gutenberg press. www.gutenberg.net
MacSwiney-Brugha, M. (2006). *History's Daughters*. Dublin: The O'Brien Press.
MacWilliams, D. (2006). *The Pope's Children.* Dublin: Gill and Macmillan.
Mahon, T. and J. Gillogly (2008) *Decoding the IRA*. Cork: Mercier Press
Manes, S. and P. Andrews (1994). *Gates*. New York: Touchstone

Manhkopf, B (1999). "Between the Devil and the Deep Blue Sea" in Pantitch et al, eds., pp. 162–177.
Mann, C. (2005). *1491: New Revelations of the Americas Before Columbus.* New York: Knopt.
McCann, A. (2003). "Irish Traditional Music and the Copyright Debate", published in *Irish Folk Festival*; www.beyondthecommons.com/iff2003.html
McCann, A. (2005). http://www.beyondthecommons.com/
Macdonald, F. and J. Nix (2006) *Chaos at the crossroads* Kinsale: Gandon
McGarvey, A. (2005). "Dr. Hager's Family Values", *The Nation,* May 30, 2005, pp 11–18.
McGraw, B. (2005). *Taking Religious Pluralism Seriously*. Waco, TX: Baylor University Press.
McGuire, R. (2003). *To Form a More Perfect Union.* New York: Oxford.
McKevitt, P., Ó Nualláin, S. and C. Mulvihill, eds. (2002). *Language, Vision, and Music.* Amsterdam: John Benjamins.
Mead, Walter Russell (2007) *God and gold* New York: Knopf
Medvedev, Z (1971) "The rise and fall of TD Lysenko" NY: anchor.
Mignolo, W. (2006). "De-Linking, the Rhetoric of Modernity, the Logic of Coloniality, and the Grammar of De-colonisation" Avenali lecture, 17 October, 2006. http://townsendcenter.be.edu.
Miller, M. Crispin(2005). "None Dare Call it Stolen," *Harper's Magazine,* August 2005, 39–46. See also www.house.gov/judiciary-democrats/ohiostatusreport/505.pdf.
Miller, M. Crispin (2007) *Fooled Again* New York: Basic books
Moloney, Ed (2002). *A Secret History of the IRA*. London: Penguin
Moody, G. (2001). *Rebel Code*. London: Penguin.
Mulcahy, N. (2005). "In at the deep end" Dublin: *Business Plus*, August 2005, pp. 32-43.
Murphy, J (1986). In De Paor, L., ed. (1986). *Milestones in Irish History.* Cork: The Mercier Press.
Needleman, J. (2002). *The American Soul.* New York: Tarcher/Putnam.
—. (1980) *Lost Christianity* NY: Harper
Nguyen, T. (2005). *We are All Suspects Now.* Massachussetts: Beacon.
Nicholls, K. (2003). *Gaelic and Gaelicized Ireland Ireland in the Middle Ages*. Dublin Lilliput Press.
Ó Duinn, S. (2000). *Where Three Streams Meet.* Dublin: Columbia Press.
—. (1990) Orthai chosanta sa chráifeacht Cheilteach Máigh Nuad: An sagart
Ó Faoláin, S. (1942). *The Great O'Neill.* Cork: The Mercier Press.
Ó Nualláin, S. (2003). *The Search for Mind, 3rd Edition.* Exeter: Intellect.

—. (2004). *Being Human*, 2nd edition. Exeter: Intellect.
—. (forthcoming). *Neural Correlates of Consciousness of What?* New Ideas in Psychology.
O Nualláin, Seán (2008) "Subjects and Objects" Biosemiotics journal, Volume 2
—. (2006). Inner and outer empiricism in consciousness research. New Ideas in Psychology 24 (1):30-40
—. (2012) "God's unlikely comeback" Cosmos and History Vol 8, No 1 (2012) The Future of Philosophy Pp 339-382
O Nualláin, Seán and T. Doris (2011) "Consciousness is cheap" Biosemiotics journal DOI: 10.1007/s12304-011-9136-y
—. (in preparation)"Ireland in crisis; Proceedings of ICIS 2012 at UC Berkeley"
O Nualláin, Seán and R. Strohman "Genome and natural language" in Witzany (ed.) Proceedings of Biosemiotics 2006. Helsinki; Umweb (2007) Pp. 249-260
O Nualláin, Seán (2008)""Remarks on the foundations of Biology" at "Cosmos and History: special issue on 'What is life?'" Vol 4 Nos 1-2
—. (2010) "Ask not what you can do for yourself: Cartesian chaos, neural dynamics, and immunological cognition" Biosemiotics Vol 3 Issue 1, 2010 DOI 10.1007/s12304-009-9070-4
Ó Riain, S. (2004). *The Politics of High Tech Growth: Developmental Network States in the Global Economy*. Cambridge: University Press.
Ó Tuama, S. and T. Kinsella, eds. (1981). *An Duanaire: Poems of the Dispossessed*. Mountrath, Ireland: Dolmen.
O'Brien, C. (1986). *The Siege*. London: Paladin.
O'Brien, E. (1984). *A fanatic heart*. NY: Signet
O'Callahan, S. (2000). *To Hell or Barbados.* Dingle/Daingean, Ireland: Brandon Books.
Orwell, G. (1949). *1984*. New York: Penguin.
Palast, G (2006) *Armed Madhouse* Penguin
Panitch, L and C. Leys, eds. *Global Capitalism versus Democracy.* Suffolk, England: The Merlin Press.
Parenti, C. (2005). "Hugo Chavez and Petro Populism", *The Nation,* April 11, 2005, pp. 15–20.
Perkins, John (2007) *The secret history of the American Empire* London: Plume
Pettibon (2004). "The Copula 'Ka' In Ixpantepec Mixtec" QP fest, CSLI, Stanford, May 28, 2004.
Pleklanou, S and D. Mazzeo, eds. (2006) *Russia.* University of Toronto Press.

Plowman, M. (2003). "Irish Republicans and the Indo-German Conspiracy of World War I", *New Hibernia Review/Irish Eireannash Nua,* 7:3, pp. 80–105.

Pocock, J. (1974). "British History: A Plea for a New Subject", *Journal of Modern History*, 47:4 (1975), 601–21 (originally published in New Zealand Historical Journal, 8 (1974), 3–12.

Quinn, Bob (2005). *The Atlantean Irish.* Dublin: The Lilliput Press.

Rees, A. and B. Rees (1961) *Celtic Heritage* London: Thames and Hudson

Rifkin, J. (1983). *Algeny*. New York: Viking.

Ritter, S. (2005) *Iraq confidential* NY: Nation books

Rivlin, G. (2005). "If You Can Make It In Silicon Valley", *New York Times magazine,* June 5 2005, pp. 64-69

Ross, S. (2006). "Google Searches Outside Ireland for Dublin Jobs", *Sunday Independent,* 19 November, 2006.

Roubini, N and S. Mihm (2010) Crisis Economics NY: Penguin

Roy, A. (2005). "The Assault on Iraq is an Assault on All of Us", *International Socialist Review,* Sept/Oct 2005, pp. 23–25.

Rutten, T. (2005). "Dublin Beyond the Blooms", *Los Angeles Times Travel* L1, L8–L9.

Ryder, S (2005) "Colony and empire in 19th century Irish nationalism" In McDonough, T. (ed.) (2005) *Was Ireland a colony?* Dublin: Irish academic press Pp. 165-185

Sakharov, A. (1990" memoirs NY: Knopf

Sargent, G. (2005). "Brand Hillary", *The Nation,* June 6, 2005 pp. 13–20.

Sargent, W. (1958). *Battle for the Mind.* Cambridge, MA: Malor Books.

Schapiro, M. (2004). "New Power for Old Europe", *The Nation,* December 27, 2004, pp. 11–16.

Schwartz, B (2005). "Managing China's Rise", *Atlantic Monthly,* June 2005 p. 27–31.

Schwenninger, S. (2005). "Reconnecting to the World", *The Nation,* July 18/25, 2005, p. 13–20.

Segal, R (1990) *Joseph Campbell* NY: Penguin

Sekyi-Out, A. (2003). "Fanon and the Possibility of Post-Colonial Critical Imagination" http://www.codesria.org/links/conferences/accra/sekyiotu.pdf.

Sharlet, J. (2008) *The Family* NY: Harper Collins

Smith, H. (2001) *Why religion matters* NY: Harper Collins

Smoley, R. (2002) *Inner Christianity* Boston: Shambala

—. (2006) *Forbidden Faith* NY: Harper Collins

Smoley, R. and J. Kinney (1999) *Hidden wisdom* NY: Penguin (Arkana)

Sokel, A. and J. Bricmont (1998). *Intellectual impostures.* London: Profile.

Sorkin, A. (2009) "The week Goldman Sachs and Morgan Stanley almost died" Extract from book, *Vanity Fair*, November 2009. The book, *Too big to Fail,* is NY: Viking/Penguin

Sri Ramanashram (1972). *The Spiritual Teachings pf Ramana Maharishi.* Boston: Shambala.

Stewart, J (1991) *Den of Thieves* NY: Simon and Schuster

Sykes, B. (2006). *Saxons, Vikings, and Celts.* W.W. Norton.

Taylor, C. (1989) *Sources of the Self.* Harvard University Press.

Teague, M. (2006). "Double Blind", *Atlantic Monthly,* April 2006, pp. 53-62.

Tipler, F. (1994). *The Physics of Immortality.* New York: Doubleday.

Titley, A. (2000). *A Pocket History of Gaelic Culture.* Dublin: O'Brien Press.

Tymoczko, M (1994) "The Irish Ulysses" California: UC Press

Tovey, H. and P. Share. (2003). *A Sociology of Ireland.* Dublin: Gill and Macmillan.

Wallace, D. (2005). "Host", *Atlantic Monthly,* April 2005, pp 54–77.

Wallis, F. (1999). *Bede: The Reckoning of Time.* Liverpool : University Press.

Washburn, J (2005). *University Inc*. NY: Basic Books.

Welsh, Frank (2002). *The Four Nations.* London: Harper Collins.

Wheatcroft, G. (2006). "Why I Now Loathe the Sporting Life", *The Observer*, 30 July 2006, p. 29.

Williams, P. (2006). *The Untouchables.* Dublin: Merlin.

Wilson, David O. (1998). *United Irishmen, United States.* Dublin: Four Courts Press.